Trilliums

Plate 1. *Trillium grandiflorum* in a Michigan woodlot. Photo by Fred Case.

Trilliums

by
Frederick W. Case, Jr.
and
Roberta B. Case

Timber Press
Portland, Oregon

Published in 1997 by

Timber Press, Inc.
The Haseltine Building
133 S.W. Second Avenue, Suite 450
Portland, Oregon 97204, U.S.A.

Reprinted 1997, 1998

Printed in Hong Kong

Library of Congress Cataloging-in-Publication Data

Case, Frederick W.
    Trilliums / by Frederick W. Case, Jr. and Roberta B. Case.
        p.   cm.
    Includes bibliographical references and index.
    ISBN 0-88192-374-5
    1. Trilliums. 2. Trilliums—Classification. I. Case, Roberta B. II. Title
SB413.T74C37 1997   96-27583
584'.325—dc20   CIP

Contents

List of Taxa of *Trillium*

Trillium albidum Freeman
Trillium angustipetalum (Torrey) Freeman
Trillium apetalon Makino var. *apetalon*
 f. *album* Samejima
 var. *atropurpureocarpum* (Makino) Samejima
 var. *rubrocarpum* Samejima
 f. *tripetalum* Samejima
 var. *viridipurpureocarpum* (Makino) Samejima
Trillium camschatcense Ker Gawler var. *camschatcense*
 var. *kurilense* Miyabe & Tatewaki
 f. *plenum* Samejima
 var. *soyanum* Samejima
Trillium catesbaei Elliott
Trillium cernuum Linnaeus var. *cernuum*
 f. *tangerae* Wherry
 var. *macranthum* Wiegand
Trillium channellii Fukuda, Freeman & Itou
Trillium chloropetalum (Torrey) Howell var. *chloropetalum*
 var. *giganteum* (Hooker & Arnot) Munz
Trillium cuneatum Rafinesque f. *cuneatum*
 f. *luteum* Freeman
Trillium decipiens Freeman
Trillium decumbens Harbison
Trillium discolor Wray ex Hooker

Trillium erectum Linnaeus var. *erectum*
  var. *album* (Michaux) Pursh
Trillium flexipes Rafinesque f. *flexipes*
  f. *billingtonii* Farwell
  f. *walpolei* (Farwell) Fernald
Trillium foetidissimum Freeman f. *foetidissimum*
  f. *luteum* Freeman
Trillium gracile Freeman f. *gracile*
  f. *luteum* Freeman
Trillium grandiflorum Michaux f. *grandiflorum*
  f. *polymerum* Victorin
  f. *roseum* Farwell
Trillium hagae Miyabe & Tatewaki
Trillium ×*hagae* Miyabe & Tatewaki (= *T. camschatcense* ×
      T. tschonoskii)
Trillium kurabayashii Freeman f. *kurabayashii*
  f. *luteum* Soukup
Trillium lancifolium Rafinesque
Trillium ludovicianum Harbison
Trillium luteum (Muhlenberg) Harbison
Trillium maculatum Rafinesque f. *maculatum*
  f. *luteum* Freeman
  f. *simulans* Freeman
Trillium ×*miyabeanum* Tatewaki (= *T. apetalon* × *T. tschonoskii*)
Trillium nivale Riddell
Trillium ovatum Pursh var. *ovatum*
  f. *hibbersonii* Taylor
  f. *maculosum* F. & R. Case
  var. *oettingerii* Munz & Thorne
Trillium parviflorum Soukup
Trillium persistens Duncan
Trillium petiolatum Pursh
Trillium pusillum Michaux var. *pusillum*
  var. *alabamicum* Freeman
  var. *monticola* Reveal
  var. *ozarkanum* Palmer & Steyermark
  var. *texanum* Buckley
  var. *virginianum* Fernald

Trillium recurvatum (Beck) Beck f. *recurvatum*
    f. *foliosum* Steyermark
    f. *luteum* Clute
    f. *petaloideum* Steyermark
    f. *shayi* Palmer & Steyermark
Trillium reliquum Freeman f. *reliquum*
    f. *luteum* Freeman
Trillium rivale Watson
Trillium rugelii Rendle
Trillium sessile Linnaeus f. *sessile*
    f. *viridiflorum* Beyer
Trillium simile Gleason
Trillium smallii Maximowicz var. *smallii*
    var. *atropurpureocarpum* Samejima
Trillium stamineum Harbison f. *stamineum*
    f. *luteum* Freeman
Trillium sulcatum Patrick f. *sulcatum*
    f. *albolutescens* Patrick
Trillium tschonoskii Maximowicz var. *tschonoskii*
    var. *atrorubens* Miyabe & Tatewaki
    var. *himaliacum* Hara
Trillium underwoodii Small
Trillium undulatum Willdenow f. *undulatum*
    f. *enotatum* Patrick
Trillium vaseyi Harbison
Trillium viride (Beck) Beck
Trillium viridescens Nuttall
Trillium ×*yezoense* Tatewaki (= *T. apetalon* × *T. camschatcense*)

Preface

No recent treatment, either technical or popular, encompassing all the accepted *Trillium* species, exists in English. Advanced amateur botanists, horticulturists, naturalists, and perhaps even trained botanists need a general treatment and field guide. The present volume is not intended to be a taxonomic revision. We have written it expressly for the amateur field botanist and interested horticulturist. Our hope is that this book will provide some of the needed general information on identification, distribution, ecology, development, and culture for anyone interested in these fascinating plants.

We have observed all the presently described American species and most of the widely accepted color forms and varieties in the wild. We have not seen *Trillium ovatum* var. *oettingerii* except as herbarium specimens, nor have we seen *T. ovatum* var. *hibbersonii* in the wild, although we grow it and have seen many specimens in Vancouver gardens. We grow or have grown all American species (but not every variety) and three of the Asiatic species in our experimental gardens at Saginaw, Michigan (U.S. Department of Agriculture hardiness zone 5) for many years, and have learned much about the species from that experience.

We have read much of the botanical literature on trilliums. In our opinion, the taxonomic revisions or treatments that can be relied upon for accurate, useful, and correct information are few. For the sessile trilliums, we recommend "Revision of *Trillium* subgenus *Phyllantherum* (Liliaceae)" by John D. Freeman (1975). This monumental work has sorted out a truly horrendous morass of misinformation and misunderstanding from previous times. Because virtually all works on sessile trilliums before Freeman's contain many errors and misunderstandings about species ranges and characters, they are unreliable. In our own field work, we find no populations or situations that seriously contradict Freeman's findings. For that reason, we rely heavily upon his information and cite Freeman's work extensively here.

For the pedicellate trilliums, "The Pedicellate Species of *Trillium* Found in the Southern Appalachians" by Lane Barksdale (1938) treats most of the pedicellate trilliums. While this work is older than Freeman's, like Freeman's work, it corresponds to what we think is the situation in the wild and we recommend it. A more recent worker, Thomas Patrick, has a great wealth of information, particularly on the pedicellate trilliums, and we have retained his treatment of *Trillium sulcatum* (1984) here. Patrick (1986a, 1986b) has published privately several identification handouts and information sheets, which we have consulted. We also follow Victor Soukup's treatment (1980) of *Trillium parviflorum*. For the Asiatic species, we follow Samejima and Samejima (1962, 1987).

We must hasten to point out that there are many other papers, particularly in recent years, that contain much excellent and useful information on individual species, groups within the genus, or on regional floristics. These works, however, do not treat the entire genus or entire subgenera or sections. References to such articles we cite will be found under our treatment of the individual species.

Some may wonder why we give nomenclatural synonymy in a book that is not a taxonomic revision. We have done so because of the great interest in trilliums to gardeners and horticulturists, and because of the vast amount of confusion over which names represent accepted species and which are synonyms of other species. For the pedicellate trilliums we follow Barksdale (1938) and Samejima and Samejima (1962, 1987); for the sessile trilliums, Freeman (1975).

The distribution maps have been generalized from a variety of regional floras, taxonomic works, and data on herbarium sheets.

Acknowledgments

F OR MUCH advice, assistance in preparation, and reading of the manuscript, we thank Drs. John Freudenstein, Rob Naczi, and A. A. Reznicek. We thank Dr. William Anderson, director of the University of Michigan Herbarium, for use of the facility and its library, and Dr. Robert Kral, of Vanderbilt University Herbarium, for use of that facility and much help while we were there.

We thank Dr. James Wells, botanist and curator of the Cranbrook Institute of Science Herbarium for help, advice, and use of the herbarium. Dr. Victor Soukup gave much helpful aid and information on trillium localities, particularly the Asiatic, western and Gulf states species. Dr. Soukup also generously supplied us with photographs of the Asiatic species and of color forms of some of the American species.

Harry Elkins helped us immensely with reference material and in checking references for us at the University of Michigan Library.

Tom Wiese, endangered species coordinator, Michigan Department of Natural Resources, provided us with the latest information on trilliums protected under the U.S. Endangered Species Act. We thank him for his generous help.

For guidance to certain trillium localities or other assistance and companionship in the field, we thank James Briggs, Lydia and G. L. Burrows III, George L. Burrows IV, David Case, Mike Champagne, Betty Cliff, Hugh and Ruth Cocker, J. Cobb Colley, Nancy Cota, P. A. Davies, Marvin Dembinsky, Honorable Tom Drake, Harry and Irene Elkins, Harold Epstein, Mrs. Fitzinger, Dr. and Mrs. Karl Flinck, Jerry John

Flintoff, Dr. John Freeman, Candido Gonzales, Darcy Gunnlaughson, Phyllis Gustafson, Don Henson, Hal and Helen Horwitz, Lehman Kapp, Irene Kleekamp, John Lambert, Dr. Richard Lighty, David Littell, Sam and Coni Maisano, D. D. Martin, Dr. and Mrs. James McClements, Max Medley, Mr. and Mrs. B. Ralph Mims, Mr. and Mrs. C. F. Moore, Tom Morgan, Mrs. Murphy, Ken and Ann Nitschke, Wayne Roderick, Janet Schultz, Al and Shirley Smith, Molly O. Smith, Louise (Weesie) Smith, Vic and Shirley Soukup, William and Mary Spiers, Mike and Polly Stone, Rob Sutter, Dan Thayer, H. S. Veltman, Dr. E. G. Voss, Dr. W. H. Wagner, Jr., Kimiko and Richard Williams (who translated the Japanese names for us), Brian Winchell, Roy and Margaret Winchell, Fred Young, and Martin Zucker.

We have pursued trilliums over many years. We thank all those whose kindness, generosity, enthusiasm, and companionship have made our experiences so rich and enjoyable. If we have omitted thanks to anyone who has helped us, it is an error of our memory and not our intent.

PART I

Introduction to Trilliums

N ATIVE TO North America and Asia, trilliums hold a special place in the hearts of naturalists, botanists, horticulturists, and outdoorsmen and outdoorswomen worldwide. Interest in these plants is manifested in their native lands by the numbers of individuals who seek them in the wild or grow them. In Europe, where trilliums are not native, enthusiasm for this fascinating genus is so great that rare species and forms sell for fantastic prices. There have even been cases of extensive theft of trilliums from the great European botanical gardens.

In Canada, the province of Ontario has named great white trillium (*Trillium grandiflorum*) its provincial flower.

On 7 June 1979, the United States Postal Service issued a series of postage stamps illustrating rare and endangered plant species. One stamp featured persistent trillium (*Trillium persistens*), an extremely local and endangered species. In 1992, the U.S. Postal Service issued a 50-stamp wildflower series. One stamp featured great white trillium (*T. grandiflorum*).

In Japan, interest in trilliums runs so high that an almost cultlike devotion to the study of these plants exists. Publications and extensive collections of forms abound.

In the United States, particularly in the Northeast and in the region of the Great Smoky Mountain National Park, most rural people know and love trilliums as the showiest of our spring woodland flowers. Thousands flock there on springtime wildflower pilgrimages to see them. Wildflower lovers and gardeners grow and enjoy these native plants. Numerous restaurants, meeting rooms, resorts, even private businesses take the name "Trillium." Conservationists seek to protect them (whether they need protection or not) with a sentimental fervor.

So great is the interest in trilliums that extensive research programs exist both in the United States and abroad to learn to propagate these plants by seed and by tissue culture methods so that they can be commercially grown for profit without impinging upon wild populations.

History and General Nature of Trilliums

Swedish botanist Carl Linnaeus in 1753 established the genus *Trillium* based upon three American species, *T. cernuum, T. erectum,* and *T. sessile*. Linnaeus apparently confused two species in his description of *T. cernuum* when he gave the type locality as "Carolina"; his plant was probably not *T. cernuum,* but rather *T. catesbaei,* for the type specimen designated today as *T. cernuum* Linnaeus is of a plant that does not grow as far south as Carolina, and its collector, Peter Kalm, never visited that region (Barksdale 1938). *Trillium cernuum* remains imperfectly understood today in spite of its vast northern range; even recent publications have attributed it to regions far south of its actual range. Because trillium structure is simple, with structural differences between taxa limited, various species collected since Linnaeus' time have been confused, misnamed, or their ranges misstated.

Traditionally most botanists have placed trilliums in the lily family, Liliaceae. Unlike lilies, the sepals and petals of trilliums are not similar in color and texture, and trilliums have net-veined leaves, while most monocots have parallel-veined leaves. For these and other technical reasons, many modern botanists place trilliums and their close relatives in a separate family, Trilliaceae. New techniques of genetic pattern analysis, especially those revealed by chloroplast DNA, suggest a relationship closer to *Amianthum* (fly-poison), *Chamaelirion* (fairy-wand), *Heloniopsis, Xerophyllum* (beargrass or turkey beard), and *Zygadenus* (death camass) than to lilies as such (Chase et al. 1995).

Relatives of Trilliums

Worldwide the genus *Trillium* has only a few recognized close relatives. Traditionally, the genera *Paris* and *Trillidium* have been considered close to *Trillium*. The genus *Paris*, native in Europe and Asia, contains several species. Vegetative growth resembles that of *Cornus canadensis* (dwarf cornel, Canada dogwood), with usually four or more leaves arranged in a whorl on a short stem. The flowers, borne much as in *Trillium* but with very narrow floral segments, are greenish and relatively inconspicuous. In Asia, the genus *Trillidium*, not recognized by all botanists, has leaves that look like *Trillium* leaves, but the flowers more closely resemble those of *Paris*. *Trillidium* differs from *Trillium* also in other significant ways. Haga and Watanabe (1966) reported *Trillidium* to contain two different genomes not found in *Trillium*. Furthermore, the pollen type and exine structure of *Trillidium* differ from that of *Trillium* (Takahashi 1983). In 1935 Tatewaki and Suto established a new genus, *Kinugasa*, based upon the structure of the plant previously called *Trillidium japonicum*. As early as 1838, Rafinesque-Schmaltz proposed the genus *Daiswa* and placed *Paris polyphylla* Smith in it. Until recently, it remained unrecognized by other botanists. A revision of *Daiswa* by Takhtajan in 1983 recognized 15 species.

In North America are found two genera that were in the past considered to be *Trillium* relatives. On the West Coast grows *Scoliopus*. The members of this genus have strange, soft leaves somewhat similar in growth habit to those of *Clintonia*, and bearing from the center of the leaf cluster, several small, yet striking green, white, and maroon flowers. The bizarre flowers produce a powerful stench to attract carrion-feeding pollinators.

In the eastern United States, usually in rich acid soils in deep shade, occurs the genus *Medeola*, with one species, *M. virginica*. A whorl of lanceolate leaves, clothed in soft short hairs tops a 30-cm-tall stem. The flowers, borne on a short scape above the leaves and often topped by a secondary cluster of leafy bracts, are yellowish-green and inconspicuous. Chloroplast DNA analyses and other studies suggest that *Medeola*, traditionally regarded as close to *Trillium*, may not be so at all and may be closely related to the genus *Polygonatum* or may belong in its own family, Medeolaceae.

Most botanists who recognize a separate family, Trilliaceae, agree that it contains at least five genera: *Daiswa*, *Kinugasa*, *Paris*, *Scoliopus*, and *Trillium*. Many modern botanists (including us) also recognize the genus *Trillidium*, which Hara et al. (1978) retained instead of the genus *Trillium* for the plant previously often treated as *Trillium govanianum*.

Taxonomic decisions on the relationships between *Trillium* and other genera lie beyond the scope and intent of this book. Here we will consider only North American and Asiatic trilliums.

Number and Provenance of Trilliums

Eastern Asia contains approximately five or six *Trillium* species (Samejima and Samejima 1987), western North America about seven, and eastern North America thirty-five (Freeman 1975). No species occurs in both North America and Asia, and none occurs both in eastern and western North America. One Asiatic species, *T. camschatcense,* the only Asiatic diploid (2n = 10), closely resembles the eastern American *T. flexipes*. All the American species are diploids (2n = 10).

There is not, and never has been, agreement among botanists about how many species of *Trillium* exist. This situation arises because trilliums possess few structural features that vary sufficiently among taxa to aid in clearly delineating species. Unfortunately, pressing the plants for herbarium specimens tends to destroy or obscure some of the differences of carriage, color, and shape that do exist. To make matters of identification worse, *T. erectum* and many of the sessile trilliums encompass a diversity of color forms or mutations. Yellowish, green, or bicolored forms appear in virtually every red-, maroon-brown-, or purplish-flowered sessile species in America. Add to this the past confusion resulting from the difficulty of communication and information exchange between early American plant explorers, and between field workers and Old World botanists and institutions; simultaneous duplications of discoveries; assignment of different names by two or more botanists to the same plant; and relegation of long-used names to synonymy, resulting in the change of a well-known scientific name, and you get a botanical nightmare of misapplied names, synonyms, confusion of ranges, and incorrect information. As a consequence, many of the older published papers contain much erroneous information.

Frequently a taxon with a widespread distribution varies continually across that range. Some botanists might choose to lump all the variations together into one variable species: others, just as strongly convinced, might split that same taxon into two or more species, subspecies, or varieties. Neither group is right or wrong; it is a matter of opinion that time and experience tends eventually to sort out. In the meantime, different individual botanists and horticulturists may choose to follow one or the other school of thought, each using a different set of names for the same plant, which utterly confuses the botanically uninformed amateur field naturalists and horticultural enthusiasts. These people frequently do not understand the problems of nomenclatural priority and the resultant synonymy. Popular publications and gardening columns are filled with complaints about name changes and why they should not have been made. Of course, the botanists are correct in their rules, but for those who do not know the reasons behind them, the system of priority engenders much confusion. One devout *Trillium* collector we know spent years trying to obtain plants of what he believed were very rare species; all were synonyms of plants already in his collection.

Pedicellate and Sessile Trilliums

All *Trillium* species consist of temperate-forest herbs that occur in the Northern Hemisphere. Taxonomists divide the genus into two sharply distinctive subgenera: subgenus *Trillium*, the pedicellate trilliums, and subgenus *Phyllantherum*, the sessile trilliums. More technical taxonomic descriptions of these appear in Part II of this book.

The pedicellate trilliums occur both in Asia and North America, while the sessile trilliums occur only in North America. Because pedicellate trilliums occur on both continents, because other *Trillium* relatives possess pedicels, and because one pedicellate taxon of eastern North America has populations with pedicellate, near sessile, and sessile flowers, botanists consider the pedicellate trilliums the more primitive type, with the sessile trilliums derived from them (Berg 1958, Freeman 1975).

The pedicellate trilliums, in our opinion, present more taxonomic and identification difficulties than do the sessiles. Because more of their ranges overlap, certain species hybridize and backcross to an extent that makes some specimens impossible to identify as to species. Failure of early *Trillium* specialists to recognize the frequency of hybridization between certain of the pedicellate species has further confused attempts to sort out this complicated group. That the North American pedicellate trilliums have been a headache is reflected in the number of uncompleted research projects extant and in the absence of a recently published taxonomic revision.

The sessile trilliums occur only in North America and grow on both the West Coast and in the eastern United States. Most species occur in the Central Lowlands, the southern Piedmont, and in the Mississippi basin. Freeman (1975) seems to have sorted out the various taxonomic problems of the sessile species. He delineated a number of "species," which he admits may, in the opinion of some, be recognized at some other taxonomic rank, but which have unique structural characteristics associated with a distinctive geographic region.

Before examining more closely the taxonomic divisions and species of these fascinating plants, let us look briefly at the general structure of the plant.

Structure of Trilliums

The Vegetative Plant

*I*N A TYPICAL plant the rootstock forms a clearly separate organ, branching into the ground. The stem is erect, deploying leaves and flowering branches along a vertical axis. Flowers arise either terminally or on separate, specialized flowering branches (peduncle or pedicels) along the axis. On or along such a peduncle may occur leaflike appendages that subtend each pedicel or flower. Botanists term these leaflike structures *bracts*. True leaves occur on stem or shoot, but not on the pedicels. With respect to internal structure, bracts and leaves show little structural difference.

In *Trillium* the adult plant arises from a subterranean or surface-creeping, horizontal stem termed the *rhizome* (Figure 1). The rhizome produces no true leaves. The axis consists of a terminal bud, compressed nodes, and internodes covered by sheathing, scalelike, papery-modified leaves, the *cataphylls*. In the axil of these scales, at the nodes, lie dormant buds that may, either naturally or if the terminal bud is injured, produce new flowering shoots. In mature rhizomes the end opposite the growing point appears bitten off (termed *praemorse*) through the decay of the oldest portion. Rhizomes in some species (for example, *T. albidum*) can be very compact, nearly erect, almost bulblike with internodes congested; in other species (for example, *T. lancifolium, T. recurvatum*) rhizomes are horizontal, thin, brittle, and elongated. While not reported to be mycorrhizal, attempts at tissue culture utilizing tissue from mature *Trillium* rhizomes have proved nearly impossible because soil fungi freely penetrate and contaminate the rhizome tissue. In the in-vitro cul-

Figure 1. A generalized pedicellate trillium plant. A, flower; B, pedicel; C, leaf or bract petiole; D, leaf or bract blade; E, stem or scape; F, developing offset rhizome and bud, a form of vegetative propagation; G, adventitious roots (feeders of current year); H, cataphyll, a dry, scalelike modified leaf; I, rhizome.

ture environment, these fungi grow much faster than the plant tissue, overwhelming and destroying it.

Except in the germinating seedling, the trilliums have no typical root system. Instead, the rhizome produces adventitious roots along its axis. New roots arise yearly along the section of rhizome at and just behind the terminal bud. Older roots along the rhizome gradually cease to function and decay.

What appears above the ground is technically not the plant's stem, but rather a flowering branch, the peduncle, with bracts subtending the flower. For this reason, plant anatomists and some recent authors refer to trillium "leaves" as bracts. Given that the reader understands this technicality, and since there is little structural difference between a leaf and a bract, and because this book is intended for a general as well as botanical readership, we shall use the term *leaf* in this book.

The mature, flowering-sized trillium plant produces three leaves at the summit of the peduncle. Young plants and weak older plants may produce one, two, or three leaves.

Flower Structure

In subgenus *Trillium* (the pedicellate trilliums), plants bear the flower on a short 1- to 6-cm-tall (as short as 0.1 in one variety) extension of the scape, the peduncle, or pedicel (most writers use the term *pedicel* to refer to the part above the point of attachment of the leaves). Additionally, flower segments spread widely (ringent, gaping), giving a flat showy display to the flower parts. The stamens and ovary are clearly displayed.

In subgenus *Phyllantherum* there is no extension of the peduncle above the bracts, with the flowers developing directly upon the point of juncture of the three bracts. The scientific term for a structure attached without a stalk is *sessile,* hence the common name "sessile trilliums" for this group. In the sessile trilliums, the petals of all but one or two species stand erect, somewhat clustered (touching each other) more or less pyramid-like in the center of the flower, overtopping and somewhat obscuring the anthers and stigmas. An exception is *Trillium stamineum,* in which the spiralled petals spread widely, fully exposing stamens much larger than the typical stamens.

Types of odor, coupled with flower color and positioning of the floral organs, suggest that pedicellate trilliums rely heavily on bees and flying insects for pollination, while the clustered petals and fetid or putrid odors of sessile trilliums suggest pollination by beetles, crawling insects, carrion flies, and such.

In *Trillium* the floral envelope consists of three leaf-textured sepals and three colored, fleshy to membranaceous petals (Figure 2). The sepals, in bud, cover and protect the other floral organs until anthesis (the opening of the flower). In most species the sepals spread widely at anthesis, but in *T. recurvatum*, they reflex strongly downward against the scape. After the flower opens, the sepals perform no known special function beyond photosynthesis.

Trillium petals serve by color and in conjunction with floral odors to attract pollinating insects. The petals and sepals serve, in some species, as a landing platform for that pollinator.

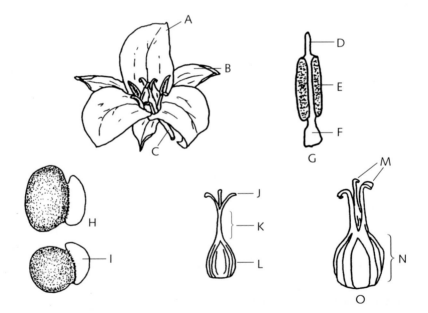

Figure 2. External flower parts and seed structure of a trillium plant. A, petal; B, sepal with folded, sulcate tip; C, pedicel; D, anther connective showing connective prolonged beyond anther sac; E, anther sac containing pollen; F, filament; G, stamen (entire structure, composed of anther and filament); H, seed; I, elaiosome; J, stigmas; K, style (formed by the united stigmas); L, ovary; M, separate stigmas; N, ovary, formed from three united carpels; O, pistil (entire structure).

Inside the ring of petals, trilliums produce six stamens, each composed of a two-chambered anther and a filament of varying length. In many species, the filament is somewhat broadened below the anther chambers (cells). The tissue between the anther cells, termed the *anther-connective,* may end at the tip of the anther cells, or extend beyond the two chambers of the anther into a short connective horn. Pollen in *Trillium* is usually yellow, whitish, or grayish-purple.

Three carpels fused into a three-chambered, three- or six-angled ovary, with three linear to subulate, separate or basally fused stigmas comprise the pistil (Fernald 1950, Freeman 1975).

Fruit

The ripened fruit consists of a fleshy outer layer, often strongly ridged or angled, containing a number of specialized seeds in each chamber (locule). *Trillium* fruit details vary from species to species, but two fundamentally different forms occur (Berg 1958). In one, most frequent among the pedicellate species, the fruit is succulent, fleshy, often reddish or purple when ripe, berrylike, and with a fruity fragrance. In the other form, the fruit is mealy, nonjuicy, and usually greenish or yellowish-white when ripe. In such species, there is little noticeable fragrance to the fruit. Such fruits frequently are much smaller than their fleshy berry counterparts, and some tend to split open weakly along the suture lines of the fused carpels. Such a fruit is capsulelike, and Berg (1958) called it such. Freeman (1975, 1995) referred to the fruit as a "berrylike capsule." Authors of most floras refer to the fruits as berries or simply as fruits.

In most species, regardless of the fruit type, the seed is dispersed not by a splitting open of the fruit along the carpel sutures, but by abscission of the tissue of the receptacle at the base of the fruit, which upon ripening rapidly becomes pulpy and weak. As the cells swell with turgor, they rupture, shedding the entire fruit. Ripening of the fruit to the shedding stage proceeds very rapidly; only a few hours elapse from firm attachment to dropping of the fruit. Escape of the seeds from the shed fruit may depend upon a chance rupture of its tissue at any point, or the deteriorated basal abscission area may simply deteriorate, the seeds falling free in clusters, of their own weight, as from a bag or sack.

Seeds

Each seed is ellipsoidal, about 2 × 4 mm, slightly curved and concave ventrally. On its concave side, a mature seed bears an appendage. This fleshy appendage, extending in all directions from its attachment, over-arches and covers about half of the seed and is equal in volume to the seed itself (Berg 1958). Berg referred to the appendage (see Figure 2), as a strophiole (sensu Sernander 1906), but more recent authors refer to it as the elaiosome. The elaiosome is fleshy, somewhat fatty or oily in tex-ture, and usually creamy white, while the ripe seed coat is firm and in various shades of brown. Internally, cells of the elaiosome are rich in oil (Berg 1958).

Seeds of trilliums are myrmecochorous, that is, attracting and being dispersed by ants. It is the elaiosome that attracts the ants. Indeed, from the reports of various researchers, the elaiosomes contain a chemical at-tractant so effective that ants become frenzied in their efforts to get at and feed upon the elaiosome tissue. Frequently, the ants cannot wait for the fruits to ripen, but cut holes into the side of the berry and extract the seeds before the fruits ripen and fall naturally. Ants eat the elaiosomes but discard the seeds, often leaving caches of discarded seeds in their tunnels where they later germinate en masse. For an interesting per-spective on myrmecochory in *Trillium*, see the discussion by Berg (1958) and that of Nesom and La Duke (1985) on seeds of *T. nivale*.

Biology of Trilliums

Pollination

WE HAVE SEEN little published information on pollinators of trilliums. Although we grow all American species in our gardens, and all set seed generously here, we have seldom seen pollinators on the flowers, except those of *Trillium nivale*. Both in the garden and in the wild, on bright sunny warm days, *T. nivale* produces a fairly strong sweet fragrance reminiscent of that of bird's-eye primrose, *Primula mistassinica* (Case 1982). At this time, the flowers are eagerly visited by small native bees and the honeybee (*Apis mellifera*). Nesom and La Duke (1985) captured honeybees on *T. nivale* at an Ohio site and found them "loaded with *Trillium* pollen." They did not, however, find direct evidence that those bees pollinated the blooms. They also observed small flies (*Phoridae*) visiting some *T. nivale* flowers.

In April 1996, in northern Alabama, we observed bumblebees and several species of swallow-tail butterflies visiting the fragrant flowers of a form of *Trillium flexipes*. While visitation was frequent and enthusiastic, we did not determine if these insects actually carried the pollen so as to effect pollination.

Particularly on those species that produce fetid or putrid odors purported to attract carrion fly and beetle pollinators (*Trillium erectum, T. foetidissimum, T. stamineum*), we have seldom observed any insects visiting the bloom. Roberta Case, in her hybridization efforts, has found that she cannot obtain pollen in almost all species except from first-day blooms, indicating that the pollen had either been shed or collected by insects. Only *T. grandiflorum* produces copious yellow pollen that may be present for a day or two.

Seed Germination

Trillium seedlings do not appear above ground until the second spring following dispersal. Many authors, including us, have assumed a type of "double dormancy" (Barton 1944). Dormancy in seeds is defined as a physiological resting period that requires some stimulus, often from the environment, to stimulate the seed into renewed growth. Seed dormancy, found mostly in species that grow in areas with strongly differing seasonal climates, prevents the seed from germinating at unfavorable times for survival (Wilkins 1984).

Double dormancy is the germination requirement of a seed for exposure to a period of mild temperatures, followed by cold and then a warming that breaks the dormancy of the seedling and causes the radicle to emerge from the seed and form a rhizome. After this, the seedling exists upon stored seed endosperm without further growth until another period of slowly falling temperatures and a cold period followed by warming again instigates growth, in this case, the emergence of the cotyledon and appearance of the baby plant above ground.

Although Goodspeed and Brandt (1916), Martin (1935), Barton (1944), Samejima and Samejima (1962), and Nesom and La Duke (1985) have reported seed dormancy in both pedicellate and sessile trilliums, published experimental documentation of the germination phenomena is surprisingly skimpy. Deno (1991) called the germination typically epigeal and stated, "This genus is notorious for extended and difficult germination." According to Deno, germination involves two steps. First, the radicle emerges to form a small corm and root the spring following the maturation of the seed. Then, after a cool period and storage of the seed at higher temperatures (70°F/21°C), the cotyledon emerges.

Hanzawa and Kalisz (1993) summarized the findings of Patrick (1973) and Kalisz and Hanzawa (unpublished) as follows:

> The seeds germinate in the spring. The seedling develops primary and adventitious roots during the first growing season, but the cotyledon does not expand and become photosynthetic until the second growing season. In the third season, *Trillium grandiflorum* produces a single true leaf.

Stephanie Solt (pers. comm. 1995), a graduate student at the University of Vermont, found that *Trillium grandiflorum* seed required a minimum of 83 days of cold (41°F/5°C) for 75-percent germination and cotyledon emergence. She further found that 100 percent of the germinated seed had produced an immature cotyledon 14 weeks after germination with or without light. From that point further growth depends upon additional vernalization (a period of cold) to break dormancy and stimulate the next stage of growth. Remarkably, Solt found that "if you harvest the seed just before they turn brown in the berry, they will germinate with no cold period." Similar results have been obtained with green, immature seed for a large number of northern terrestrial orchids and other plants which, when mature, require a cold stratification to break the seed dormancy, but will germinate rapidly without stratification from immature seed.

Several authors, including Deno (1991), maintain that *Trillium* seeds stored dry for any amount of time either fail to germinate or give a very low percentage of germination. This appears to be generally true for most species. However, we purchased seed of *T. rivale* from a collector in the United Kingdom, who had stored the seed dry for about six months prior to our purchase. The packet was further mislaid on our desk for nearly a year. When planted, the seed germinated profusely after the usual cold period. *Trillium rivale* grows in a region that is seasonally quite arid and, like many arid-soil plants, may have adapted to a different germination regimen. We have seen some evidence that seed of *T. nivale* may also tolerate dry storage, at least for a brief period.

In light of the horticultural demand for trilliums, the rather serious conservation problems involved with obtaining rare species, and the difficulty of propagating trilliums by tissue culture, manipulation of the seed germination and seedling development process offers, at present, the best promise for the production of large numbers of plants quickly.

Seedling Growth and Maturation

Once the seed has germinated, trillium plants produce only one shoot per season, at least while immature. The one-leaf stage continues to appear for two to four or more years, but under good growing conditions, the plant and leaf will increase in size and surface area each year. When a certain critical size and rhizome volume have been attained, the nonflowering seedling produces three leaves and continues to accrue stored food energy. A season or two later it will commence flowering. Older, vigorous plants, in many species, may produce two or rarely three flowering shoots from a single terminal growth. Exactly how many years the process of maturation to first flowering requires seems to depend more upon leaf area and rhizome volume (accumulated food?) than chronological age (Hanzawa and Kalisz 1993).

Several authors have attempted to estimate the age at which trilliums first flower using a variety of methods. Some observers counted the number of rhizome segments (nodes) (Martin 1935), others counted sheath scars or used estimates based upon number of leaves, and still others measured biomass in the rhizome. Estimates based on such data (for example, Hanzawa and Kalisz 1993), we believe, yield too long a time before most plants reach flowering age.

Based on scientific observations, gardening experience, or conservation zeal, various authors have suggested that trilliums require 10 to 20 years to achieve flowering size. Fully mature flowering size is achieved, in nature, after only four or five years of growth, depending upon available light and nutrients at the site (Deno 1991). Nesom and La Duke (1985) estimated commencement of flowering at four years for *Trillium nivale*. This corresponds well with our observations of seedlings of *T. nivale* in our gardens.

Dr. Richard Lighty, director of the Mt. Cuba Center for the Study of Piedmont Flora, Greenville, Delaware, and his staff grew *Trillium grandiflorum* from seed in "a frame under natural conditions." The soil was quite heavy and rich. Lighty (pers. comm.) reported the following results:

> We planted approximately 10,000 freshly collected and cleaned seed, 20 of which germinated the spring following sowing. The following spring approximately 2,000 seeds germinated. Three years later, we had 14 plants bloom. We don't know if these were from the 20 plants which had germinated precociously (which would make them four years old), or if some of them had been growing for only three years. At any rate, we were delighted to think that *Trillium* might be produced from seed to blooming plant in five to six years.

We have grown many species to flowering from seed in five to seven years in our experimental beds, and others appear regularly on our lawns and in flower beds that did not exist 10 years previously.

There is a wide disparity in age at flowering of siblings from a single berry. Soil fertility, available light, seasonal moisture, and whether or not the leaves of the young plant persist without damage the entire season appear to be more important than chronological age per se. Perhaps under difficult competition in the wild, maturation takes 15 or more years, but under conditions of good growth and rich soil, most species mature much earlier. Because trilliums are perennial plants, they can, in theory, live indefinitely. The age of a given rhizome is not determinable, however, because the older portions of the rhizome decay.

Disease, herbivores, and successional change are the natural enemies of wild trilliums. Today, the bulldozer used for massive development of subdivisions, shopping centers, and highways far outstrips digging or picking by collectors in destroying both plants and available habitat.

Growth Bud Dormancy

Like the seed, the bud tissue of trillium possesses dormancy. Buds cannot commence growth unless they have been subjected to a period of cold, near but not necessarily at, the freezing point for an extended period of time (Solt, pers. comm. 1994, Barton 1944). Even so, dormancy is more complex for trilliums than for most other plants.

In many plants, even those with bud dormancy, once growth commences for the season and the terminal buds of each shoot have started to develop, bud growth along the stems is inhibited by the diffusion of hormones away from the terminal bud meristem tissue. Growth of each branch therefore is more or less in a straight line. If the terminal bud or buds are removed, the source of the inhibiting hormone is removed and lateral buds develop, resulting in much branching that season. Branching is dependent upon the presence or absence of the terminal bud and its hormones.

In *Trillium*, branching is more complicated. Once a terminal bud commences growth, all other buds along the rhizome, dormant or new that season, become dormant. We do not know at present the mechanism that initiates this dormancy. Removing the terminal bud on the rhizome changes the hormone balance, resulting in the formation of some or many small bulblike rhizome branches with enlarged buds (see Figure 3). Unlike other plants in which the terminal buds are removed, *Trillium* rhizome buds remain dormant and cannot commence growth until subjected to a period of cold between 33 and 68°F (1 and 20°C) (Wilkins 1984, Solt, pers. comm. 1995). This fact has given rise to the very widely quoted, although incorrect, statement that "picking a trillium will kill it." After picking, no new shoot appears that season, but a new scape will appear next season.

We have seen no research dealing directly with how long a cold period is necessary to break the bud dormancy in trilliums older than germinating seedlings. Solt (pers. comm. 1995) found that 83 days of cold temperature were necessary to initiate first germination in the doubly dormant seed. It seems likely, though, that the necessary cold period will be similar in length to the time required to break the first dormancy of the germinating seedling. Similar dormancy in some other plant seeds or shoots can be broken by application of gibberellins (Wilkins 1984, Solomon and Berg 1995). In some plants, including asparagus, foliar sprayings with the cytokinin benzyladenine released bud inhibition and resulted in axillary shoot development without disbudding the growing point on the rhizome (Mahotiere et al. 1993). Whether or not rhizome buds of trilliums will respond to such treatments we do not know. Given

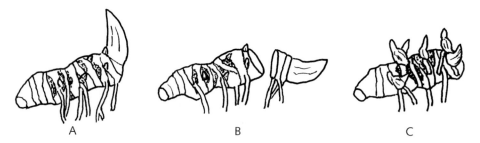

Figure 3. A trillium rhizome, showing a means of vegetative propagation. A, basic rhizome, showing the large terminal bud (with primordia of coming season's stem, leaves, and flowers) and the smaller dormant buds along the rhizome; B, rhizome with terminal bud and a very short piece of rhizome cut and removed to be planted separately (the back section of the cut rhizome is treated with fungicide and planted); C, the same rhizome at the end of the season or following spring after cutting, showing development of several small offsets from the previously undeveloped rhizome buds.

the problems with tissue culturing rhizomes of trilliums, propagation by inducing the growth of lateral rhizome buds may be the necessary technique to multiply choice clones. Use of gibberellins or cytokinins to remove the dormancy and therefore speed the cloning process would be the ideal approach.

In some but not all seasons, our potted *Trillium albidum*, *T. angustipetalum*, and *T. chloropetalum* plants send up small lateral shoots without a period of cold, *if* the pots have been subjected to severe drying for some time and were then well watered. These species, which occur in a very mild and seasonally dry region of California, like some other species of mild regions (Wilkins 1984), may respond to drought as strongly as to temperature. For practical purposes, ordinary temperate-zone winter temperatures break the bud dormancy for trilliums in the garden or in the wild.

Mutations and Abnormalities

Few genera produce as many "abnormal or mutant" forms as *Trillium*. Anomalies appear in almost all species, but are most frequently reported in *T. grandiflorum*. Let us look at these in detail.

Unusual variants, forms, or mutants of *Trillium grandiflorum* have been described many times in the literature. Most of these variants have appeared in New York, Michigan, and Quebec, but have been reported elsewhere also. They consist of plants with green stripes or other markings upon the petals, often accompanied by abnormally petiolate leaves, extra whorls of leaves, or no leaves at all. Other variants include all green petals (see Plate 2, Fernald 1950, Stoutamire 1958, Hall 1961, Pringle 1967, Hooper et al. 1971), no petals at all, knots of sepals, or tufts of petal-like leaves. We have even seen plants with green-striped petals and with abnormal leaves that sprouted miniature petals from the distal ends of several stamens.

Some of these peculiar forms seem to be stable and reappear with slight variations for several to many years. Others, however, become more and more fantastically deformed each year, have their leaves turn deep burgundy and go dormant early, and gradually deteriorate and die over a period of a few years. At a state game area in southeastern Michigan, we observed large colonies of *Trillium grandiflorum* and smaller

Plate 2. Mycoplasma-infected flowers of *Trillium grandiflorum* from the wild, showing some but by no means all the various forms infected plants take. Photo by Fred Case.

colonies of *T. erectum* for more than 20 years. After the petal-greening condition appeared in a large colony, it seemed to spread rapidly for a few years until a large portion of the plants carried the condition. In ensuing years, several large colonies of the infected plants declined in size and health, and eventually disappeared. Clearly, the condition seemed to be pathological.

To determine if, indeed, a pathogen caused the strange greening condition, Hooper et al. (1971) collected and prepared tissue samples from normal white and deformed green plants for examination under the electron microscope. In every case where greening or structural abnormality was present, they found in the conducting tissues of the trilliums strange ultra-microscopic membrane surrounded organisms termed *mycoplasmas*. No such organisms were found in the tissues of normal plants without petal greening or deformity.

Mycoplasmas are subcellular organisms midway in size between viruses and bacteria. Scientists find mycoplasmas to be ultimate parasites that cannot exist independently of a living host. In some as yet poorly understood manner, they induce in their host plant mutation-like changes as described above. They cause tissue-greening, lumping and distortion of petal tissue, such as occurs in parrot tulips, and cause aster-yellows disease of certain plants. In some mycoplasma-infected plant groups, such as carnations and citrus trees, the infected host has been cleared of these organisms through the use of certain antibiotics or with heat treatments. How mycoplasmas get from trillium to trillium is not proved, but we suspect that they may be vectored by leafhoppers or some other sucking insect. We have found mycoplasma-infected plants of *Trillium undulatum* and *T. erectum* in woods where *T. grandiflorum* is extensively infected.

Some infected *Trillium grandiflorum* plants can be very attractive, and many uninformed gardeners desire them or collect them. At times such plants have actually sold for high prices to collectors. This is a bad situation in all respects, for the plants themselves will usually decline, but until then become a potential source of infection for other trilliums and perhaps other plant species in the garden. They should not be grown.

In west-central Upper Michigan, in deciduous forests on limestone soils there occurs, with normal *Trillium grandiflorum,* a very dwarf form. This plant, first brought to our attention by botanist/artist Don Henson, was also described and written up in an Escanaba, Michigan, newspaper article as a possible new species. Careful examination of the plant, however, reveals that the condition is also pathological. Although dwarfed without distortion of leaves and petals, the ovaries are elongated, often completely without ovules, and the stamens have little or no pollen. Plants seldom mature any seed. Usually a large rhizome that has partially rotted and diminished in size will be found near the growing end from which the dwarfed flowering stem sprouts. The nature of the pathogen causing this dwarfing of *T. grandiflorum* has not yet been discovered, nor have we seen this condition except on limestone soils.

In almost any large population of *Trillium grandiflorum*, one can find individual plants with two or four leaves and/or petals. Such anomalies, we suspect, result from developmental errors induced perhaps as the result of mechanical injury to the bud meristem tissue for that season.

If collected and maintained, most of these forms, not being genetic changes, revert the following season to a normal plant.

Double forms, that is, plants in which all the reproductive organs have mutated to petals, occur with some frequency in *Trillium grandiflorum* (Plates 3, 4), but have been reported only rarely for most other species. Such forms possess great beauty, and gardeners and collectors seek them out with fervor. Most double forms are sterile and must be propagated by slow, asexual division. Thus, if available at all, they command very high prices. Further discussion of double forms in *T. grandiflorum* occurs under that species treatment.

Plate 3. Hose-in-hose (stacked petal) mutation of *Trillium grandiflorum* found wild in Michigan. This is an unusual and outstanding form but a slow grower. Photo by Fred Case.

Plate 4. Outstanding double *Trillium grandiflorum* mutation known unofficially as "Smith's double." This is the form most frequent in cultivation. Photo by Fred Case.

Natural Hybrids

Some *Trillium* species hybridize with others, while some do not. As a general rule, trilliums appear to crossbreed with each other, in nature or in the garden, only within closely related groups.

Among Asiatic species, hybridization has been well documented between several of the Japanese species, with three named hybrids, *Trillium* ×*hagae* (*T. camschatcense* × *T. tschonoskii*) (see also *T. channellii*), *T.* ×*miyabeanum* (*T. apetalon* × *T. tschonoskii*), and *T.* ×*yezoense* (*T. apetalon* × *T. camschatcense*). Samejima and Samejima (1987) also cited cytological evidence that *T. smallii* arose as an allopolyploid hybrid between *T. apetalon* and an unknown (perhaps extinct) diploid species.

Haga and Channell (1982) crossed the Asiatic *Trillium camschatcense* (2n = 10) with various pedicellate and sessile American species (2n = 10). Only members of the *T. erectum* group produced plump, apparently viable seed. Haga and Channel raised a few seedlings of the cross *T. camschatcense* × *T. erectum* to flowering. Crosses outside the *T. erectum* group produced watery, undeveloped seed, with either pedicellate or sessile species.

In North America, where all *Trillium* species have the same chromosome number (2n = 10), one might expect all species to be interfertile and to cross easily. This is not true. Literature reference to *Trillium* hybridization among the American species in nature is rare (Peattie 1927, Barksdale 1938, Case and Burrows 1962, Case and Case 1993). We have found almost no experimentally documented information on crosses between members of other American *Trillium* groups in the wild or in the garden.

In spite of the lack of published information, our field and garden experience leads us to believe that sympatric *Trillium* species of the *T. erectum* group hybridize regularly. We have observed hybrids between *T. erectum* and *T. cernuum* in Michigan's northern peninsula and between *T. erectum* and *T. flexipes* in southeastern Michigan, southern Ohio, and Kentucky. In Tennessee and North Carolina we have found mixed populations of *T. sulcatum* and *T. flexipes,* and *T. vaseyi* and *T. rugelii,* with many intermediate and distinctively marked plants present. The color patterns and structural features exactly paralleled the patterns of hand-pollinated crosses we obtained in our garden plots. We consider our finds to be hybrid swarms between the various species. It is in the *T. erectum* group that most of the confusing species and difficult-to-identify *Trillium* populations occur. It is our view that most of the confusion is due to the frequency of hybridization in the wild.

In California, we have observed putative hybrids between *Trillium chloropetalum* var. *giganteum* and *T. albidum.*

In our garden we have cross-pollinated *Trillium nivale* with the distantly related *T. undulatum,* a cross unlikely to be found in nature. The parent species are isolated from each other by soil preference, season of bloom, and extremely limited range overlap, if any. From this cross we obtained plump, healthy-appearing seeds, which are currently planted in our cold frames.

Petal Color and Color Patterns

At the time of opening (anthesis), trillium petals are colored maroon, red-purple, greenish-purple, yellow, yellow-green, white, or blends of these. White-petaled forms, particularly in the species related to *Trillium grandiflorum* and *T. pusillum,* may fade to a deep pink or purplish-red with age. In *T. ovatum* in the Smith River Canyon area of northern California, southern Oregon, and locally elsewhere, the white petals become almost barn-red before petal tissue deterioration becomes apparent. Only in selected individuals of a few species do the flowers open pink. In the *T. erectum* complex the petals do not change color; rather they slowly brown along their margins or windburn into deterioration.

The petals of the sessile trilliums are thicker in texture and tend to remain in good condition on the plant for a longer time than those of the pedicellate group. Colors gradually fade, the redder tones of the fresh flowers receding, leaving bronze tones or duller purplish-greens.

Genes for color production and color expression produce the pigments that color many flower petals. Presence or absence of a particular allele, or a mutation of it, may alter the petal color. Environmental factors may also affect petal coloring. Color or tone of some of these pigments may change at different acidity or alkalinity levels (pH) in the cell. Intensity or occurrence of some colors may be influenced by external factors, such as light, temperature (especially during bud development), and soil pH. Coloring in a single flower results from interaction of all the above factors operating in concert.

Reds, maroons, and some blues in many flowers result from the presence of pigments called anthocyanins. In a general way, anthocyanins reflect red colors in an acid pH environment but blue colors in an alkaline environment. Other flower pigments include carotenes (orange) and xanthophylls (yellow). Yellow plastids containing xanthophylls (chromoplasts) frequently occur in petals. Green chloroplasts may or may not be present in petals to varying degrees.

Botanical literature shows few studies on the exact nature of trillium petal colors. A study by Les et al. (1989) on a mixed color population of *Trillium sessile* found that coloring in the three phenotypes (appearance types red, pink-yellow, or yellow) resulted from the presence or absence of anthocyanin compounds, and secondarily by quantitative differences in the concentration of several flavonol glycosides (other pigments). Les et al. (1989) found red *T. sessile* contains both cyanidin 3-arabinoside and 3-diarabinoside. Pink phenotypes contained only cyanidin 3-arabinoside. Petals of yellow phenotypes lacked cyanidin entirely. Other pigments found in all three of their phenotypes (red, pink, yellow), were quercetin 3-O-glucoside, quercetin 3-O-arabinoglucoside, quercetin 3-O- arabinogalactoside, and quercetin 3-O-arabinogalactosyl, 7-O glucoside. Petals of yellow phenotypes contained mostly quercetin 3,7-O triglycosides. These authors quote extensive research findings that the "presence or absence of a particular floral pigment is usually a single-gene difference." Except for an unpublished master's thesis by S. S. Asbury (1973), little other direct research on trillium petal coloring appears in the literature.

Based upon the known presence of anthocyanin pigments in *Trillium sessile,* the findings of single-gene control, and known inheritance patterns in other plants, we may speculate on the nature of certain trillium color forms, at least in the *T. erectum* complex. In many populations of normal red *T. erectum* occur yellow, greenish-yellow, pink, or white individuals. If these colors result from single-gene mutations, we believe that what we see as the maroon-red color of the petal is actually the result of a series of separate pigment and plastid colors blended together, each factor controlled by a different gene. Together, these produce the deep red coloring we see in the typical plant.

If one or more deletions or mutations occur, one or more colors could be dropped or the cell chemistry altered, resulting in a change in color tone or absence of one or more of the colors present. Loss of the gene for anthocyanin would shift the color towards the yellow tones (Les et al. 1989). If yellow plastid pigments occur in that individual, a yellow petal color would intensify (Plate 35). This simple gene mutation change in color can occur anywhere within a species' range, and such forms occur occasionally throughout, but petal coloring in certain *Trillium* species is still more complicated.

Many insects see mostly reflected ultraviolet (UV) light wavelengths that are largely invisible to humans. What we see and what the insect sees are quite different. Ultraviolet photography has shown that many flower petals that appear unicolored to us actually absorb and reflect UV light in patterns forming guidelines, or targets, visible to their insect pollinators. These patterns or guidelines lead the pollinator into the critical area of the blossom where it then effects pollination. Position and shape of the pattern is genetically controlled. In numerous orchids the pattern and lip colors are inherited independently from other flower petal colors. Although not experimentally tested, such a situation appears to exist in the *Trillium erectum* group. Indeed, in *T. erectum* f. *blandum* and *T. sulcatum* one can often observe a faint, slightly darker "bull's-eye" pattern formed in the center of the flower (Plate 34).

When hybrids occur between two different species, genetic materials controlling dominance and recessiveness of pattern and petal color from each parent recombine. The result is that the central target area or "bull's-eye," formerly indistinguishable to our eyes, may be recombined with a visible pigment in the hybrid, producing flowers with a dark center against a lighter background. When *Trillium erectum* is one parent and the other is a white-petaled species, the most common hybrid form bears a central dark red-maroon bull's-eye spot with the distal half of the petals white (Plate 5). If the *T. erectum* parent is itself a color variant, then the dark bull's-eye appears against a pink, yellow, or greenish background. Backcrossing to either parent or between hybrids results in myriad patterns and shades.

Phenomena such as chromosome crossovers, fracture and inversion of chromosome sections, and deletions or translocations of chromosome segments occasionally produce drastic changes. Although we do not know the precise nature of the genetic aberration in certain trilliums, we have seen forms bearing a reversal of the hybrid petal color pat-

Plate 5. Hybrid swarm between *Trillium erectum* and *T. flexipes* in the Case garden. Photo by Roberta Case.

tern, the center white, the distal portion dark; a speckled overlay of a dark pigment against a light colored background, or the bleeding of the darker bull's-eye color distally along the main petal veins (Plates 6, 7).

A particularly attractive variant similar to that of some picoteed tuberous begonias has occurred in our hand-pollinated *Trillium* hybrids. In these, the petal margins have colored darkly, while flecks of dark color appear scattered across the face of an otherwise pale petal. The effect is dramatic and lovely (See Plate 10).

Plate 6. Hand-pollinated trillium hybrid (*Trillium erectum* × *T. flexipes*) showing the bicolored pattern so often encountered in these hybrids. Photo by Fred Case.

Plate 7. Spontaneous garden hybrid involving the yellow form of *Trillium sulcatum*. Note the dark center and radiating dark lines of this outstanding flower. Photo by Fred Case.

We have found wild hybrid populations between *Trillium erectum* and *T. flexipes* at the contact between their ranges in Michigan, southern Ohio, southern Kentucky, and at several locations in Tennessee, and between *T. sulcatum* and *T. flexipes*, *T. rugelii* and *T. vaseyi* in Tennessee and North Carolina. In Michigan's Upper Peninsula, we have observed a large hybrid swarm of *T. erectum* × *T. cernuum*. Regardless of the species involved, the almost identical color patterns suggest that we are correct in our reasoning on the hybrid origin of the color variation. With few exceptions, it is only when two compatible species appear in the same vicinity that the bicolored forms and unusual color patterns abound. Even the uniform petal color forms we interpret as single-gene mutations rather than hybrid recombinations seem more abundant in regions of species overlap and extensive hybridization. For species whose ranges make contact but do not extensively overlap, color variations tend to appear only along the zones of contact of the two species (Case and Burrows 1962).

We have selected plants of *Trillium erectum* (red) from central Michigan and of *T. flexipes* (white) from near Louisville, Kentucky, where coloring in each species was uniform and without unusual colors or patterns present, and hand pollinated them using precautions to prevent contaminating pollen. From these crosses flowered the exact same range of color patterns as those we have found in wild populations of the two species. Therefore, we are convinced that the unusual variation in coloring and color patterns found in some wild populations results, in part, from hybridization.

Ecology of Trilliums

Compared to North American terrestrial orchids, trilliums are much more adaptable in their soil and habitat requirements. Most species grow ubiquitously across the forest floor of the proper habitat within their natural range. Less particular about the successional stage they occupy than many plants, species such as *Trillium grandiflorum* or *T. cuneatum*, characteristically associated with mature deciduous forests, may invade old fields and brushy early forest stages adjacent to mature forests where parent colonies already grow. The largest colonies of *T. grandiflorum* in the Great Lakes region develop in maturing second-growth timber, but in southwestern Michigan and along the Blue Ridge Parkway, we have seen extensive stands in very old timber. Apparently mature plants can maintain themselves over long periods under conditions of deep shade, but we see few seedlings in the deeper forest situations.

Only a few species demand a specific soil or niche. Of these, *Trillium undulatum* seems most particular. It grows only in very acidic, deep humus in cool soils across its range. *Trillium nivale* occurs on neutral to somewhat alkaline soils where natural geological processes create a very critical type of disturbance, usually gravelly alluvial deposits or continually eroding rock and slumping soils. In the wild, *T. rivale* grows in peaty, gravelly soil adjacent to streams and banks, moist in spring, bone-dry later. One would expect it to be difficult in cultivation, but it is not, adapting well to a well-drained peaty soil.

Under cultivation, adult plants of most *Trillium* species may persist for many years, even in the wrong soil conditions. Many plants, however, require more exacting conditions for seedling survival. Proper soil temperatures, soil pH, and moisture to which the particular species has adapted must prevail. Seeds of most *Trillium* species may germinate prolifically, but survive best only in raw, exposed soils free from most plant competition. Under conditions of heavy leaf mold or other plant competition, seedlings rarely establish. Given freedom from smothering competition, proper soil type, and good soil drainage, most species respond well in the wild and in cultivation.

For those species that truly demand a special soil condition, such as *Trillium undulatum,* seedlings appear only where the deep humus, temperature, and acid conditions exist. Few gardeners can cultivate and long maintain this species except those who garden in its natural habitat.

Some of the western and Gulf coastal trilliums, although they, too, require cold to break dormancy, in cultivation in northern areas commence growth in such early mild spells that later frosts or freezes kill the new growth. Then, of course, their rhizome buds require a new period of cold to break dormancy before they can recommence growth. Since frost damage may occur season after season and exhaust the plant's stored food, these species are difficult to grow in the open in the North.

Although trilliums may not be considered safe and edible for human consumption (indeed they were used as a nerve tonic and as a drug to relieve labor pains in earlier days), certain wild animals graze them into oblivion. Woodchucks and deer have done major damage to our trillium plantings. Deer eagerly seek out the young sprouts of most species. Repeated grazing over several years results in failure of the plants to produce and store food, and so they starve. Districts where deer abound or rapidly increase suffer a simultaneous decline in populations of trilliums. At one 300-acre estate in North Carolina, deer destroyed a very large population of several *Trillium* species, particularly *T. erectum,* over a period of just a few years (C. F. Moore, pers. comm.).

The Asiatic trilliums grow, according to various authors, predominantly in mixed deciduous forests on river terraces, hillsides, and mountain slopes. Such habitats closely approximate those of the trilliums of the eastern United States, even to many of the same tree genera.

Details of the ecological conditions under which a particular *Trillium* species occurs in nature can be found under that species' treatment.

Horticulture of Trilliums

M ANY *Trillium* species possess desirable horticultural proper-
ties: showy flowers, longevity, tolerance of deep shade or sun,
and good winter or summer hardiness. In addition, especially in eastern America, trilliums are among the most showy and abundant of spring woodland flowers, known and beloved by many. As one's
horticultural interest grows, often a deep sentimental or nostalgic desire
develops to grow the trilliums of one's youthful memories. The plants
also have intrinsic interest—color forms, mutations, colorful hybrids,
and many species—that feeds the desire to grow them. Trilliums are
worthy horticultural subjects.

Cultivation

Most *Trillium* species grow readily in the garden. Their major requirement is a good rich, loamy or humusy, lightly shaded, well-drained soil.
For the majority of species, a neutral pH reaction seems ideal. A few species grow in the wild only upon limestone. Such species may benefit
from the addition of ground limestone to the soil bed. However, there
are those who do not believe that addition of lime for the so-called calciphile species is necessary. The Royal Botanic Garden, Edinburgh, Scotland, does not add lime to soils in which it grows calciphile plants (A.
Evans and R. McBeath, pers. comm.). Upland Appalachian species grow
mostly in neutral to moderately acid soils, usually well-drained. *Trillium
undulatum* requires strongly acid soil rich in forest duff or peat.

The Asiatic trilliums, which tend to be miffy in American gardens, in the wild grow in sites wetter than those in which most American species grow, and they often grow with various skunk cabbages (*Lysichiton* sp. and *Symplocarpus* sp.). These plants may require more moisture at their roots to do well here.

Horticulturist Judy Glattstein, in the August 1988 issue of *Fine Gardening*, discussed her methods of cultivating trilliums. She gardens on a property shaded by tall oaks with an understory of dogwoods and black birch. The soil is a "good rich loam, rich from the long-term deposits of fallen leaves," mildly acid. Glattstein, wisely, we think, recommends that purchased rhizomes be planted in late September or early October. These (at present) will most likely be wild-collected rhizomes, no matter what the dealer states (see "Conservation of Trilliums") about this situation. In fall, these rhizomes will be quite dormant, and unlike the same rhizomes in spring, will not commence growth in shipment. For all species, Glattstein mixes a tablespoon each of muriate of potash and superphosphate into the bottom of the planting hole about 3 to 4 inches deep. Over this she adds 0.5 inch of untreated soil to insulate the rhizome from any possible burn effects of direct contact with the fertilizers. After placing the rhizome in the planting hole, she fills the hole with a mixture of leaf mold and soil and uses natural oak leaves and/or a coarse compost as a mulch. Glattstein fertilizes her plants twice a year, as shoots appear and as the flowers fade, with a 10–30–20 (nitrogen–phosphorous–potassium) liquid fertilizer.

Digging in leaf mold or adding fertilizer benefits the plants. We have a rather large woodland area, making use of liquid fertilizer on many widely scattered plants a chore. Instead, we scatter regular farm quality 12–12–12 dry fertilizer around our plants. The fertilizer should be spread in late winter or very early spring, before growth commences. Grains of fertilizer on the tender unfurling leaves can cause burn and damage spots. These injured spots seem to be loci for a later invasion of *Botrytis* (fungus) infection in a wet, humid summer. Too heavy a fertilization regimen produces over-sized, soft plants prone to physical injury and fungal disease. We prefer a single application yearly, just before spring growth commences.

For species such as *Trillium nivale* that grow on limestone outcrops or basic soils, we use crushed limestone chips mixed into ordinary garden soil. Our plants have responded by seeding on this soil in great abundance. Where we have such a soil adjacent to a rather acid, peaty bed, the limestone region abounds in seedlings. Where the acid soil commences, seedlings do not appear, and the lack of *T. nivale* seedlings there is startling. Surely this indicates that this species appreciates the limed soil.

Trillium rivale responds, in cultivation, to a cool, peaty, sandy soil, moist in spring but drying considerably about the time the plants deteriorate in July. Its response to a cool peaty soil in the Michael and Polly Stone garden at Loch Ness, Scotland, is phenomenal. Here a selected clone, planted as a few-stemmed plant, has formed an enormous clump (Plate 29).

Most gardeners struggle and ultimately fail with *Trillium undulatum*. We have had limited success under two sets of conditions. If we plant the rhizomes about 6 inches deep under spruces (*Picea* sp.), pines (*Pinus*), or other conifers in a deeply shaded peaty, moist soil, a percentage of the plants will survive, at least for a few years, without soil amendments. Better success with *T. undulatum* for us, however, has been with prepared beds located in an area heavily shaded in summer. We excavate an area at least a yard square to a depth of 6 or 7 inches. Into this excavation we pour a layer of silica sand (washed silica sandblasting sand purchased from a building supply store) at least 2 to 3 inches deep. On this sand we place the rhizomes. We then take the excavated soil, if sandy and somewhat acid, and add Canadian peat and fir bark chips such as are sold for potting tropical orchids. If the excavated soil is not acidic, discard most or all of it, and concoct a soil of peat, silica sand, pine bark, or fir bark. This should be used to cover the rhizomes to a depth of about 6 inches. In such a situation we can keep *T. undulatum* happy at least for a few years until the soil decomposes and changes chemically. Our happiest results with *T. undulatum* have been the seeding by plants from our prepared beds into a naturally acid woodland site nearby.

Trilliums are woodland plants; most species may be grown easily in moist woodland or humus-amended soils. Plant them in scattered, naturalistic clumps with other native woodland plants in a wildflower garden or woodland border for most effective results.

Trillium species from western North America and Japan may grow more vigorously in mild maritime climates than some of the eastern and northeastern North American species. With present knowledge and availability, one must do individual experimentation with available material. Successes and failures should be reported in horticultural publications.

Additional comments on culture can be found under the individual species treatments.

Propagation

Propagation of trilliums from seed, while not difficult, is a slow and commercially expensive process at present (see "Seed Germination"). If one can obtain fresh seed of the desired species and has the patience for the project, seed planted when ripe will usually appear in the second spring after planting.

John Gyer (pers. comm.) writes that ripe seed with the elaiosome attached is prone to mold infections and rot. He asserts that failure to remove the elaiosome has caused a substantial seed loss in some nurseries. Gyer removes the elaiosome by soaking the fresh seed about 15 minutes in a 3-percent hydrogen peroxide solution as obtained from drug stores. He suggests that after the peroxide treatment, seed be stored about five days on moist toweling in a plastic bag, then removed and gently rubbed in a sieve under running water. Sterilize the seed again in hydrogen peroxide briefly and plant.

Once the seed has germinated, normal weeding, watering, and mild fertilization will speed seedling growth. Because maturation takes four to seven years, seeds in pots are at risk of neglect, drying out, or other fatal hazards. We recommend, therefore, that trillium seeds be planted directly into the soil of a cold frame or into the location where you wish your plants to flower, provided the area will not be subject to cultivation or plant competition.

If you are an experimenter, it may be possible further to speed trillium seedlings toward maturity. Almost ripe green seed apparently will germinate without a dormant period (Solt, pers. comm.) thus eliminating the 83-day waiting period of cold to break the dormancy. If you plant the seed in pots, you may be able to mature *Trillium* seedlings, once germinated, as we do *Arisaema* seedlings. After each cycle of growth, as the seedlings begin to go dormant, we allow the pots to dry. When the pots have been dry for two to three weeks, we remove the tiny rhizomes or bulblets, place them in a sealed plastic bag, and put them in the vegetable crisper (do not freeze) of a refrigerator for a cold period. While 6 weeks works well for *Arisaema,* Solt's findings (see "Seed Germination") indicate that *Trillium* seed needs to be kept near freezing for a minimum of 83 days for initial germination. Because of the genetic requirement for breaking bud dormancy before a new growth cycle can commence, it may be necessary to cool the seedlings also for 83 days between each subsequent resting cycle. (We know of no published information on the length of cold period required to break dormancy in trilliums beyond the seedling stages). At the end of the cooling period, remove the seedlings, plant them in pots, and allow them to come into growth. Growing under fluorescent lights on a 16-hour day, regular weak fertilization, and repeating the drying and cold resting process should, as with our *Arisaema* project, reduce the interval between initial germination and first flowering of the trillium seedlings by one to several years. Undoubtedly such a process has been tried in some research process. If it has been published we have not seen it.

Some trilliums form clumps naturally, while others seldom do. Even within a species there are genetic strains that proliferate freely, while other strains continue a straight-line single growth pattern for years. There is an astounding statement in a recent research paper (Hanzawa and Kalisz, 1993, p. 405) on *Trillium grandiflorum* that the species does not reproduce clonally (vegetatively). This may be true for individuals of the particular colony under study, but we wish those authors could see some of the massive clumps certain of our clones, including the sterile double ones, produce.

Dr. Richard Lighty and staff of Mt. Cuba Center for the Study of Piedmont Flora, Greenville, Delaware, are currently experimenting with *Trillium grandiflorum* 'Quicksilver', so named because of its rapid multiplication of offsets. This form will eventually be released to the nursery trade. We have several hybrids of *T. flexipes* × *T. erectum* and *T. flexipes* × *T. sulcatum* as well as *T. cuneatum* and other species, which produce clonal offsets rapidly. Even when the flower size is not large, these massive clumps make a real show in the garden. For commercial propagation, such rapidly reproducing clones offer much. Growers should look for such forms.

Certain individual trillium clones, while outstanding for flower quality, refuse to produce offsets naturally. Some of the finest forms and doubles we have seen are of this sort. Since such forms will not come true from seed, other means must be utilized to multiply them. The rather recently perfected methods of tissue culture seem the obvious route to go. Unfortunately, tissue culture of adult trilliums has not worked well. While the plants are not symbiotic with soil fungi, such fungi do invade and contaminate the rhizome. Under conditions of *in-vitro* cultivation, it has proved difficult or impossible to obtain trillium meristem tissue free from the contaminating fungus. *In vitro,* the fungus multiplies faster than the trillium tissue, overwhelms it, and destroys it. Once this problem has been solved, tissue culture will provide the fastest method of propagation. Recently, a New Zealand nurseryman informed us that he had successfully tissue-cultured trilliums. If what he told us proves practical, we should soon see a radical change in rare trillium availability to gardeners, and a change in the attitude of conservationists to growing these plants.

In the meantime, one can slowly multiply recalcitrant plants by other methods. One cited in several older books recommends girdling the rhizome a short distance behind the current terminal bud (Foster 1968). Girdling done after the flowering season, with replanting the rhizome, causes dormant buds behind the girdle to develop into small lateral offset plants by the following spring. These can then be removed immediately or left for a year to gain additional strength. This method carries an inherent danger: the girdled area may become infected by a fungus or bacteria that causes a fatal rot of the entire rhizome.

We prefer to disbud the terminal bud from the rhizome rather than girdle it. There are two techniques in use and well publicized in popular gardening articles. In one we simply cut out and discarded the terminal bud. We then dried the scar on the rhizome in air for a day and dusted it lightly with a garden fungicide before replanting it. If done just after flowering, before the plant makes up the new terminal for the coming year, many buds along the rhizome may develop, forming small but healthy offset plants (Case 1988).

An alternative method cuts off the rhizome about an inch or so behind the terminal bud (Figure 3). After fungicide treatment and a little drying, both pieces are replanted. The terminal bud and youngest rhizome resume growth, frequently even blooming again the next season.

The back portion of the rhizome, like in the method described above, gives rise to a few to several small offset buds. All these offsets, of course, are clonal, genetically identical with the original plant unless a mutation of cells at the growing point has taken place.

The second method, removing some rhizome with the terminal bud and replanting it, offers some insurance against loss of a valuable form, should the older, less vigorous portion of the rhizome rot instead of growing. In both cases, only a few plants can be produced yearly compared to the high yield of successful tissue culture, but it is better than no method at all and provides exact copies of the original prized plant. These offsets typically mature and flower much faster than do seedlings.

Margery Edgren (1993) detailed a method, after removal of the terminal bud and part of the rhizome as described above, for inducing "more shoots faster than with the usual treatment." Her variation involves stimulation of the rhizome with cytokinins and gibberellic acid, both plant or cell growth hormones. Her use of these chemicals removes the plant's cold dormancy requirement. With the use of long-day artificial light, she can cycle the plant growth two times per year and hasten maturity. She does not state conclusively whether or not the treatment resulted in higher production of offshoots, but after seven seasons the offsets had not yet flowered.

Several researchers continue to work on a rapid asexual propagation method practical for commercial plant production. If developed, it will make many species available to the horticultural and landscape industry and eliminate the threat to wild populations from commercial collecting.

Diseases and Pests

Like most plants, trilliums suffer from parasites and disease. Fortunately, trilliums are hardy plants and serious problems are few.

Seedlings and very young plants can be susceptible to damping off or rot fungi in the soil. This seems to be much less a problem in prepared beds in the ground than in pots or flats on a greenhouse bench or windowsill. Soils used to grow trilliums from seed can be sterilized by various horticultural products available at garden supply stores, drenched with liquid fungicides, or heat-sterilized. If chemical controls are used, they should first be checked to be safe for human contact. Second, they should not pollute the soil or ground water as the old mercury anti-damp off compounds did.

For small amounts of soil, a pot or two can be heat-sterilized in a microwave or an oven. We have found that under our greenhouse conditions, heat-sterilized soils seem later to favor a proliferation of algae and slimy soil growths that can cause as much trouble as the damp-off organisms themselves.

In most instances, we find that, if we prepare a soil bed or a suitable soil in pots, water it well, and leave it for a while before planting, the various parasitic organisms will run their course and disappear naturally. From such "cured" soil we have had better seedling growth and few damp-off problems.

More serious than seedling damp-off is *Botrytis* disease, a superficial, that is, not systemic, fungus parasite. The disease appears on leaves or flowers in early summer, usually after a period of very humid or rainy weather. At this time tree leaves shade the plants from any beneficial fungicidal action of ultraviolet rays. Plants that have been stressed are most susceptible. In trilliums, the leaves suffer. At first tiny brown spots appear scattered across the leaf's upper surface. Over a period of several weeks these enlarge, coalesce, and gradually destroy the season's leaves. With the progress of the fungus comes a decline in good leaf tissue, and therefore photosynthesis and food storage. The process weakens rather than kills, but if the plants become infected for several years in a row, they may cease to flower or even die.

If detected early and the plants sprayed with a fungicide, *Botrytis* can be stopped in its tracks. Repeated spraying may be necessary as indicated on the fungicide's instructions. Systemic fungicides, if not toxic to trilliums, offer the best protection, for they become absorbed into the plant's tissues throughout, preventing the invasion of the fungal hyphae at any point. Do not spray all your plants with any one fungicide until you have tried it experimentally on a few for signs of phytotoxicity.

Lilies harbor both *Botrytis* and various virus diseases. Once a planting of lilies becomes infected, it is very difficult to clean it up except by removal of all the lilies and starting anew with healthy stock in a different soil. Trilliums, which are closely related to lilies, are certainly as susceptible to *Botrytis*. Whether or not lily viruses will transfer to trilliums, if vectored, has not been established, but because of the close family relationships such a possibility must be considered. We do not grow hybrid or exotic lilies, only those native in the same habitats as trilliums.

Soggy, poorly drained soils can favor rot fungi, which quickly destroy trillium rhizomes. No fungicide can protect against moisture-clogged, oxygen-poor soils. Likewise, trillium rhizomes stored in a sealed plastic bag and accidentally overheated perish quickly.

Most serious, in our opinion, of the trillium diseases is the greening disease caused by mycoplasma organisms (see "Mutations and Abnormalities"). This strange malady, which we suspect to be vectored by leafhoppers, spreads in wild populations sometimes until whole colonies seem infected. Many bizarre flower patterns and forms result (Plates 2, 8), some quite attractive at first. Eventually, nearly all infected plants slowly decline and disappear. Most disturbing is that some people collect these bizarre forms and some dealers sell them around the world. The potential for destruction of collections and fine forms or rare species is great.

Although mycoplasma infections of certain ornamental and crop plants have been cured by heat and antibiotic treatment, it is an elabo-

Plate 8. Mycoplasma-infected *Trillium erectum* on South Manitou Island, Michigan, showing extreme distortion of petals and deformity of stamens characteristic of this disease in this species. Photo by Fred Case.

rate and costly treatment developed for commercial producers and industries, not a remedy easily available to the individual gardener.

Whether or not the as-yet-uninvestigated dwarfing disease of *Trillium grandiflorum* in Michigan's Upper Peninsula presents a serious problem or is a local one confined to limestone districts (see above) we do not know.

In 45 years of growing many *Trillium* species, we have encountered very few bothersome insect pests. In woods and gardens we encounter almost none. In cold frames, where there is more dampness and a closed atmosphere, aphids may build up and can damage and even abort developing flower buds or deform expanding leaves. Scale insects seldom cause any problem. In the confines of a frame or greenhouse, white flies may develop colonies on the undersides of leaves, but they are rare. We have seen almost no slug or snail damage. Should any of these pests appear, spray with an appropriate and environmentally safe insecticide or slug and snail poison. Follow manufacturer's directions exactly.

Creating Hybrids

Hybridization occurs in wild populations where closely related species overlap. In cultivation, related forms that might never make contact to hybridize in the wild can be caused to do so artificially. Selective hybridization, using selected superior forms, offers an opportunity for the hybridizer to produce some new and outstanding trilliums for garden and landscape use.

The red-maroon pedicellate trilliums produce several color forms (see "Petal Color and Color Patterns"). These forms result from genetic variations and mutations. Used in hybridization they increase the possibilities for producing new and different colors. There is also a color pattern in the flower generally visible to insects that perceive ultraviolet light. This pattern is not visible normally to the human eye (see "Petal Color and Color Patterns"), but when species bearing this pattern crossbreed with other species, random gene assortment may link the color pattern to a visible pigment. The result is bicolored flowers. Breeding between these forms and between various compatible species can produce outstanding garden flowers. Occurrence of mutations during the hybridization process can produce picotee, colored, branched venation,

Plate 9. Complex spontaneous garden hybrid of *Trillium flexipes* ancestry in the Case garden. Photo by Fred Case.

Plate 10. Garden hybrid (*Trillium erectum* × *T. flexipes*) showing a picotee color pattern. Photo by Fred Case.

and other new color-patterned blooms, some of great beauty (see Plates 9, 10).

The sessile trilliums, too, produce several color forms. Most of the sessile species have dark purple, red, or maroon-brown petals. A few produce yellow or green petals. Nearly all the dark red-purple species have yellow or pallid forms, although white-petaled forms occur only in the western species *Trillium albidum* and *T. parviflorum* and more rarely in forms of *T. chloropetalum*. A few species, such as *T. maculatum* and *T. viridescens,* have bicolored forms, with the base of the petal dark maroon-purple and the distal half pale yellow or yellow-green. Some of these forms are quite attractive. Although some wild hybrids among sessile species have been reported, almost nothing is known of crossing compatibility or deliberate attempts by hybridizers to produce sessile trillium hybrids. The close similarity between some of the sessile species, particularly the eastern ones, may limit their hybridization potential.

Controlled Crosses

Making a hybrid is simple. Collect fresh pollen from the proposed male parent just as the flower opens. If the female parent is not yet in bloom, the pollen can be stored in a folded paper envelope; do not use waxed paper. Place the pollen in a sealed bottle in the refrigerator until time of use. For long storage, use a desiccant such as silica gel to keep the pollen very dry.

Just before or as the female parent flower opens, cover it with a bit of nylon mesh or stocking material to keep out pollinating insects while allowing air circulation to prevent molding. Either force open the petals with forceps and remove the stamens before they ripen, or very carefully remove them as the flower opens. Then, place the selected, stored pollen on the stigmas of the plant. Remove the petals so as not to attract insect pollinators and tie a label on the plant's stem with either both parent names or an identifying number also recorded in your hybridizing notes. Flowers pollinated successfully in April or May ripen fruits from late July to early September. Harvest fruits and plant seeds before they dry. Keep careful records so that the genetic history of any outstanding hybrid that might result can be traced in future years.

Breeding Goals

Those undertaking to hybridize trilliums ought to have a breeding plan of goals and standards towards which to work. Of course there will be surprises along the way, both serendipitous and otherwise, but work toward a plan. As a starting point, we suggest the following as desirable qualities to develop in garden trilliums:

1. Good floral display: erect flower carriage with outfacing or up-facing blooms.
2. Clear colors, with smooth pigment distribution, not the granular colors found in some *T. erectum* forms.
3. Variety in color pattern of the petal center, edging, and venation.
4. A strong clumping habit with many offsets: larger clumps make better garden displays and the faster propagation makes desirable clones available sooner.
5. Disease resistance.
6. Hardiness.

Conservation of Trilliums

O PINIONS on the conservation of trilliums encompass many diverse problems and perceptions. Some are valid concerns while some, emotionally based, are not grounded upon sound scientifically determined facts. In this chapter we will examine several threats to wild *Trillium* populations and the legal protection of trilliums in North America.

Threats to Wild Populations of Trilliums

Picking Wild Trilliums

It is popularly believed that picking a trillium even one time kills the plant. This is not true. Trilliums, like all green plants, obtain their food from the process of photosynthesis, the manufacture of carbohydrates from carbon dioxide and water using the energy of sunlight. The organs of food-making are the green leaves, the light energy capturing and converting agent the green pigment chlorophyll. Naturally, anything which deprives the plant of its leaves injures it. Once picked, trilliums cannot produce another set of leaves until their cold dormancy requirement is satisfied, but trilliums have large, heavy rhizomes which store a considerable amount of food. If the plant picked is of reasonable health and size, it will appear the following season. If the rhizome is large and healthy enough, it may even bloom. There simply is no truth to the statement that picking a trillium once kills it. However, our experience from our many lecture appearances and what we have written in the past indicates that some zealots ignore the facts and go right on believing the "facts" they want to believe.

Grazing by Wild or Domestic Animals

It is true that repeated picking of the same plant, season after season before it can manufacture enough food to maintain itself, will eventually kill it. A far greater threat to most wild *Trillium* populations than human picking is grazing by wild or domestic animals. Deer have done serious damage to trilliums in our gardens, so much so that we have had to use electric fences to maintain any trilliums. On the estate of C. F. Moore near Brevard, North Carolina, large populations of *Trillium erectum* varieties and *T. grandiflorum* have almost totally disappeared. The Moore estate, part of a civic watershed, has been closed to the public, vehicles, and other agents which might possibly have destroyed the trilliums for many years. Disappearance of the plants coincided with the redevelopment and rapid increase in the deer herd following its near extermination by pioneer hunters (C. F. Moore, pers. comm.). A similar history has occurred elsewhere, many times. Repeated grazing, unlike the one-time picking of an individual plant, takes the same plants season after season, depleting their food reserves until they die. Maintaining wild deer herds at reasonable levels will save more trilliums than all the "education" not to pick. This is not to say that we advocate or approve of wanton picking, but there simply are not that many people out picking trilliums, and young children and the uninformed will pick a few no matter what people say.

Commercial Digging of Wild Trilliums

Commercial collecting from wild trillium populations is not a good situation, as repeated collecting of a given area can deplete parental stocks or eliminate a rare species. Nursery propagation certainly is preferable and a better conservation practice.

Some propagation techniques are available, but present methods are slow, tedious, and commercially unprofitable. Several large research projects to propagate trilliums by various means are under way. Stephanie Solt (pers. comm.), University of Vermont, currently researches methods for rapid seed germination and maturation of *Trillium grandiflorum* on a commercial, horticultural level. The Mt. Cuba Center for the Study of Piedmont Flora, Greenville, Delaware, is developing propagation methods for choice trillium clones (R. Lighty, pers. comm.). Various wildflower societies and commercial nurseries also seek to propagate trilliums profitably in quantity. Tissue culture, if it can be perfected for trilliums, probably offers the best and quickest route to mass production of trilliums.

Some native plant dealers offer trillium rhizomes in quantity lots at wholesale and retail. Most do not state the origin of their plants; some call them "nursery stock." To our knowledge, no true commercial quantity "propagation" takes place at the present time. The reader must realize that the term "nursery stock" may be misleading. In some states or other legal districts, wild-collected material can be kept in beds or rows for a specified period of time and then be classed as nursery stock. If no laws covering the situation exist, dealers can call these plants what they may. Most trilliums offered today were collected in the wild. When taken legally from areas slated for development, we have no objection. In fact, we encourage legal rescue operations where the plants will otherwise be destroyed anyway. It is better that the gene pool be maintained in cultivation than totally destroyed. What we object to is illegal mass collecting from wild lands.

On the other hand, the amount of wild trillium material collected and sold or exported does not, so far as we can determine, approach the numbers given by zealous conservationists, conservation lobbyists, and those who seek to block export of all trilliums or to make a political issue of collecting them. We know of a situation where one zealot queried a number of wildflower dealers as to how many trilliums they exported. Out of a large number only a handful replied, so the person simply extrapolated the number by multiplying the amount exported by the few by the total number of dealers queried. Of course many did not export trilliums, and the number was entirely too large.

Many conservationists oppose any collecting of wild plants for any purpose, scientific or other. These people do not want trilliums grown in gardens, exported, or otherwise taken from the wild. Frequently these vocal groups loudly condemn anyone who does seek to obtain them. It is strange, we think, that all too often, these same groups make no comment whatsoever about the opening of new shopping malls, housing or industrial developments, or cut, slash, and herbicide lumbering techniques, which truly destroy far more trilliums or other wild plants than any collector or nursery operation possibly could.

All our garden plants were at one time wild native plants somewhere. So were our food plants. Had they not been brought into cultivation we would possibly not have them today. It is our position that we ought to be able to grow wild species if we desire to, but it is also our position that, first and foremost, wild populations should be maintained, protected, and managed if necessary so that the species' existence is not endangered or threatened anywhere.

To do this, we must first know and understand the species. This may involve learning how to cultivate them, but it also may involve development of new techniques to multiply individuals of a species, such as the relatively new tissue culture techniques used to increase the stock of selected fine nursery clones. If such a technique does not work on a particular group, as is the current situation with tissue culture of trilliums, we ought to expend more money and effort to develop such a technique.

We do not condone mass commercial collecting from the wild. Threatened and endangered species of all wildlife should be protected by law, but we also believe there should be legal means by which properly qualified, trained botanists and horticulturists can bring into cultivation seed or selected, choice individuals of desired species, multiply them, and make them available to commercial sources so that anyone interested in these beautiful and worthy garden subjects can obtain them. We do not think that laws intended to protect a species should be so entangled in excessive regulations and red tape as to make any possession or obtaining from the wild impossible, especially if regulations prohibit horticultural taking or possession from the wild but do not protect the plants from commercial development or other private or public agency development of the land. Export of plant species that are endangered or threatened in the wild should be carefully but not impossibly regulated. Properly certified and licensed routes to export and import for commercially propagated stock should be available. To do otherwise is to encourage massive black-market traffic in trilliums.

Commercial Lumbering Techniques

The type of commercial lumber harvesting utilized can have a big influence upon native wild plant populations. An older method, selective timbering, once widely used and favored, is now out of vogue. In that method, only selected individual trees were harvested. Disturbance to the forest floor, while considerable, did not alter the basic conditions enough to kill all the herbs, or in the case of trilliums, to destroy them. The following growing season, the trillium plants emerged and continued growth. At times the forest was opened enough to allow entrance to grasses and meadow herbs. Sometimes the trilliums suffered, but rarely did an entire population disappear with this timber-harvesting method.

Clear-cutting of selected tracts within a forest, a practice widely utilized on state or federal public lands, also affects trilliums. Typically, timber on a site within a larger forested area is sold and promptly clear-cut. Within the cutting area, the soils are disturbed by heavy lumbering machinery. All forest cover is removed. Many plant species cannot survive the changes wrought in the lumbered area and thus disappear. Some survive in small numbers. Trilliums can sometimes survive such a practice in small numbers, or if the tract is small and surrounded by larger timber, may actually thrive in the cutover area. This method can be damaging, but is seldom totally devastating to the plants of the forest floor.

A new and, to many biologists, disturbing lumbering practice has appeared and is widely utilized in the southern United States and now in northern large private lumber company lands. In this method, the area is clear-cut. All sizes of timber may be utilized: anything not of high quality is chipped for chipboard. No trees are left. Then, the land may be burned to kill brush and eventually sprayed with herbicide "to kill weed trees." Finally, special trees, often hybrids or exotic species, are planted for a future timber harvest. This cut, slash, burn, and herbicide practice takes an enormous toll upon some native plants, alters the paths of natural succession, and may exclude the return of some native plants. For the more delicate natives, lady's slippers and other wild orchids, as for trilliums, the full effect on their populations is unknown. Any practice that totally alters a habitat usually takes out all individuals of a species dependent upon it, both adults and seedlings. With today's technology, massive machinery, and aerial spraying of vast areas with powerful herbicides, we are concerned about the impact on trilliums and other native plant populations.

As human populations increase and demands for forest products increase, these clear-cut, burn, and herbicide lands will increase, while old-growth forests with trilliums to act as seed sources will decrease in numbers and become more widely separated. Even if the cut lands are

allowed to go back to forest in a natural succession, if populations become too widely separated, can trilliums reseed and populations recover
fast enough to survive before the next round of forest cutting takes
place? While we believe in habitat management generally and understand that fires and some lumbering practices can favor certain wild species, we believe that modern massive clear-cut lumber practices pose one
of the greatest threats to extant wild plants (including many *Trillium*
species)ʻand many species of wildlife, and must be addressed as a con-
servation/moral issue.

National forest policy in the United States requires collecting permits
for any taking of native plants for any purpose on national forest lands.
All commercial collecting is illegal unless specially permitted. All U.S.
threatened and endangered species are rigorously protected. Plants of
"special concern" also receive protection and monitoring.

In Michigan, wild game animals are considered the property of the
state and enjoy its legal protection on public and on private lands. They
may not be taken without permits or hunting licenses. A private land-
owner does not own the wild game on his land and may not kill game
animals on his land except with the same licensing permits as would be
required on state land. The Michigan Department of Natural Resources
views protected plants in the same way and protects them similarly on
public land.

Unfortunately, on both state and federal lands some timber is auc-
tioned or tracts leased for lumbering. Private lumber corporations own
vast areas of timber land in many states. Should native legally protected
plants growing on these leased public or private lands be burned and
herbicided out of existence indiscriminately while the game or protected
animals and the same plant species are rigorously protected on adjacent
unleased public lands? This is a difficult issue of conservation morality
that must eventually be faced.

Legal Protection of North American Trilliums

Two *Trillium* species, *T. persistens* and *T. reliquum*, each of extremely local distribution, enjoy protection as endangered species under the U.S.
Threatened and Endangered Species Act. Both species are sufficiently local and rare as to deserve such protection. A third variety, *T. pusillum* var.
ozarkanum, part of what we treat in this book as a single species, *T. pusil-*

lum, is listed federally as a C-2 species of medium priority at this writing. Such a listing means the plant is under study for possible listing at either the threatened or endangered level, if the study determines that the plant requires protection (U.S. Fish and Wildlife Service 1994, and Tom Wiese, Michigan Endangered Species Coordinator, Michigan Department of Natural Resources, pers. comm.).

Many species enjoy legal protection under state laws. In Michigan, for example, the Christmas Tree Act protects, among many other showy wildflowers, all species of *Trillium* on state lands. Most state park and all national park regulations protect native plants within their boundaries. Some, not all, county and city parks protect native plants.

In addition to the federal Threatened and Endangered Species Act, many states have enacted their own threatened and endangered species protection laws. In most cases, state and federal, there are regular mandatory reviews of the status of the protected species and those of special concern. As conditions indicate, species are added, dropped, or their level of protection changed. This is as it should be, and wise and sensible persons hope to see this type of protection of our wildlife resources continued.

In spite of all the dire talk and a few problem situations, most American *Trillium* species seem to be holding their own at present. Within the sometimes limited distributional ranges, if one enters the proper habitat, the species will be present, usually frequent, and, in the case of *T. grandiflorum, T. erectum, T. sessile,* and *T. recurvatum,* and many others, locally abundant. Many species thrive not only in mature forest, but also in second-growth forest and brushland, and some can invade fallow fields. Except for the species identified under the U.S. Endangered or Threatened Species Act, just a few *Trillium* species of very limited natural distribution may, at present, be in trouble. Only in urban areas, developments, some commercial lumber tracts, and areas of excessive human or deer population do most trilliums truly suffer and their numbers decline.

With continued human population growth and all its demands upon the land, we can expect that wildflower populations of all types will be increasingly stressed and damaged. We ought to set about now, before they become endangered, to protect our native plant treasures for the future.

PART II

Trillium Taxonomy

What Is a Species?

EXTBOOKS (Solomon and Berg 1995, Villee et al. 1985) define a
species as a "group of organisms with similar structural and
functional characteristics that in nature breed only with each
other and have a close common ancestry." Because of the nature of sex-
ual reproduction in animals, that definition works well for them. But in
plants that are rooted to the ground, the help of a pollinating insect may
be required. Bees and flies have on occasion made mistakes: cross-pollination and hybridization between different species have served to blur
species distinctions.

When a population occurs over a vast area, as does *Trillium cuneatum,* natural selection pressures may affect the plants in one part of that
range differently than those of another, resulting in gradual differences
in the structure of the species from one region to another. Depending on
the botanist, the differences may be interpreted as one gradually chang-
ing cline or a series of adjacent subspecies, or the population may be
divided arbitrarily into two units. Species demarcation is in part, at least,
a matter of personal opinion.

If the organisms involved have few or obscure structural differences,
just where to split up a population or how to treat it becomes a problem.
Trilliums, beyond the features that distinguish the two great subgenera,
possess few sharply different structural features. The features that do exist, unfortunately, also tend to be obscured or destroyed when the plants
are made into herbarium specimens. Not everyone agrees with the naming of all *Trillium* species, and not all "species" are equally different from

each other. Therefore, determination of what is a species and how to identify it can be very difficult.

When the ranges of two closely related species overlap, hybridization may occur. If it does, distinguishing traits of each species may be blended in the hybrids, further obscuring differences between them. While the two populations may appear quite different at the opposite ends of their respective ranges, in and near the area of overlap, determining exactly to which species a given individual belongs may be very difficult. Some botanists (the lumpers) solve the problem to their own satisfaction by combining the two populations into one variable species. Others (the splitters), just as positive that they are correct, maintain the populations as two species and their hybrids. Neither is wrong, since what constitutes a species is a matter of opinion, but when differences are few, as in trilliums, it can make identification problems great for the beginner horticulturist or field naturalist. Identification of some *Trillium* species can be very difficult.

Description of the Genus *Trillium* and Its Two Subgenera

Trillium Linnaeus, Sp. Pl. 339. 1753: Gen. Pl. ed. 5. 158. 1754.
Perennial, somewhat fleshy herbs, from a horizontal subterranean or surface rhizome. Rhizome compressed-shortened, praemorse in most species, and bearing a large terminal bud, numerous cataphylls, and ringed and contractile adventitious roots. Stem (scape) bearing a whorl of 3 net-veined, short-petiolate or sessile, uniformly green or mottled leaves (foliaceous bracts) at the summit. Flowers single, terminal, pedicellate or sessile, perfect. Sepals 3, foliaceous, persistent, green or with maroon markings. Petals 3 in the American species, absent, or 1 to 3, sometimes deformed, in the Asiatic species. Red, purple, pink, white, yellow, green, or combinations thereof, erect, spreading or recurved, shriveling after anthesis. Stamens 6, anthers mostly equal to or longer than the filaments, hypogynous. Stigmas 3, subulate and sessile or with a short style, spreading, twisted, or erect, persistent. Superior ovary 3- to 6-lobed. Fruit a berrylike many-seeded capsule with obscure sutures, not or only rarely dehiscing along its sutures, but shed as a unit from an abscission layerlike zone at its base. Seeds ellipsoid, 2–4 mm long, bearing a large, oily, myrmecochorous elaiosome on

one side. Native to Asia and North America. All American species are diploids, 2n = 10, plus 0–7 beta chromosomes; the Asiatic species range from diploids to hexaploids (Freeman 1975, Samejima and Samejima 1987). The genus is divided into two subgenera.

Trillium subgenus *Trillium*

Leaves uniformly green except in one form, flowers pedicellate (except subsessile to sessile in one subspecies); petals spreading.

Trillium subgenus *Phyllantherum* Rafinesque

Leaves usually variously mottled, flowers terminal, sessile, petals more or less erect.

Within the subgenus *Trillium* there appear to be several natural groupings of more closely related species. Barksdale (1938) considered that these smaller subgroups number three:

1. Erectum group, distinguished by rhombic leaves, a globose to flask-shaped, six-angled ovary, and separate, recurved stigmas.
2. A second group, characterized by elliptic to broadly ovate leaves and green (to whitish, our words), six-angled ovary. Barksdale singled out only *Trillium catesbaei* and *T. pusillum* as having a short style, but most members of this subgroup have the stigmas united at the base, if very shortly so.
3. Undulatum group, bearing petiolate leaves and three-angled ovaries.

Haga and Channell (1982) investigated species groups in American trilliums through attempts to cross them with the diploid Asiatic *Trillium camschatcense*. The crosses with *T. erectum, T. gleasonii* (synonym *T. flexipes*), and *T. vaseyi*—all members of Barksdale's Erectum group—produced solid, seemingly viable seed. Seeds of the cross between *T. camschatcense* and *T. erectum* flowered in 9 to 10 years. Crosses involving *T. camschatcense* and *T. grandiflorum* produced soft, "liquid" seed that never developed. While ability to cross or not to cross with a common parent does not necessarily prove close relationship, Haga and Channell's results tend to support two of Barksdale's groups as natural groupings.

Utech (1980) and Samejima and Samejima (1987) suggested dividing the pedicellate trilliums of North America into two subgroups in subgenus *Trillium:*

1. Grandiflorum subgroup, with about eight species including *T. grandiflorum, T. ovatum, T. rivale,* and *T. undulatum.*
2. Erectum subgroup, with about six species including *T. cernuum, T. erectum, T. rugelii,* and *T. sulcatum.*

Kato et al. (1995), using chloroplast DNA restriction site mapping, a recently developed and highly informative technique to show relationships, found that the pedicellate trilliums "did not form a distinct monophyletic group." Rather, they found that all the pedicellate species they examined and all sessile species belonged to one "weakly supported clade," except *Trillium undulatum* and *T. rivale,* which were found to be paraphyletic. Kato et al. (1995) concluded that there is good evidence for recognizing the sessile trillium subgenus *Phyllantherum.* They found that the pedicellate subgenus consisted of three differing groups. Kawano and Kato (in preparation, cited in Kato et al. 1995), using their data and that of others (such as Utech 1980, Samejima and Samejima 1987), stated that the pedicellate trilliums can be divided into at least two major subgroups:

1. The Erectum subgroup, including *T. catesbaei, T. cernuum, T. erectum, T. flexipes, T. grandiflorum, T. ovatum, T. rugelii, T. sulcatum,* and *T. vaseyi.*
2. The Undulatum subgroup, including *T. nivale, T. persistens, T. pusillum, T. rivale,* and *T. undulatum.*

The Erectum subgroup species show a close relationship to each other in their similarity of flower structure and interfertility. Indeed, it is within this group (excepting *Trillium catesbaei, T. grandiflorum,* and *T. ovatum*) that nearly all the complex hybridization we have observed occurs, and it is in this group that taxonomists have least agreed about species delineation, because, we believe, much natural hybridization and backcrossing has obscured the species limits. The Undulatum subgroup contains species which the authors consider to have diverged early in the history of the genus. The subgroup is clearly composed of individual species not so closely related to each other as in the Erectum group.

Freeman (1975) recognized no sections within the sessile trillium subgroup, but proposed three groups of species that "demonstrate affinities perhaps worthy of informal recognition." His three groups, we think, have merit:

Group I. The *Trillium recurvatum* group
Characters: basally recurved sepals, incurved anthers, slender, elongated rhizomes. Most likely closer to group III than II. Two species: *T. lancifolium* and *T. recurvatum*.

Group II. The *Trillium sessile* group
Characters: prominently prolonged anther connectives, introrse or extrorse anther dehiscence, sharply angled ovaries, usually linear stigmas, and thick compact rhizomes. Seven species native to the eastern United States: *T. decipiens, T. decumbens, T. discolor, T. reliquum, T. sessile, T. stamineum,* and *T. underwoodii*.

Group III. The *Trillium maculatum* group
Characters: lateral anther dehiscence, anther connectives little or not at all prolonged, stigmas subulate or thickly subulate. Thirteen (or fourteen species): *T. albidum, T. angustipetalum, T. chloropetalum, T. cuneatum, T. foetidissimum, T. gracile, T. kurabayashii, T. ludovicianum, T. luteum, T. maculatum, T. petiolatum, T. viride,* and *T. viridescens. Trillium parviflorum* Soukup, described after Freeman's paper was published, probably belongs to this group, as it is closely related to *T. albidum*.

Freeman (1975) considered Group III "a residual group including species not referable to groups I or II, . . . taxa that nevertheless exhibit close intragroup affinities."

Regarding the second subgenus in *Trillium*, Berg (1958) suggested that subgenus *Phyllantherum* was monophyletic, based on fruit and pollen structure. Kato et al. (1995) found strong molecular support for the distinctness of subgenus *Phyllantherum* as a single, closely related natural subgroup; chloroplast DNA analysis indicated that the sessile-flowered group's closest relatives among the pedicellate species are *Trillium ovatum* and *T. grandiflorum*.

Use of Identification Keys

A dichotomous identification key offers the simplest method of identifying unknown trilliums. It consists of a series of paired couplets, each contrasting the other's statement. The unknown plant is compared to each of the statements, and the user of the key chooses one or the other.

By a series of these choices the user is led to a species name. From there, the user compares the plant in hand with the description of that species, to available illustrations of it, and to the distribution map of the species. If all details fit, it is likely the plant has been identified correctly. If the details do not fit, the user must go back over the key and recheck the decisions made.

To use a key with facility, one must first learn the vocabulary necessary to understand the comparisons and differences the key points out. Consult the diagrams of a *Trillium* plant and flower (Figures 1, 2), and use the glossary of terms carefully. Too many people fear keys because they appear difficult and confusing. With practice, keys become easy to use and offer the surest way to quickly name an unknown specimen. No key, however, is perfect or equally good in all parts. In the genus *Trillium*, the structural features necessary to differentiate between species are limited. Not every individual *Trillium* plant will key out correctly, nor is each species equally distinct from its congeners. Hybrids will usually not key satisfactorily, nor will deformed, unusually large or small individuals. The key presented in this book is intended for use with fresh, living, typical material at full bloom.

Because nothing delineating the sessile trilliums written before Freeman's work (1975) can be considered fully accurate, and because several sessile species were not described until then, it has been necessary to rely very heavily on Freeman's study for information. The following key was written using information from these sources: Barksdale 1938, Case and Burrows 1962, Johnson 1969, Freeman 1975, Patrick 1984 and undated, and our own field work and cultured material. In addition, we examined and measured the trilliums in the University of Michigan Herbarium and those of Vanderbilt University before constructing this key and writing our descriptions.

Our nomenclature follows Freeman (1975) and Soukup (1980) for the sessile trilliums, Barksdale (1938) and Patrick (1984) for the pedicellate trilliums.

The North American Trilliums

A Key to the North American Trilliums

1. Flowers borne on a pedicel above (but may nod or bend below) the usually unmottled, uniformly colored green leaves. Subgenus *Trillium*. 2

1. Flowers sessile, borne directly upon the usually mottled leaves.
. . . . 19

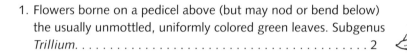

2. Stigmas uniformly thin throughout, united at least at the base into a short or long style, or grouped closely upon a slight to prominent raised pedestal at top of ovary. Ovary at anthesis small or inconspicuous, green, greenish-white, white. 4

2. Stigmas fleshy, separate, often basally thickened. Ovary prominent, 6-angled, often maroon, dark purple, pink, creamy white, or white with red or purple markings. 3

3. Stigmas short, fleshy but uniformly thick basally, recurved and more or less lobed on adaxial surface. Leaves ovate-lanceolate, mostly less than 7 cm wide, strongly petiolate. . . . . 10. *T. rivale*

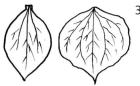

3. Stigmas of various length, usually basally thickened, gradually tapered, erect, reflexed or coiled, not lobed on adaxial surface. Leaves elliptic, obovate to rhombic, mostly more than 7 cm wide, blade tapered basally, sessile to subsessile. 12

4. Plants typically 15–30 cm or more tall. 8

4. Plants typically short, delicate, usually less than 20 cm tall in anthesis (often less than 15 cm). 5

5. Ovary 3-lobed or -angled, leaf tips round-obtuse, bluish-green. Stem hexagonal in cross section. Plant blooming very early in season.. . . . . 6. *T. nivale*

5. Ovary 3- to 6-lobed or -angled, leaf tips acuminate (generally) to blunt- to acute-tipped, rarely obtuse but not clearly round-obtuse, green or bronze-green. Stem round in cross section. 6

6. Pedicel recurved beneath leaves, or rarely leaning above leaves to nearly horizontal. Petals strongly arcuate-recurved, undulate-margined, opening white or pink.
. . . . 1. *T. catesbaei*

6. Pedicel essentially erect at flowering, variable in length (rarely only 1–2 mm long). Petals erect-spreading to widely spreading, not recurved. 7

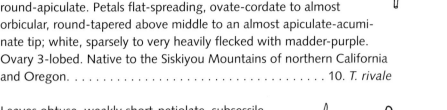

7. Leaves long-acuminate, strongly petiolate, weakly to strongly cordate at base, glossy, dorsal surface bluish-green, sometimes with a lighter silver-green pattern on or near the main veins: petiole 3–8 cm long, rarely longer. Sepals shorter and narrower than petals, round-apiculate. Petals flat-spreading, ovate-cordate to almost orbicular, round-tapered above middle to an almost apiculate-acuminate tip; white, sparsely to very heavily flecked with madder-purple. Ovary 3-lobed. Native to the Siskiyou Mountains of northern California and Oregon. . . . . 10. *T. rivale*

7. Leaves obtuse, weakly short-petiolate, subsessile, or sessile, or with leaf blade tissue narrowed into a petiole-like base, green, with maroon undertones. Sepals round to blunt-tipped, about as large and prominent as the petals, widely erect-spreading. Petals spreading-ascending, oblong to narrowly lanceolate, recurved in upper half, strongly undulate, white, aging to deep rose on backs. Ovary 6-lobed. Native to eastern United States. . . . . 9. *T. pusillum* varieties, including var. *texanum*

8. Stigmas united into a style 2–6 mm long. Leaves elliptic-ovate, ovate-lanceolate to lanceolate, usually 2–8 cm wide. 11

8. Stigmas barely united at base, rarely separated. Leaves ovate to rhombic, usually 8–20 cm wide. 9

9. Fresh petals with a distinct red inverted V-shaped mark near base, leaves strongly petiolate, ovary 3-lobed or -angled. . . . . 14. *T. undulatum*

9. Fresh petals uniformly white, pink, or with faint pink blush, no distinct V-shaped marking. Leaves subsessile, or sessile, ovary 6-lobed or -angled. 10

10. Petals erect or strongly ascending, petal margins near their bases overlapped, rolled, lower half of overlapped petals forming a tube, spreading widely in upper half and often there, with undulate-wavy margins, obovate to lanceolate, 1.5–7 cm long, 1–4 cm wide, opening white or rarely pink, aging to pink-purple. Native to eastern North America. . . . . 5. *T. grandiflorum*

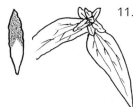

10. Petals erect-ascending, upper margin plain to strongly undulate, scarcely touching at base to strongly overlapping and forming a tube, widely spreading in upper half, linear to obovate, 1.5–7 cm long, often with pink or blush markings on fresh petal face; old flowers turning deep rose-pink, purple or barn red. Dwarf and mottled-leaf forms occur. Native to western North America. . . . .
. . . . 7. *T. ovatum*

11. Peduncle erect or only slightly leaning. Petals erect-spreading, linear to narrowly elliptic, white at anthesis, fading to deep pink with an inverted V-shaped white base. Leaves lanceolate to lanceolate-ovate, 1.6–3.3 cm wide. Anthers straight. Plant confined to a few square miles at head of Tallulah Gorge, South Carolina, and Georgia. . . 8. *T. persistens*

11. Peduncle leaning almost to horizontal or clearly recurved and declined beneath the leaves. Petals arcuate-recurved, distally undulate, oblong-lanceolate, narrow or broad, opening white or pink. Leaves often slightly raised exposing the flowers beneath at anthesis. Anthers curved, bright yellow. . . . .
. . . . 1. *T. catesbaei*

12. Anther and filament of about equal length, pale lavender- gray. Petals oblong-lanceolate, recurved-reflexed from the base, extending behind the plane of the sepal bases for more than half their length, white, rarely pale pink, usually thin-textured, upper surface veins not appearing conspicuously engraved. . . . . .
. . . . 2. *T. cernuum*

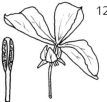

12. Anthers longer or shorter than filaments, (rarely equal, but if so, dark purple, red-maroon, yellow, or cream). Petals ovate to obovate, flat, spreading, or if recurved, in distal half only, red, maroon-purple, rose, cream, or white, rarely bicolored, upper surface veins appearing conspicuously engraved. 13

13. Ovary dark purple or maroon. 15

13. Ovary white or white with red-purple stains. 14

14. Pedicel short, 2–3 cm long, strongly recurved below leaves. Anthers dark purple, anther sac about 2× longer than the filament. Petals ovate-elliptic to almost orbicular, apex abruptly acumi-nate, white, rarely bicolored. Ovary conical-pyramidal. Stig-mas shorter than ovary. Native to the southern Appalachians. . . . . 11. *T. rugelii*

14. Pedicel usually 4–12 cm long, erect, leaning, or recurved. Anthers thick, creamy white, about 4× longer than the fila-ments. Ovary strongly pyramidal to flask-shaped, widely attached at base. Stigmas nearly equal to ovary. Plant mainly of the interior central lowlands and valleys. . . . . 4. *T. flexipes*

15. Pedicel erect, or leaning from base, not recurved, flower erect or dangling but not distinctly below the leaves. 17

15. Pedicel recurved or declined to carry flower below leaves. 16

16. Pedicel declined below leaves, usually 2–13 cm long. Stamens 1.5 to 2 times taller than the small, more or less spherical ovary. Anther sacs maroon to yellow. Petals usually maroon, broad, spreading to recurved, longer than the sepals. . . . . 15. *T. vaseyi*

16. Pedicel recurved below leaves, usually short, 1–7 cm long. Stamens about as long or no more than one-third longer than the prominent conical-pyramidal ovary. Anther sacs dark purple. Petals usually white or bicolored, distally white, oval to broadly oval, recurved, about equal to the sepals. . . . . 11. *T. rugelii*

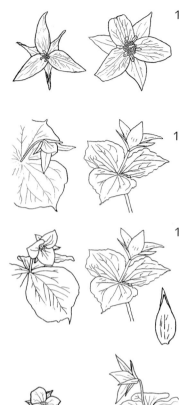

17. Flowers open, usually flat, petals carried in same plane as sepals. Petals spreading, not recurved, lanceolate to ovate, up to 2 times the width of the sepal (wider in Great Lakes populations). Sepals flat to somewhat sulcate at apex. Odor faintly fetid, of a wet dog. . . . . 3. *T. erectum* and varieties

17. Flowers gaping, strongly three-dimensional. Petals erect-spreading, or recurved in distal half, much wider than the sepals. Sepals sulcate-tipped. Odor musty or fruitlike. 18

18. Petals ivory-white, very large, 1.5 times longer than sepals, not recurved to weakly so at tip, flowers at attachment to pedicel not strongly reflexed, flower therefore facing upward. Sepals mildly sulcate-tipped. Stem usually 1.5 times longer than leaf, plant not appearing tall in proportion to flower size. Odor sweet, applelike. . . . . 12. *T. simile*

18. Petals dark maroon-red, moderately wide in proportion to length, less than 1.5 times longer than the sepals, often recurved in distal half; more or less erect pedicel reflexed at tip to carry the flower facing outward at right angle to shaft of the pedicel. Sepals strongly sulcate. Stem usually 2 to 2.5 times longer than leaf, plant appearing very tall in proportion to flower. Odor funguslike. . . . . . . 13. *T. sulcatum*

19. Stigmas united basally into a short style, the tips widely spreading and threadlike. Petals spreading, exposing stamens and ovary, thin-textured, of short duration, margins undulate. Leaves unmottled. . . . . 9. *T. pusillum* var. *virginianum*

19. Stigmas separate, sessile, linear to subulate. Petals erect, more or less connivent, more or less concealing stamens and ovary (except in *T. stamineum*), thick-textured. Leaves (bracts) variously mottled (greens, bronzes) at flowering; mottling sparse and/or becoming obscure with age, especially in the western North American species. Subgenus *Phyllantherum* 20

20. Plant typically erect, scape straight, leaves held well above ground, or leaf tips only, touching the ground in early anthesis. 23

20. Plant with petioles arising from scape apex at or near the ground surface, or plant decumbent or semidecumbent, the leaves resting near or on the ground. 21

21. Plant scape more or less erect, but largely subterranean; long-petiolate leaves attached to scape at ground level, obscurely or not at all mottled; individual leaves plantainlike. Native to western United States. . . . . 31. *T. petiolatum*

21. Plant decumbent or semidecumbent by an S-shaped curve of scape. Leaves heavily mottled; without a significant petiole. Native to southeastern United States. 22

22. Anthers opening toward outside of flower (extrorse), upper stem below leaves distinctly puberulent. Petals lanceolate-oblanceolate, 40–80 mm long or longer, filaments 2–5 mm long. 21. *T. decumbens*

22. Anthers opening towards ovary (introrse), stem glabrous throughout. Petals 25–55 mm long, filaments very short, 1–2 mm long. . . . . 33. *T. reliquum*

23. Sepals displayed above leaves, spreading or somewhat erect. Anthers erect, straight. Rhizomes thick, horizontal or somewhat compressed-thickened erect and superficially bulblike, not brittle, surface brown below the dead scales. 25

23. Sepals strongly reflexed at their bases, often below leaves, and parallel to scape, or adpressed to downward turned leaves. Anthers erect, curved inward. Rhizomes horizontal, elongated, slender, very brittle, surface white below the brownish, dead scales. 24

24. Petals short, lanceolate-ovate, about 2 times longer than broad, leaves with a definite petiole. . . . . . . 32. *T. recurvatum*

24. Petals elongated, linear to barely lanceolate, at least 4 times longer than broad, leaves sessile or subsessile. . . . . 26. *T. lancifolium*

25. Petals maroon, red-brown, bronze, yellow, or green. 28

25. Petals white, rarely tinged pale pink. 26

26. Anther dehiscence introrse. Petal tips obtuse-blunt or erose. Ovary purple. . . . . 18. *T. chloropetalum* var. *giganteum*, in part

26. Anther dehiscence latrorse. Petal tips obtuse-rounded to acute, Ovary green or greenish-white, rarely purple at base. 27

27. Plant 30–55 cm tall. Petals oblanceolate to obovate, 48–80 mm long, clear white to very pale pink or pinkish at base. . . . . 16. *T. albidum*

27. Plant 15–30 cm tall. Petals linear to linear-lanceolate, 25–48 mm long, white, greenish-white, rarely purplish at base. . . . . 30. *T. parviflorum*

28. Petals maroon, red-brown, greenish-maroon, purplish-bronze, or brown throughout (except in pigment-free mutant individuals whose petals will then be pale green or yellow-green). 34

28. Petals yellow, pale yellow, greenish, or bicolored green with a purplish base. 29

29. Petal bases clearly not clawed. 33

29. Petal bases prominently to obscurely clawed. 30

30. Petals mostly narrow, linear to linear-spatulate. 32

30. Petals mostly wide-spatulate. 31

31. Petals widely spatulate, 30–48 mm long, with a broadly cuneate basal claw; claw obscurely marked with purple or green. At least one petal with an apiculate nipplelike apex, pale sulfur-yellow fading almost to cream. . . . . 22. *T. discolor*

31. Petals narrowly to linear-spatulate, 40–70 mm long, obscurely to clearly narrow-clawed at base, the tips round-acute to obtuse, green, bicolored, green with a purplish base (very rarely all purple) lacking an apiculate nipple (robust individuals and color varients of species 37, 38). 32

32. Upper surface of leaf (under magnification) with numerous stomates across entire surface. Carpels two-thirds the height of stamens. Anther dehiscence introrse/latrorse. Petals green or yellowish-green (rarely all purple) above a weak purplish claw. Odor of rotten fruit. . . . . 37. *T. viride*

32. Upper surface of leaf without stomata or with a few near leaf tip only. Carpels half the height of stamens. Anther dehiscence latrorse. Petals green or yellow-green above a distinct purplish claw (petal rarely purple throughout). Flower odor musty. . . . . 38. *T. viridescens*

33. Petals pale lemon-yellow or greenish-yellow, elliptic-obovate, or oblanceolate to lanceolate, apex acute. Anther connective extending 0.5 mm or less beyond anther sacs, stamens slightly longer than the carpels or about equal. Flower odor strongly of lemon. Native to southeastern United States. . . . . 28. *T. luteum*

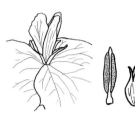

33. Petals yellow, or yellowish-green, bronze green or brown above a yellow base; oblanceolate to obovate, apex truncated, erose, or obtuse. Anther connective extending 1–1.5 mm beyond anther sacs, stamens about 2 times longer than the carpels. Floral odor spicy, of roses. Native to California Bay region. . . . .
. . . . 18. *T. chloropetalum* var. *chloropetalum*, in part

34. Anther extrorse, stamens erect, thick, fully exposed, large and conspicuous, more than half the petal length. Petals spreading to horizontal, with 1 or 2 spiral twists, linear to elliptic, deep maroon to blackish-red. . . . . 35. *T. stamineum*

34. Anther introrse or latrorse, stamens at least partially obscured by petals. Petals erect to divergent and slightly spreading, not spirally twisted, shape and color variable. 35

35. Anther dehiscence predominantly latrorse. 42

35. Anther dehiscence introrse. 36

36. Stamens equal to, less than, or very slightly taller than carpels. 38

36. Stamens about 2 times as tall as carpels. 37

37. Petals oblanceolate to obovate, 65–100 mm long, 14–25 mm wide, garnet-red, rose, pink, purple, lurid brown. Anther connective prolonged I.0–I.5 mm beyond anther sacs. Native to California. . . . .
. . . . . . 18. *T. chloropetalum* var. *chloropetalum,* in part, and *T. chloropetalum* var. *giganteum*

37. Petals linear-elliptic to linear-oblanceolate, 21–40 mm long, 3–8 mm wide, dark purple or maroon. Anther connective slightly prolonged 0.I–I.0 mm beyond anther sacs. Native to eastern Texas and western Louisiana. . . . . 24. *T. gracile*

38. Anther connectives not prolonged beyond anther sacs, or if prolonged, rarely to 0.5 or 1 mm. 41

38. Anther connectives prolonged 1.0 mm or more beyond anther sacs. . . 39

39. Anther connectives prolonged beyond anther sacs into a beak 2–5 mm long, ovary subglobose. . . . . . .
. . . . 34. *T. sessile*

39. Anther connectives prolonged beyond anther sac about 1–1.5 mm. . . 40

40. Stem 25–50 cm tall, petals linear, 50–100 mm long, surface glossy, dark purple to red purple, quilling with aging, 8 to 10 times longer than wide. Leaves 10–20 cm long, 8.7–15 cm wide, blade base contracted into a narrow petiole-like isthmus; leaves obscurely and sparsely mottled or spotted in darker green, rarely plain. Native to central and southern California. . . . . 17. *T. angustipetalum*

40. Stem 8–28 cm tall, petals elliptic to linear-lanceolate, 25–50 mm long, weakly incurved, dark red-purple. Leaves 6.7–12 cm long, 3.8–6 cm wide, blade base evenly tapered to a broad attachment, leaves strongly mottled in several shades of green or bronze-green. Native to eastern Louisiana and southwestern Mississippi. . . . . 23. *T. foetidissimum*

41. Stem 19–39 cm tall. Leaves 7–15 cm long, 4.5–7 cm wide. Petals oblanceolate-spatulate to linear-spatulate, divergent-erect, 45–70 mm long, clear dark red, red-purple, rarely yellow above a purplish base, margins upraised from about the widest point to petal base, apex round-acute. Ovary ovoid, 3-angled to smooth. Native to southeastern United States. . . . . 29. *T. maculatum*

41. Stem 25–48 cm tall. Leaves 10–18 cm long, 7–17 cm wide. Petals oblanceolate, 60–100 mm long, 30–35 mm wide at widest point, erect, widest at about the middle, cuneate basally, round-acute apically, glossy dark maroon-red or purple ("lurid purple" per Freeman 1975). Ovary ovoid, rounded 6-angled. Native to northern California and extreme southwestern Oregon. 25. *T. kurabayashii*

42. Connectives scarcely, if at all, prolonged 0–0.5 mm beyond anther sacs, very rarely longer. Margins of distal third of leaves convex-rounded to leaf apex. 43

42. Connectives prolonged 1.0–2.0 mm beyond anther sacs. Margins of distal third of leaves straight to leaf apex. 44

43. Petals 40–70 mm long, usually more than 9 mm wide, oblanceolate to elliptic-obovate, narrowed to a cuneate but not clawed base, maroon, brown-purple, bronze (fading to browner tones with age), ovary ovoid. . . . . . . 19. *T. cuneatum*

43. Petals 35–55 mm long, rarely more than 8 mm wide at widest point, linear-oblanceolate, erect-spreading, dark maroon-brown, purplish, or commonly dull greenish above a narrowed purplish, weakly clawed base, ovary triangular-ovoid. . . . . 27. *T. ludovicianum*

44. Stem 1.5 times longer than leaves (hence "short" appearing), leaf tips at anthesis often touching ground. Petals 3 to 4 times longer than wide. . . . . 36. *T. underwoodii*

44. Stem 2.5 to 3 times longer than bracts (Freeman 1975) (hence "tall" appearing), leaf tips at anthesis held well away from ground. Petals about 2 times longer than wide. . . . . 20. *T. decipiens*

The Pedicellate Trilliums: Subgenus *Trillium*

1. *Trillium catesbaei* Elliott

Synonymy: *Trillium cernuum* Linnaeus, in part, *Trillium nervosum* Elliott, *Trillium stylosum* Nuttall, *Trillium affine* Rendle

Common Name: Catesby's Trillium, Rosey Wake-robin, Bashful Wake-robin (Small 1933)

This widespread species grows in a variety of habitats, from fairly open laurel thickets and well-lighted hillsides to deeply shaded, rich coves and stream flats. It varies somewhat in flower size and stature, but less so through its range than some other nodding species. The specific epithet *catesbaei* honors the early American naturalist Mark Catesby, noted for his explorations of the Virginia Tidewater area.

Habit

Stem 2–4.5 dm tall, slender.

Leaves elliptic-ovate, 6.5–15 cm long, including petiole-like elongated base, 4–8 cm wide at anthesis, enlarging somewhat after flowering, green, often underlain with a purplish-maroon tone in well-lighted plants, usually raised somewhat exposing the flower below them, veins on upper leaf-surface prominent, deeply engraved; petiolate leaf base 4–15 mm long.

Plate 11. *Trillium catesbaei* in cultivation. Photo by Fred Case.

Pedicel 2–4 cm, rarely 5 cm long, angled, deflexed, or recurved, flowers opening at the leaves or below them; an erect-flowered form occurs in forests below Caesar's Head, Sout Carolina, and perhaps elsewhere.

Sepals linear-lanceolate, 2–4.5 cm long, to 7–8 mm wide, falcate-recurved, green or purple-streaked.

Petals opening white, pink, or rose, occasionally very deep rose; elliptic-oblong to oblong-lanceolate, margins often undulate-wavy, 3.5–5 cm long, 1–2 cm wide, occasionally wider; petal bases somewhat imbricated, forming a funnel-like tube basally, recurved distally; plants from the deep coves in South Carolina tend to open deeper pink and have larger, wider petals than many other forms.

Stamens prominent, recurved, 1.6–2.5 cm long; anthers bright yellow; anther sac slightly shorter than the white filament.

Ovary white, deeply 6-angled at anthesis; stigmas prominent, strongly curled (circinate) to erect.

Fruit a pulpy berrylike capsule, greenish or whitish, ovoid, angles less prominent, 1–1.5 cm in diameter.

Season
Late March in Alabama and outer Carolina Piedmont to June in mountains, very rarely later.

Distribution
Central and northern Alabama, upper piedmont of Georgia, northward through the Piedmont and mountains of North and South Carolina and eastern Tennessee, to southern Virginia. Very local in some districts, abundant in others.

Habitat
Acid soils, mountain laurel (*Kalmia latifolia*) and rhododendron (*Rhododendron* sp.) thickets, dry open woodland, deep maturely forested coves in mountains, woods and thickets of the

Map 1. *Trillium catesbaei.*

Piedmont, often particularly abundant on flats along small streams. Grows in sun or shade.

Varieties, Forms, Hybrids
None.

Comments

This species within its range is more cosmopolitan than some species and may grow in almost any brushy or wooded cover. Yet it can be absent where an experienced person might expect to find it. Upland and mountain forms tend to be white-flowered, smaller, and narrower-petaled than the cove and piedmont forms. Plants usually occur as single or double stems, rarely more, as this species does not regularly form the large clumps characteristic of some pedicellate species.

Elliott, author of *Trillium catesbaei,* apparently separated out one of its forms as *T. nervosum.* This name is still mentioned in British horticultural and botanical literature, but is almost unmentioned in U.S. literature. North American botanists treat *T. nervosum* as a synonym of *T. catesbaei.*

While easy to cultivate in a humusy acid soil, *Trillium catesbaei* does not respond with vigor nor does it tend to seed about as do species such as *T. grandiflorum* or *T. erectum.*

2. *Trillium cernuum* Linnaeus

Synonymy: *Trillium cernuum* var. *macranthum* Wiegand
Common Name: Nodding Trillium

Seldom a showy plant because it hides its flowers beneath a tight crown of leaves, *Trillium cernuum* nevertheless gets much mention in the botanical literature. It was the name on which Linnaeus founded his genus *Trillium,* but botanists are uncertain which plant should carry that name. Linnaeus appeared to include in his description features of both *T. cernuum* and *T. catesbaei.* He gave as the type locality, "Carolina." Since *T. cernuum* does not grow that far south, Barksdale (1938) concluded that Linnaeus actually intended his name for *T. catesbaei.* After

Plate 12. *Trillium cernuum,* showing the nearly equal length of the anther and filament, and their characteristic lavender-gray color.

much confusion, botanists have settled on the name *T. cernuum* for the northern plant from Linnaeus' description, but even today many are confused by this species. South of its true range in the southern Appalachians and environs, several superficially similar species are often confused with *T. cernuum..* Although still included in some southern floras, evidence of its occurrence from Virginia southward is limited. The specific epithet *cernuum* means "nodding."

Habit
Stem or commonly 2 to 3 stems from a single rhizome crown, 1–4 dm tall, rarely taller, bearing the 3 leaves so close together that they almost overlap umbrella-like.

Leaves bright green without red tones, broadly rhombic-ovate to suborbicular, acuminate-tipped, widest near the middle, narrowed toward the point of attachment, with or without a barely noticeable petiole-like base, 5–15 cm long, 6–15 cm wide, sometimes larger in both dimensions.

Pedicel 1.5–3 cm long, strongly recurved or declined, flower nodding and usually hidden beneath leaves; reports of longer and shorter peduncles are usually based upon abnormally small flowering specimens or southern plants that actually represent other species.

Sepals lanceolate, acuminate, green, margins slightly raised, equalling the petals.

Petals 1.5–2.5 cm long, 9–15 mm wide, oblong-lanceolate, acuminate-tipped, usually strongly recurved, opening white or rarely pale pink, thin-textured.

Anthers 2–6.5 mm long, pale lavender-pink, or gray, about equalling the slender filament.

Ovary at anthesis white to pinkish, pyramidal, strongly 6-ribbed; stigmas stout.

Fruit a large, ovoid-pyramidal, fleshy, dark red berry, its bruised tissue fruitily fragrant, juicy; as the fruit matures, the leaves become raised, exposing the fruit to view.

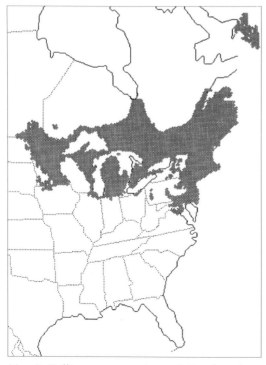

Map 2. *Trillium cernuum.* A population found on southwestern Newfoundland is not shown.

Season
Late April to early June, possibly July in Newfoundland and northern Manitoba.

Distribution
Most northern of all North American trilliums, this species thrives in swamp cover southward in its range, but grows in both wet and drier cover northward. Newfoundland across Canada to Manitoba, southward through the Great Lakes States to Wisconsin, Indiana, Ohio, Pennsylvania, New York, New England south to West Virginia and Virginia, perhaps very rarely southward at higher eleva-

tions. Reports south of Virginia represent *Trillium rugelii, T. catesbaei,* or *T. flexipes* forms.

Habitat

Prefers cool, low, moist to swampy woodlands, streambanks among alders (*Alnus* sp.) and pond borders in deep deciduous forests in southern part of its range. Northward it grows also in upland woods of conifers mixed with deciduous trees. In Michigan, frequent along trout streams and conifer-hardwood swamps, often with Canadian yew (*Taxus canadensis*).

Varieties, Forms, Hybrids

var. *cernuum*. The typical variety described above.

var. *macranthum* Wiegand. Older authors and floras commonly list two varieties, var. *cernuum* (see above) and var. *macranthum,* based primarily upon size differences: the smaller var. *cernuum* is found from Delaware and eastern Pennsylvania northward to Newfoundland, and the larger var. *macranthum* (large-flowered) is found mainly farther inland into the Midwest, or at the southern area of its range as formerly given into the southern Appalachians where *T. cernuum* does not grow. The areas ascribed to var. *macranthum* are those sympatric with *T. flexipes* and *T. rugelii,* both robust species with which *T. cernuum* may hybridize. Even in areas it occupies alone, *T. cernuum* varies considerably in size not only with fertility of the soil, but also with stage of development that season. Although there is a tendency for the eastern seaboard plant to be somewhat smaller and more delicate, and the midwestern and far northern plants to be more robust, there is much variation largely dependent upon soil nutrients. Although there are regional size trends, we do not believe, based upon our experiences with this plant in Newfoundland, Michigan, Wisconsin, and Minnesota, that the two varieties can be maintained.

forma *tangerae* Wherry. Flowers deep roseate (Fernald 1950). Named for its discoverer, Louise F. A. Tanger. This deep rose-colored form, in our opinion, represents a hybrid with *Trillium erectum* (see below).

Although hybrids of *Trillium cernuum* with other species are not, to our knowledge, reported in the literature, Fred Young, Janet Schultz, and the authors observed a hybrid swarm between *T. cernuum* and *T. erectum* in Upper Michigan in which all possible combinations of form, structure, and color occur, exactly paralleling the hybridization of *T. erectum* and *T. flexipes* in Michigan woodlands and in the controlled pollination experiments in our garden (see Case and Burrows 1962; Case 1991, 1993). We are convinced that the plant known as *T. cernuum* f. *tangerae* described from Quebec represents one of these hybrid forms, as both parents occur together there, and many deep rose individuals occur in our Michigan hybrid swarm.

Comments

Trillium cernuum, while an interesting species, has little to recommend it horticulturally. Its small and thin-textured flowers usually remain hidden beneath the leaves. Only the fruit is moderately conspicuous. Furthermore, *T. cernuum* frequently sulks under garden conditions, dwindling and disappearing after a few years. Naturalized on our land in low wet ground in a thicket, it fares better but does not truly thrive as most species do. Its hybrids with *T. erectum* grow much better in the garden.

3. *Trillium erectum* Linnaeus

Synonymy: *Trillium rhomboideum* Michaux, *Trillium foetidum* Salisbury, *Trillium erectum* var. *atropurpureum* Pursh, *Trillium purpureum* Kin, *Trillium nutans* Rafinesque, *Trillium atropurpureum* Curtis ex Beck, *Trillium erectum rubrum* Clute

Common Name: Red Trillium, Wake-robin, Stinking Benjamin, Stinking Willie, Purple Trillium, Squawroot, Birthwort, American True Love

This widespread American trillium flowers very early in the spring, heralding the onset of the spring wildflower season. Indeed, it is not unusual for the plants to suffer considerable frost damage, even to the extent that the stem freezes below the leaves and snaps off, ending the appearance of the plant for that season (see "Growth Bud Dormancy").

While it cannot be described as showy in the sense of *Trillium grandiflorum*, the flowers of *T. erectum* or some of its local varieties can be

Plate 13. *Trillium erectum*, a Michigan form. Flowers fade to a duller red-purple tone with age. Photo by Fred Case.

quite striking, especially since this species tends to form large clumps. Throughout its wide range, this species varies considerably. Many locally distinct populations exist, considerable individual variation (either from mutation or hybridization), within populations occurs, and consequently, taxonomic confusion reigns. Some local populations may deserve subspecific or specific rank, others may best be treated as forms or varieties. The specific epithet *erectum* refers to the stiffly erect pedicel in some forms of this species. In many populations, however, the pedicel leans or almost declines, making the name somewhat inappropriate.

Habit

Stem 1.5–6 dm tall, southern populations tend to be tallest, several stems often arising from the same rhizome, bearing 3 sessile leaves.

Leaves broadly rhombic to ovate-rhombic, about as broad as long, widest near the middle, base acute, acuminate-tipped, 5–20 cm long and wide, bright green without much trace of dark pigments.

Pedicel straight, erect or dangling, or somewhat declined below leaves but not strongly recurved below leaves as in *T. cernuum* or some forms of *T. flexipes;* 1–10 cm long, rarely longer; flowers typically open dark red-maroon, fading to dull purple-brown.

Sepals lanceolate-acuminate, about equaling petals, 1–5 cm long, green, often streaked or overlaid with maroon, occasionally entirely dark maroon, leafy-textured.

Petals lanceolate, ovate-lanceolate, occasionally ovate, 1.5–5 cm long, 1–3 cm broad, heavy textured, with major veins prominent, appearing somewhat engraved, dark red-brown, maroon, purple, or white; pale yellow-green or white mutants occur in nearly all populations, occasional deeper yellows; bicolors and speckled forms occur especially in mixed populations with *T. cernuum, T. flexipes, T. rugelii,* and *T. sulcatum,* suggesting to us that these forms are of hybrid origin (see discussion pages 38–44); northern forms tend to have rather longer lanceolate-acuminate petals than those farther south and the petals tend to be directed somewhat forward, rather than being widely spreading, with one petal often carried in a somewhat asymmetrical position relative to the other two—a condition much rarer southward; occasionally, local, almost linear-petaled forms predominate.

Stamens dark maroon, gray-maroon or yellowish, strongly yellow with exposed pollen, 5–9 mm long; filament as long or longer than the anther, but variable with race.

Ovary oval to spherical, 6-angled, the angles forming very low ridges when fruit is ripe, dark purple to maroon, even in white-flowered forms; stigmas short, stout, recurved, about half the length of ovary at anthesis, or less.

Flower odor fetid, like a wet dog.

Fruit, when mature, a juicy and fragrant almost spherical to slightly pyramidal dark maroon berry.

Season
Early to late April and May; into early June in northern part of range, depending upon latitude and elevation.

Distribution
Quebec including Gaspe Peninsula, eastern and southeastern Ontario to Michigan (where distribution is irregular and local, including one recently discovered Upper Peninsula colony) south through Nova Scotia and New England to Ohio, Pennsylvania, Delaware (Fernald 1950) and in the mountains southward to Kentucky, North Carolina, and upland Georgia. We have found typical *Trillium erectum* on shaley outcrops near Liberty, Kentucky, at the south of the Bluegrass (limestone) area some distance west of the Appalachian region. Populations at lower elevations southward, especially around the Great Smoky Mountain National Park region tend to be mostly the white-petaled *T. erectum* var. *album,* while the plants of higher elevations are dark red flowered. Reports of *T. erectum* from west of the stated distribution in Ohio, Michigan, and Illinois may represent *T. flexipes* f. *walpolei,* introgressive hybridization between outlying colonies of *T. erectum* and various species (see comments under each species and Case and Burrows 1962), or escapes from gardens.

Habitat
Prefers a humus-rich, cool, moist, somewhat acid soil. Occurs in upland deciduous forest and under hemlocks (*Tsuga* sp.) rhododendron (*Rhododendron* sp.), and laurel (*Kalmia* sp.) thickets, mixed white pine-deciduous forests, often where there is a ground cover of Canadian yew

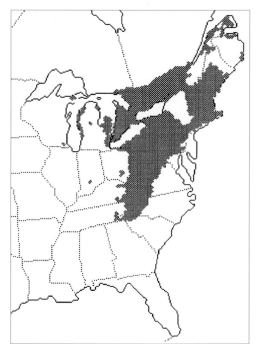

Map 3. *Trillium erectum.*

(*Taxus canadensis*) northward. In lower Michigan grows frequently in low, swampy woodlands and brushy thickets along streams, especially in margins of old, somewhat disturbed white cedar (*Thuja occidentalis*) swamp. Southward becomes increasingly a plant of higher elevations (especially the typically colored dark red flowered forms), occurring in almost any forested cover on neutral to acidic soils unless very dry. The white-flowered populations (*Trillium erectum* var. *album*) seem to occur in somewhat more neutral and richer soils.

Varieties, Forms, Hybrids

var. *erectum*. The typical variety described above.

var. *album* (Michaux) Pursh. Occasional throughout the species' range, but the predominant form at lower elevations surrounding the Great Smoky Mountains (Plate 14). This form, white-petaled, with the globose, dark maroon ovary, seems clear-cut *T. erectum,* but may be confused with some plants essentially identical except for a more pyramidal dark ovary. Patrick annotated some of these confusing specimens at Vanderbilt University as a dark ovaried form of *T. flexipes.* He published nothing on them, to our knowledge, and never formalized or typified his treatment. We do not regard this plant, with its flower form so typically that of *T. erectum,* to be *T. flexipes.* Rather, we think there has been much hybridization in the area where its populations are so frequent, and that the pyramidal ovary of *T. flexipes* and others has introgressed into *T. erectum* var. *album.* In some districts var. *album* is the only form of *T. erectum* present, while in other districts it is present only as an occasional albino mutation.

Many other colors occur. Most frequent is a soft pale yellow, but white with pink overlay, or paler forms of the red-maroon coloring also appear. None of these forms seems to have been named and typified in *Trillium erectum.* This is probably to the good, because some of these forms may represent interspecific hybrids, not true forms.

Trillium erectum hybridizes with *T. cernuum, T. flexipes, T. rugelii,* and possibly other species, in regions where their ranges overlap. Many spectacular and unusually colored individuals result. These are discussed elsewhere in this book (see "Natural Hybrids").

Plate 14. *Trillium erectum* f. *album* in cultivation. Photo by Fred Case.

Comments

Trillium erectum varies more in color, size, and ovary shape than any other pedicellate *Trillium*. Because it intergrades with almost all related species, many specimens are impossible to key or place with confidence. That these confusing forms are hybrids we have verified by duplicating them with hand-pollinated crosses from selected typical plants of each species involved. The resulting offspring show the same range of color and shape variation as we have observed in the confusing wild populations.

Horticulturally, this species in its finer forms is an outstanding garden plant for the woodland and wildflower garden. Propagating easily from division of clumps, and spreading spontaneously in the garden from seed, it can be had in numbers without decimating wild populations. Its tendency to produce fine hybrids and many color forms makes it an ideal plant for the geneticist to work with in producing exceptional trilliums for garden use. (See "Petal Color and Color Patterns" and Plates 5, 6, 10).

4. *Trillium flexipes* Rafinesque

Synonymy: *Trillium erectum* var. *declinatum* A. Gray, *Trillium album* Small, *Trillium declinatum* Gleason, *Trillium gleasonii* Fernald
Common Name: Bent Trillium, White Trillium

Some authors list no common name for this widespread, somewhat confusing species. Although declined trillium or Gleason's trillium might at first seem appropriate common names, many forms of this species do not decline, and *Trillium gleasonii* was applied to the predominately declined northeastern forms of *T. flexipes*. Freeman (1995) and Patrick (1986B) called the plant bent trillium or white trillium. The specific epithet *flexipes* means "with bent or flexed foot-stalk" (Fernald 1952). Rather than referring to the sometimes declined pedicel itself, we think Rafinesque must have been referring to the kneelike bend at the summit of the pedicel, which is usually flexed to cause the flower to face outward at right angles to the pedicel.

Trillium flexipes superficially resembles *T. cernuum*, *T. rugelii*, and some forms of *T. erectum* var. *album*. Over its vast range, the species varies considerably, and because it hybridizes with related species, it has confused more botanists than any other pedicellate *Trillium*, resulting in several synonymous names and a myriad of incorrect locality reports. At times, misidentified hybrids have obscured the distribution information for other species and added to the confusion surrounding *T. flexipes* and its relatives.

Plate 15. *Trillium flexipes* at home on a calcareous slope in Kentucky. Photo by Fred Case.

Plate 16. *Trillium flexipes,* erect-flowered form from Kentucky. Note the heavy petal texture.

Trillium flexipes is the common white-flowered *Trillium* of the east-central U.S. lowlands west of the Appalachian mountains and south of the southern Great Lakes States. Only in the Lakes states, extreme southern Ontario, along the Cumberland Plateau and in the vicinity of the Great Smoky Mountains does its range overlap that of the showier *T. grandiflorum* to any extent. Physically a robust, tall plant, its flowers are smaller than those of *T. grandiflorum,* but of a creamier white with much heavier textured petals. Erect-flowered forms can be very showy. Blooms remain in good condition longer than those of *T. grandiflorum* and do not turn pink with age. The large-petaled very fragrant form from northern Alabama from a distance can scarcely be distinguished from some forms of *T. grandiflorum.*

Habit

Stem robust, 2–5 dm tall, one to several from a single rhizome.

Leaves sessile, rhombic, 7–25 cm long and wide, frequently wider than long, acuminate-tipped, tapering from just above the middle to the sessile base, light to medium green without red or maroon undertones.

Pedicel stiffly erect, angled or carried horizontally, or declined beneath leaves, but rarely curved (recurved), 4–12 cm long (be suspicious of the identity of plants with shorter and strongly recurved peduncles); flowers of erect forms reflexed about 90 degrees on the peduncle to face outward rather than upward, or variously carried on strongly declined peduncles; flowers creamy white (brown-maroon, grizzled tan or pinkish in what may be introgressed hybrid forms, see discussion elsewhere in this book).

Sepals green, lanceolate, barely equalling petals, weakly recurved.

Petals heavy textured, veins weakly engraved, ovate-lanceolate to broadly ovate, 2–5 cm long, 1–4 cm wide.

Anthers thick, cream-yellow, at least twice as long as filament, often longer.

Ovary pyramidal, strongly 6-angled, white or pink flushed at anthesis; stigmas short, thick and strongly recurved.

Fruit very large, juicy, berrylike, strongly angled, rosy-red to purplish, fruity-fragrant where bruised, persistent into early autumn.

Season

April in southern part of range, early May over most of its range, into early June in Great Lakes states and their islands.

Distribution

New York to southern Minnesota, southward to Missouri, Arkansas, Alabama, and the central lowlands from Alabama, Tennessee, and Kentucky where locally abundant, to New York. Occurs along the edges of the Cumberland Plateau in Kentucky and Tennessee, on limestone soils. Only recently discovered in southern Ontario.

Habitat

Rich wooded slopes on limestone-derived soils, especially along stream valleys, upper alluvial plains in sandy-alluvium, rich woods on higher flood plains.

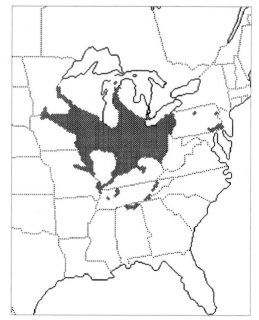

Map 4. *Trillium flexipes.*

Varieties, Forms, Hybrids

forma *flexipes.* The typical form described above.

forma *walpolei* (Farwell) Fernald. A form, usually with a declined pedicel and bearing reddish-brown or maroon petals and a white ovary. This form occurs frequently in Michigan and southeastern Ohio, and very locally in Kentucky. Case and Burrows (1962) mapped the occurrence of this form for Michigan and found it to occur only along the contact zone between *Trillium flexipes* and *T. erectum.* Case and Case (1993) crossed typical *T. erectum* and *T. flexipes* to produce identical color variations as occur in these wild mixed species populations. We consider this form to be a hybrid expression.

forma *billingtonii* Farwell. A bicolored form, red at the petal base and white distally. Authors have ignored this name. Because this form is identical with another common expression found in our controlled hybrids, we believe this form and other related forms to be introgressed hybrids with *T. erectum* on the contact zone of their ranges. Frequently these plants possess white petals with a dark red-brown base. Dried specimens, hastily examined, superficially resemble *T. undulatum,* and probably bear the responsibility for the reports of *T. undulatum* from locations near Ann Arbor, Michigan, and various places in Indiana and Illinois, since these are from areas of soils completely unsuitable to *T. undulatum.*

Comments

While some authors consider *Trillium flexipes* a form of *T. erectum,* they must have worked entirely from dried herbarium specimens. The plant is undoubtedly closely related to *T. erectum,* as it hybridizes freely, producing fertile hybrids, but in life the two plants and their behavior differ considerably. *Trillium flexipes* is a plant of circumneutral to alkaline soils, often those derived from weathering of limestone; *T. erectum* prefers acidic, humus-rich soils. *Trillium flexipes* prefers lower slopes, flood plains, and alluvial soils, while *T. erectum* grows most frequently in upland deciduous or mixed forests in humus. Northward it grows also in the borders of old, much oxidized peaty soils of white cedar (*Thuja*) swamps. *Trillium flexipes* is generally a plant of the interior lowlands (the central lowland of Fenneman 1938), while *T. erectum* is a plant of the Appalachian uplands, Cumberland Plateau, and northern hardwood forests on glacial soils. The ovary of *T. flexipes* at anthesis is white or white streaked with rose-pink, and strongly pyramidal with prominent ridges; that of *T. erectum,* at anthesis is dark maroon-red or purple-black, almost orbicular with shallow ridges. Hybrids, of course, are intermediate, making positive identification difficult. Typical *T. flexipes* petals are white with the flower carried at right angles to the peduncle, while typical *T. erectum* flowers are dark red-maroon, with flower carried facing outward or upward from the peduncle attachment (except in the plant known variously as *T. sulcatum,* or *T. erectum* var. *sulcatum*). *Trillium flexipes* blooms emit a faint to strong odor of old garden roses, or no odor at all, those of *T. erectum* have a faint to fairly strong (at close range) fetid odor resembling that of a wet dog.

Northern forms of *Trillium flexipes* tend to produce declined or recurved peduncles, thus carrying the flower at or below the leaves. Such forms lack the showiness of the stiffly erect-flowered forms prevalent in the Central and Southern states. Many of the northern forms also produce strongly recurved petals. Such forms closely resemble large plants of *T. cernuum* with which they are frequently confused. In such cases, one must carefully examine the stamens: those of *T. cernuum* are slender, lavender-pink or purplish, with anther and filament about of equal length, while those of *T. flexipes* are thick, cream or yellow, with the anther greatly exceeding the length of the usually very short filament. Since both these species may grow in proximity in some northern habitats, the possibility that some plants with strongly recurved petals may be hybrids should not be overlooked. Plants of *T. flexipes* along the bluffs of the Mississippi River in the Driftless Area of Minnesota and Wisconsin emit a strong and very pleasant fragrance, but the strongest and most pleasing fragrance is found in the forms of *T. flexipes* from the Bankhead forest region of northern Alabama.

For horticultural purposes, *Trillium flexipes* is an outstanding species. It hybridizes readily with *T. erectum* and *T. sulcatum.* We have produced viable seed in hand-pollinated crosses with *T. vaseyi.* It seems likely it will also cross with *T. rugelii* and *T. simile.* We have seen putative hybrids with *T. cernuum.* As selected *T. flexipes* clones can impart erect flowers, heavy-textured petals, long-lasting blooms—all desirable garden characteristics—to its offspring and also produces a percentage of bicolors (see "Petal Color and Color Patterns"), it is an ideal parent for a horticultural breeding program.

5. *Trillium grandiflorum* (Michaux) Salisbury

Synonymy: *Trillium rhomboideum* var. *grandiflorum* Michaux, *Trillium grandiflorum* Salisbury, *Trillium erythrocarpum Curtis's Botanical Magazine*, *Trillium grandiflorum* f. *viride* Farwell, *Trillium grandiflorum* f. *roseum* Farwell

Common Name: White Trillium, Great White Trillium, Large-flowered White Trillium, White Wake-robin

This species, the most showy, best known and loved of all the trilliums, is the provincial flower of Ontario, Canada, and, in European gardens, one of the most highly prized woodland or shade flowers. No other *Trillium* can match this species' abundance and flowering spectacle as it occurs in the heart of its range. The specific epithet *grandiflorum* means "large-flowered." See Plates 1, 17, 18.

Habit

Stem 1.5–3 dm tall, occasionally taller, especially under cultivation or in particularly fertile soil, with typically 3 subsessile leaves; occasional 2- or 4-leaved anomalous forms appear, usually persisting only one season then reverting.

Leaves ovate to somewhat rhombic, tapered to an acuminate tip, widest near the base, dark green with maroon overtones when first emerging, rich dark green later, persisting until late summer or early autumn; leaves commonly 12–20 cm long, 8–15 cm wide, the veins appearing prominently engraved on upper surface; local populations can be smaller or larger in general size.

Pedicel erect-ascending to strongly erect, 2–8 cm long, occasionally longer, often much longer in mycoplasma-infected plants.

Sepals 2–5.5 cm long, 1.2–2.3 cm wide, acuminate, green, occasionally streaked with maroon purple.

Petals variable; size depending upon age, vigor, health, and genetics of the particular population, 4–7.5 cm long, 2–4 cm wide, lanceolate to oblong, obovate, or rarely suborbicular, sides often parallel, but tapering to a more or less acuminate tip; petal bases erect, flaring and recurving somewhat above the middle to produce a strongly funnelform flower; inner surface of the petal with the veins appearing deeply

Plate 17. *Trillium grandiflorum* in early bloom. Photo by Fred Case.

engraved; petal tissue opening white to rarely deep salmon-pink, strongly opaque at first, becoming somewhat transparent with age, fading to a dull, pinkish-purple, occasionally almost to red.

Stamens with filaments much shorter than the anther, stout; anthers long, slender, pale-colored, recurving, strongly yellow with exposed pollen in anthesis, shriveling and persisting with the ripened fruit.

Ovary 6-angled, pale green even when mature, ovoid, 8–18 mm long; stigmas slender, erect, becoming spreading, equal or exceeding the ovary at anthesis.

Fruit pale green, obscurely 6-angled, with many large brown seeds in a mealy, moist but not juicy pulp when mature; falling from plant with seeds inside.

Season

Late April into early June, depending upon latitude or elevation, opening just after *Trillium erectum* in shared habitat.

Distribution

Maine, New Hampshire and southern Quebec, across southern Ontario to Michigan, Wisconsin and northeastern Minnesota. In the South, locally along the Appalachian mountains to Georgia but absent from some districts. Common in parts of Smoky Mountain National Park.

Habitat

On well-drained soils in rich deciduous or mixed woods, favoring woods of sugar maple (*Acer saccharum*) and beech (*Fagus* sp.) in the north, on subacid to neutral soils. Occasionally found on floodplains, in thickets or fencerows, or old fields adjacent to woodland. Adversely affected by grazing: large populations have disappeared after repeated grazing by deer. Populations most vigorous in young to early maturity stages of second-

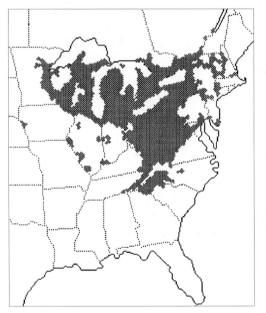

Map 5. *Trillium grandiflorum.*

growth forests, declining with the increased shading of old-growth woodlands.

Varieties, Forms, Hybrids

forma *grandiflorum*. The typical form when other forms occur.

forma *roseum* Farwell. Flowers opening light to deep pink. Occasional throughout, but locally frequent along the Blue Ridge Mountains of Virginia (Plate 18). The epithet *roseum* means "pink flowered."

Although named by various authors as taxonomic forms, the following (and many others, not all of them named forms) almost certainly represent stages in a mycoplasma infection (for a discussion of the mycoplasma problem, see "Mutations and Abnormalities"; for an illustration, see Plate 2):

> forma *chandleri* Farwell
> forma *dimerum* Louis-Marie

Plate 18. *Trillium grandiflorum* f. *roseum* in the wild on the Blue Ridge Mountains in Virginia. Photo by Fred Case.

forma *elongatum* Louis-Marie
forma *lirioides* (Rafinesque) Victorin
forma *petalosum* Louis-Marie
forma *striatum* Louis-Marie
forma *viride* Farwell

We examined some of Farwell's types and many of his specimens in the Cranbrook Institute of Science and University of Michigan Herbariums. They were clearly representative examples of stages of the mycoplasma infection we studied (Hooper et al. 1971).

forma *polymerum* Victorin. A multipetaled mutant occurring rather frequently in this species.

Most double and multipetaled forms are stable, healthy, sterile plants of great beauty (Plates 3, 4). Horticulturally, such forms have been designated form *floro plenum* or form *multiplex,* meaning "many petaled." Neither of these names is a formal one typified and with a proper Latin diagnosis, and thus both are botanically invalid. Horticulturists will likely ignore that fact and continue to use the variety or forma *floro plenum* for convenience to indicate doubles, as they have for years. Individual clonal names (horticultural) have been applied to some individuals of the double and other unusual forms.

No hybrids of *Trillium grandiflorum* have ever been documented.

Comments

With a rather vast range, it is natural that this species should show considerable variation, which it does. The usual floral variations—larger and fuller petals, smaller than normal floral segments, and narrow-petaled forms—all occur. But additional variations also appear. Some arise from genetic mutation, some result from disease.

Two- or four-petaled forms occur, often accompanied by two or four leaves and sepals. These forms most commonly result from cell division errors in the bud, perhaps induced by physical injury; the following year the same plants revert to normal three-petalled, three-leaved plants. Only rarely are such forms genetic and permanent.

Other startling forms occur. Occasionally, a plant will appear with green leaflike tissue down the middle of each petal. Other variants include all green petals, abortive and distorted green or green and white petals, no petals at all, only knots of sepals, and doubling of petals accompanied by greening and distortion of petal shape (see Plate 2). Changes in leaf shape accompany these aberrant forms, the most frequent being long petioles on the normally sessile leaves or no leaves at all. Some of these forms seem to stabilize and reappear with slight variations for several years. In others, the plants become more and more fantastically deformed each year, finally to deteriorate and die. These peculiar forms, formerly thought to be mutations (see Hall 1961, Stoutamire 1958), result from infection of the plant by mycoplasma organisms (Hooper et al. 1971).

Over most of its range, *Trillium grandiflorum* produces white flowers that fade to a dullish pink-purple with age. Occasional plants produce almost red-maroon petals just as they collapse, but none we have seen approach the flat, barn-red of aging *T. ovatum* along the Smith River in northern California. All these aging flowers appear tired, with thin-textured petals as the flower gradually withers. However, along the Blue Ridge Mountains in Virginia occurs an outstanding form that opens from light to deep pink, with salmon or peach undertones. Horticulturist Richard Lighty has a form that he avers to open almost a cerise-red. Some plants actually open white and develop their color within a day or so upon exposure to light. This color is much warmer and more attractive than the pink induced by aging. The correct epithet for this pink-opening form appears to be *T. grandiflorum* f. *roseum* (Plate 18).

In these *roseum* forms, the leaves frequently have deep wine-red undertones superimposed upon the normal green, perhaps indicating some genetic tendency to overproduction of anthocyanin pigments. This is further indicated by the variation of individual pink clones depending upon type of soil, mineral content, soil pH, and soil and air temperatures. Plants from the Royal Botanic Gardens, Edinburgh, Scotland, sometimes fail to produce the deep pink coloring when transplanted to warmer climates (Alfred Evans, pers. comm.; Harry Elkins, pers. comm.) The late botanist Edgar T. Wherry (1974) claimed this color to be strongly influenced by iron content of the soil, more iron producing deeper colors.

The pink forms occur either in pure stands or mixed with typical white-flowered forms along at least 100 miles of the Blue Ridge Mountains in Virginia. The clones of forma *roseum* widely grown in Europe may have come from populations east of Chesapeake Bay in Maryland (Wherry 1974).

Perhaps the most spectacular of the *Trillium grandiflorum* forms are those with extra petals, such as forma *polymerum*. A wide variety of double and multipetaled forms, both genetic and disease-induced, occur. Some of these are spectacularly showy and highly desirable for garden use. Most are completely sterile plants, their reproductive organs completely replaced by additional petals. Consequently, these forms must be propagated by asexual means, a relatively slow process. Such forms bring a high price in the garden market. If these or other outstanding forms of *Trillium* could be tissue-cultured, it would make outstanding plants available to all in a short time. Rare species, too, could be propagated in this manner without impinging upon wild populations.

According to a popular misconception, *Trillium grandiflorum* is rare, local, or endangered in parts of eastern New England, New York and the East Coast because it has been overpicked, dug, and collected. This is simply not true. The maps of Patrick (1973) show that the species never grew there abundantly. Its center of distribution is farther west, along the Appalachian Mountains, across western New York, southern Ontario, Michigan, Wisconsin, eastern Minnesota, and northeastern Ohio. The abundance of this species within this region is legendary and breathtaking. In much of this area, *T. grandiflorum* colors the spring woodland floor with drifts of white. Thousands of plants per acre flower in May. Almost every unpastured, undisturbed woodland harbors large populations.

6. *Trillium nivale* Riddell

Synonymy: None
Common Name: Snow Trillium, Dwarf White Trillium

Like the eastern skunk cabbage (*Symplocarpus foetidus*), snow trillium, a true harbinger of spring, blooms so early that it regularly gets buried in snow. The specific epithet *nivale* means "of the snows, snowy." The plant can withstand freezing solid night after night and yet continue to ma-

Plate 19. *Trillium nivale*, with photographer's fingers to show size scale. Photo by Fred Case.

Plate 20. *Trillium nivale*, a clump of an Indiana form. Photo by Fred Case.

ture, bloom, and fruit without serious damage. The dwarf stature and early season of bloom impart a special charm to this species, enhanced by its often very rare or local distribution in parts of its range.

Habit

Stem, at onset of anthesis, 3–5 cm tall, continuing to expand after anthesis until 4.5–9 cm tall, hexagonal in cross section (Deam 1940).

Leaves elliptic-ovate, obtuse to weakly acuminate, distinctly petioled, blue-green, with prominent veins, 1.5–4.5 cm long, continuing to expand after onset of anthesis.

Pedicel short, erect at first, strongly recurving beneath the leaves in fruit, 1–2 cm long.

Sepals shorter than the petals, lanceolate, blue-green.

Petals very showy, white, thin-textured and recurved to firm-textured and erect-spreading, ovate-elliptic to oblong, obtuse-acuminate tipped, 1.5–3.5 cm long, 8–15 mm wide.

Stamens slender, 5–18 mm long; anthers 2.5–11 mm long, slightly longer than the filaments.

Ovary obtusely 3-angled, white, nearly globular when ripe; common style slender, elongate, the tips spreading.

Fruit ripening in mid-June, greenish-white, pulpy, quickly deciduous.

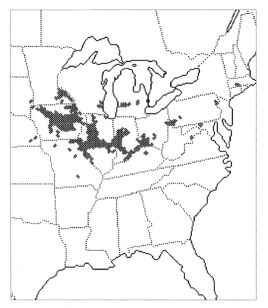

Season

Early to mid-March to early April; varies by one to two weeks from season to season depending upon the specific spring warmup. Seed matures in mid-June, much earlier than that of most species, and the leaves wither and die at the same time.

Distribution

Primarily at south edge of Pleistocene glaciation from West Virginia (Dobberpuhl, pers. comm.) and Pennsylvania across south-central

Map 6. *Trillium nivale.*

Ohio, southern and western Indiana, Illinois, and up the Mississippi Valley to southern Minnesota, with outlying more or less disjunct stations in Maryland, northern Ohio, Indiana, south-central Michigan, Wisconsin, and locally west to Nebraska. Locally abundant in a narrow habitat to locally rare and endangered.

Habitat

Occurs on limestone-derived soils, alkaline glacial drift, or loess. Habitat of two distinct types, at least in outward appearance. In one, plants grow in crevices of limestone outcroppings, talus, and bare, creeping soil at base of ledges, sliding soil at top of cliffs, or in debris at base of weathering large rocks and boulders. Soil must be raw, open, with little or no leafmold or live plant competition. In the other habitat, plants grow along moderate to large rivers, on the floodplain or riverbank at the point of highest inundation deposits, where soil is gravelly-sandy, alkaline, but not hardpacked clays (see Case 1982). Very large, crowded colonies may form in a limited area, and then the plant may be absent for miles along the river only to reappear in another suitable niche. The species may appear in both types of habitat at the same location if conditions permit. Many of the disjunct stations out of the main range of the plant are of the floodplain raw gravel type, or in specialized neutral to alkaline soils such as on forested deposits of loess in Minnesota and Iowa.

Varieties, Forms, Hybrids

None listed in the literature; however, we have noticed a difference in flower size, texture, and plant vigor between plants from limestone outcrops in southern Indiana, and those of riverbank gravels in Ohio, Michigan, and Minnesota. The Indiana form, more vigorous in growth with very large flowers, cultivates easily, and seeds abundantly in our garden. The Michigan stream-floodplain form, with more recurved, thinner-textured petals, lacks vigor, does poorly, gradually disappears in cultivation, and seldom seeds in our garden. Whether these two forms deserve any taxonomic recognition is debatable, but certainly the Indiana form is a superior one for horticultural purposes.

Comments

Although locally frequent in the heart of its limited range, *Trillium nivale* can also be rare, local, and a challenge to find. In Michigan it was thought to be extirpated in 1938 and for 40 years thereafter. For most of those 40 years, we hunted diligently for it. With the help of Candido Gonzales, who found the first plants, and others, we rediscovered first a few plants, then several thousand on several riverbanks of a major river system in Michigan. Publication of an article by us on its very special habitat resulted in others discovering outstanding stations as well (Case and Case 1982). Considering that the species was not seen at all for 40 years, yet, when relocated, grew in very local colonies of hundreds, even thousands of plants, it is possible that colonies wax and wane with the vagaries of flooding and its soil deposition. *Trillium nivale* does not compete well with other vegetation and requires a raw, open soil, kept so by flood deposits or the action of rock weathering and gravity.

Horticulturally, *Trillium nivale* is an outstanding rock garden plant, of appropriate size, showy, and relatively easy to cultivate if given limestone soil. It propagates easily and quickly from seed and produces large amounts of seed in the wild or in the garden. Its early bloom makes it doubly desirable. It seems closely related to, but biologically isolated from painted trillium (*T. undulatum*). We have hand-pollinated *T. undulatum* with *T. nivale* pollen and obtained what appeared to be good seed.

7. *Trillium ovatum* Pursh

Synonymy: Synonymy for *T. ovatum* follows Munz (1959). *Trillium californicum* Kellogg, *Trillium crassifolium* Piper, *Trillium scouleri* Rydberg, *Trillium venosum* Gates, *Trillium ovatum* var. *stenosepalum* Gates
Common Name: Western White Trillium, White Trillium

The most widespread of western North American trilliums, *Trillium ovatum* varies greatly within its range. Although it closely resembles the eastern *T. grandiflorum* in general aspect, it varies more in size and flower fullness, both within a given habitat and from area to area of its

Plate 21. *Trillium ovatum* in the wild in Washington. Photo by Fred Case.

range. The specific epithet, *ovatum* (egg-shaped), refers to the shape of the petals, oval, not strongly overlapping or imbricated as in *T. grandiflorum.* Nevertheless, there are many plants, which out of the normal geographic location, could not be distinguished from the eastern *T. grandiflorum* with its broad, overlapping petals. *Trillium ovatum* is a beautiful species that is exciting to encounter in the wild. It blooms early; if grown together, when *T. grandiflorum* is fully open, *T. ovatum* is already fading.

Habit

Stem 1.3–7 dm tall, occasional plants slightly taller.

Leaves continuing to expand during anthesis: ovate-rhombic, medium green, blotched and spotted in dark green or maroon in one variety, 0.5–2 dm wide, 0.7–1.2 dm long, acuminate, main veins prominent.

Pedicel erect to leaning, 3–6 cm long.

Sepals lanceolate, green, 1.5–5 cm long, 6–20 mm wide.

Petals thin-textured, white, fading to rose-pink, often with darker pink markings near petal base and midrib (or in forms along the California-Oregon border, fading to dark barn-red), nearly linear to widely obovate, widest at or above the middle, margins flat to undulate, 1.5–7 cm long, 1–4 cm wide.

Stamens prominent, slightly reflexed-spreading, bright yellow in anthesis, 10–18 mm long, the anther exceeding the filament.

Ovary 6-angled, 5–12 mm tall; stigmas 6–10 mm long, recurved.

Fruit a berrylike capsule, green or white when ripe, usually deciduous from the base without the capsule splitting, pulpy.

Season
Late February in southern part of range, March and April elsewhere.

Distribution
South-central California north to British Columbia, inland to southwestern Alberta, Montana, and Colorado. Locally abundant in coastal mountains.

Habitat
Redwood (*Sequoia* sp.) forests, mixed coniferous-deciduous forests, moist, brushy thickets. At Lolo Pass, Montana, grows under spruce (*Picea* sp.) and Douglas fir (*Pseudotsuga menziesii*) in ravines along mountain streams.

Varieties, Forms, Hybrids

var. *ovatum.* The typical variety described above.

forma *hibbersonii* **Taylor.** On Vancouver Island, British Columbia, grows a dwarf form of what is apparently *Trillium ovatum* (Plate 22). According to D. Gunnlaughson (pers. comm.) there is a larger and smaller dwarf form of this plant in cultivation. Plants range from 3 to 10 cm tall, with all parts proportionally diminished. Petals open clear pink, fading to white. Some horticulturists who grow this form aver that it is a distinct species: some even consider it allied closely to *T. rivale* (not true). We have not seen this

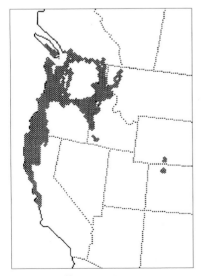

Map 7. *Trillium ovatum*

Plate 22. A stem of typical, normal-sized *Trillium ovatum* with a plant of *T. ovatum* var. *hibbersonii* to show its dwarfed stature. Photo by Fred Case.

form in nature. The plants we have seen in Victoria, in Scotland, and in our garden appear to us to be a genetically dwarfed form of typical *T. ovatum*. Forma *hibbersonii* grows on exposed cliff and bluff faces among rocks and may be comparable to local dwarfed races of other plants that develop from the rigorous natural selection of wind and strong light in exposed habitats (as for example *Cypripedium calceolus* var. *planipetalum* (Fernald) Victorin & Rousseau, on exposed limestone shores and barrens in northern Newfoundland). They are essentially typical plants except that they become genetically dwarfed to survive in the windiest habitats. Taylor, in his treatment of forma *hibbersonii* (Taylor and Szczawinski 1974), states that the dwarf form occurs occasionally throughout the range of *T. ovatum*. We have seen herbarium specimens from Montana in the University of Michigan Herbarium of a somewhat dwarfed form. It was, however, larger than the plants of forma *hibbersonii* that we have seen.

forma *maculosum* F. & R. Case, *forma nova*. Type: California, Mendocino County: Fish Rock Road, north of Gualala. Locally abundant with lesser numbers of plain green-leaved plants along and deep into the forests along Fish Rock Road for at least two miles. 23 March 1996, F. & R. Case, s. n. (holotype: MICH; isotype: US). *A forma typica foliis maculosis et flore parviore differt.* Flowers small, petals narrow, linear-lanceolate to ovate. Leaves blotched or spotted with dark maroon or maroon-green markings on upper surface (but not on lower) (see Plate 23) in the manner of the sessile trilliums, especially in the mid-section of entire leaf. This is the first instance, to our knowledge, of the report of maculate leaves in a pedicellate trillium. Many sizes, including tiny seedlings, with the dark leaf markings were present. The blotching does not appear to be a pathological condition. This remarkable form was first brought to our attention by Wayne Roderick and later by Jerry John Flintoff, who thoughtfully sent us a living plant for study. We later visited the region and were amazed at the numbers of this form at this site; clearly it was more abundant than the typical form.

var. *oettingerii* Munz and Thorne. Salmon Mountains Wake-robin (Hickman 1993) has distinctly petiolate leaves and more or less nodding and smaller flowers, with linear to linear-lanceolate petals only 0.5–2.4 cm long, 2–6 mm wide. This variety occurs in the Salmon and Siskiyou Mountains region of the California-Oregon border. Like the typical variety, it grows in moist mixed deciduous and evergreen forests. From the few herbarium specimens we have examined, one could make a good case for recognizing this form as a distinct species.

Plate 23. *Trillium ovatum* var. *maculosum*, showing a unique leaf spotting in pedicellate trilliums. Photo by Fred Case.

Double forms of *Trillium ovatum* have been reported in the horticultural literature. We do not believe that any has been properly named botanically. Such forms would be highly prized by gardeners and horticulturists within the region where the plants are fully hardy.

Comments

Trillium ovatum is in many ways the showiest of western trilliums, and certainly the most widespread and abundant. As with the eastern great white trillium (*T. grandiflorum*), individual plant and blossom size depends upon not only the genetics of the plant, but also on the age, vigor, and nutrition of the plant. A given plant can, when weak, produce inferior flowers, while at another blooming, if plant health has improved, the flower can be impressively large and showy. In most *Trillium* species, there will be some genetically limited small-flowered forms and individuals.

In spite of its great beauty *Trillium ovatum* is not a satisfactory garden plant in the colder northeastern states and eastern Canada, for it lacks the winter hardiness of *T. grandiflorum*. That fact, coupled with its very early commencement of growth and consequent repeated damage from frost, usually leads to its early death.

8. *Trillium persistens* Duncan

Synonymy: None
Common Name: Persistent Trillium

Trillium persistens was the first *Trillium* species to be listed by the United States as an endangered species. It was also the first *Trillium* species to be pictured on a U.S. postage stamp. It has the smallest range of any valid species and is exceedingly rare within that range. The specific epithet *persistens* means "persistent" and describes the leaves, which remain in good condition well into the autumn, much later than the leaves of most other species. Similar in aspect and general appearance to *T. catesbaei*, *T. persistens* might easily be confused with it.

Habit

Stem 1–2.6 dm tall.
Leaves essentially sessile, ovate-lanceolate to lanceolate, 3- to 5-veined, 3–8.5 cm long, occasionally longer, 1.5–3.5 cm wide, upper surface dull dark green, acuminate.

Plate 24. *Trillium persistens* in the wild in Georgia. Photo by Fred Case.

Pedicel 1–3 cm long, one-fourth to one-half length of the leaves at anthesis (Duncan 1971), leaning to erect.

Sepals weakly divergent, elliptic to narrowly ovate, acute, 11–22 mm long, 5–6 mm wide.

Petals erect in basal half, spreading in distal portion, linear-elliptic to occasionally linear, 20–35 mm long, 5–10 mm wide, undulate, at least in outer portion, acute-tipped, white fading to a light to medium reddish-purple *with an inverted V-shaped basal portion remaining white.*

Stamens erect to mildly divergent, straight, 9–14 mm long; anther and filament approximately of equal length, the anther dehiscing toward the center of the flower (introrse), the connective barely longer than the anther sacs.

Ovary obovate, very sharply 6-angled, 2.5–6 mm long; stigmas united into a short, 2–6 mm long, (Duncan 1971) style, erect, slightly divergent at tip.

Fruit a green or greenish-white, pulpy but not juicy berrylike capsule.

Season
Early March into mid-April.

Distribution
Approximately 4 mi² of forest at the head of Tallulah Gorge and surrounding lands, on South Carolina–Georgia border in Rabun and Habersham Counties, Georgia, and Oconee County, South Carolina. Very rare and local.

Habitat
Mixed deciduous-pine woodlands, along stream flats, and at edges of rhododendron (*Rhododendron* sp.) and mountain laurel (*Kalmia latifolia*) thickets, usually well shaded and in humusy soils. Occasionally in more open, brushy situations with *Vaccinium* sp. and trailing arbutus (*Epigaea repens*) ground cover. Extremely rare and local, even within its small range.

Varieties, Forms, Hybrids
None.

Comments
Unlike typical forms of the related *Trillium catesbaei*, *T. persistens* carries its relatively small flower above the leaves. In *T. persistens*, the petals are erect-spreading, slightly boat-shaped, not recurved as those of *T. catesbaei*. If the petals of *T. persistens* are removed at their point of attachment, they leave an inverted V-shaped scar on the receptacle (not to be confused with the inverted V-shaped white base of an aging

Map 8. *Trillium persistens.*

petal in this species). The leaves are glossier, with the veins less engraved on the upper surface, and the leaves are generally more lanceolate–long acuminate. It also differs in possessing a far more sharply ridged ovary at anthesis. Although some authors consider this plant to be a local mutation of *T. catesbaei,* careful comparison shows many differences. We have seen several colonies of *T. persistens* in the wild, growing with or near *T. catesbaei.* We believe it to be a distinct species.

Very local, rare, and well-collected early, the occurrence of *Trillium persistens* has been fully documented by botanists, and no further herbarium specimens need be taken for documentation, unless botanists discover new colonies outside the presently known range. Under no conditions ought it to be collected from the wild for horticultural purposes. This species lacks the showy character necessary to be a good garden subject. Rather, it should be left and enjoyed in the wild. If collectors must have the plant, it should be propagated from seed.

9. *Trillium pusillum* Michaux

Synonymy: *Trillium pumilum* Pursh, *Trillium texanum* Buckley, *Trillium virginianum* (Fernald) Reed
Common Name: Dwarf Trillium, Least Trillium

One of the most interesting trilliums, *Trillium pusillum* occurs as a series of widely disjunct populations across the Southeast. It is absent from extensive areas of seemingly suitable habitat between populations where it would be expected to grow. Much like species isolated on islands, these small disjunct populations interbreed among themselves and, with local mutations, become slightly different from one another. As a result, botanists have named many varieties, even considering some local forms distinct species. In growing these various forms in our garden, we find the differences so inconsistent and so affected by plant vigor that it is difficult to distinguish the various forms. The exception to this is var. *virginianum,* which has sessile or nearly sessile flowers. The specific epithet *pusillum* means "small" or "dwarfed."

Plate 25. *Trillium pusillum* var. *pusillum* in cultivation. Note the pedicel and undulate petal margins. Photo by Fred Case.

Habit

Stem 0.7–2 dm tall, expanding after onset of anthesis.

Leaves of most forms dark green underlain with dark maroon or wine coloring, minutely petioled to subsessile, oblong to lanceolate-obtuse, with 3 to 5 major veins from the base, 2.5–8 cm long, occasionally longer, 1–3 cm wide, narrowest in var. *texanum*.

Pedicel 0.5–2 cm long, stiffly erect, or absent to much reduced in var. *virginianum*.

Sepals oblong-lanceolate, obtuse to strongly rounded at tip, spreading and conspicuous, 1.5–3 cm long, 0.5–1 cm wide at base.

Petals white, deep rose-pink backed with aging, margins strongly undulate, oblong to narrowly lanceolate, quite variable between individuals and populations, 1.5–3 cm long, 0.5–1.5 cm wide, generally narrowest in var. *texanum*.

Stamens 8–10 mm long; anthers pale lavender, usually completely obscured by the copious bright yellow pollen at anthesis, about equalling or slightly longer than the white filaments.

Ovary ovoid, obscurely 6-angled, white, 2.5–8 mm long; stigmas ascending as a common stalk, distally long-spreading, curved, 3–12 mm long.

Fruit a white berry, pulpy, many-seeded, rapidly deciduous about 1–1.5 cm long, ovate.

Season
March in Deep South; April and May, rarely into early June, in mountain (West Virginia) stations.

Distribution
See under varieties.

Varieties, Forms, Hybrids
The following varieties seem to be generally accepted by botanists. Some are more distinct than others. None except var. *virginianum* seems consistent in comparative cultivation.

var. *pusillum*. The typical variety described above (Plate 25).

Distribution. From the Carolinas on Coastal Plain and Piedmont to Alabama, where there are several colonies in northern Alabama (these may represent Freeman's var. *alabamicum*, in press) and Tennessee.

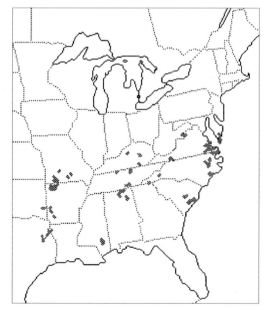

Map 9. *Trillium pusillum* varieties.

Habitat. Most colonies of this variety occur in low swampy woods, floodplain swamps, pocosins, occasionally sphagnous swamp borders in acid soil. Companion plants include red maple (*Acer rubrum*), red buckeye (*Aesculus pavia*), trailing arbutus (*Epigaea repens*), laurel (*Kalmia* sp.), Virginia bluebells (*Mertensia virginica*), flowering fern genera, twisted trillium (*Trillium stamineum*), and blueberry (*Vaccinium* sp.).

var. *alabamicum* Freeman. Mentioned as "in press" in Freeman's 1995 listing of southeastern trilliums, with no other information. We have seen Alabama plants at two disjunct stations. Like all other highly localized populations, there appear to be some minor differences between them. While we do not yet know what characters Freeman uses to segregate var. *alabamicum*, he is an astute and very capable botanist and no doubt these plants do have subtle but significant, differences at the variety level. The epithet *alabamicum* indicates the variety's native state, Alabama.

Distribution. Must await Freeman's publication of this variety.

Habitat. Assuming all Alabama material belongs to this variety, low floodplain soils under deciduous trees, ground very wet in springtime.

var. *monticola* Reveal. Similar to var. *virginianum* in having sessile to subsessile flowers, less variable in peduncle length than var. *virginianum* (0–8 mm long), petals undulate to wavy-margined, leaves elliptic, 2–4.5 cm long, 1.5–3 cm wide. The epithet *monticola* means "mountain loving," for its known habitats.

Distribution. At present, known to occur only very locally on mountain crests along the Virginia–West Virginia state line at elevations of 1190 m (3900 ft.) (Bodkin and Reveal 1982). Apparently very rare and local.

Habitat. Grows in woodland and at borders of openings, in rocky, shaley soil. Frequent plant companions, according to Bodkin and Reveal (1982), consist of mountain laurel (*Kalmia latifolia*), fetter bush (*Pieris floribunda*), hickory pine (*Pinus pungens*), white pine

(*Pinus strobus*), chestnut oak (*Quercus prinus*), and eastern hemlock (*Tsuga canadensis*).

var. *ozarkanum* Palmer and Steyermark. Generally larger than typical var. *pusillum,* and according to authors, with five major veins per leaf instead of three as in var. *pusillum.* This is a highly variable feature depending upon age and vigor of plant. We are not certain that such differences can be maintained. In comparative plantings in our garden, most plants of var. *pusillum* (from Alabama or North Carolina) cannot be distinguished from those of var. *ozarkanum* (from Arkansas) unless labeled. Variety *ozarkanum* is almost entirely an upland plant, while most of the other varieties grow in low wet ground. The epithet *ozarkanum* means "of the Ozark Mountains."

Distribution. Variety *ozarkanum* occurs in the Ozark Mountain areas of southern Missouri and Arkansas (Steyermark 1963), with disjunct stations in Kentucky south of Louisville and near Liberty. We have found three small stations south of the well-known one near Liberty. Here the plants grow in beech-oak (*Fagus-Quercus*) forest, on ridges and steep slopes, almost entirely on highly weathered shaley rock in locations with considerable subsurface moisture at bloom time. These plants are large and vigorous in cultivation.

Habitat. Occurring on coarsely cherty, rock soils in beech-oak (*Fagus-Quercus* spp.) and mixed deciduous forest.

var. *texanum* Buckley. Differs from var. *pusillum* in its narrower leaves with more rounded tips, and its narrow, almost linear (but variable) petal shape (Plate 26). Otherwise, its behavior is like the swamp forms of var. *pusillum,* that is, very local but forming massive colonies in a small area. Variety *texanum* blooms in mid-March to early April. The epithet *texanum* indicates "native of Texas."

Distribution. Rare and local in the Big Thicket region of southeastern Texas.

Habitat. Confined to low swampy floodplains of small streams, in acid, often lightly sphagnous habitats, in deciduous or mixed pine,

Plate 26. *Trillium pusillum* var. *texanum,* showing the characteristic narrow petals and rather round-tipped leaves. Photo by Fred Case.

deciduous forest. Plants often form dense ring-shaped colonies about the bases of trees.

var. *virginianum* Fernald. Generally slightly smaller than typical var. *pusillum;* flowers sessile to very short petioled, 2–4 mm; otherwise like *pusillum* (Plate 27). This is the only form found in Tidewater country of Virginia. The epithet *virginianum* indicates the area of primary occurrence, Virginia.

Plate 27. *Trillium pusillum* var. *virginianum,* showing the sessile flower of this variety. Photo by Fred Case.

Distribution. Southeastern Virginia, Delmarva Peninsula, and extreme northeastern North Carolina. Frequent in the vicinity of Williamsburg, Virginia.

Habitat. Grows in acid soils in low swampy woodlands along streams, red maple (*Acer rubrum*) swamps, very wet in spring, the plants often grouped on hummocks. Sphagnum moss may be present.

Comments

With so many isolated local populations, *Trillium pusillum* lends itself to an "island effect" pattern of variation, and indeed many of its populations can be identified by minor structural variations. This has led to the naming of these populations as forms, varieties, or as separate species. Fernald (1943) first named the var. *virginianum,* perhaps the most discrete variety of *T. pusillum,* since the majority of individuals (but not every one) from its region are either sessile or subsessile. Reed (1982) elevated var. *virginianum* to species status and included var. *monticola* in his concept of var. *virginianum.* He also retained var. *pusillum* and var. *ozarkanum,* and elevated var. *texanum* to species rank.

Roe (1978) first reported a Virginia mountain population that he considered to be var. *virginianum.* Bodkin and Reveal (1982) "rediscovered" Roe's station, and after comparing the plants with var. *virginianum* from the Delmarva Peninsula, named the mountain population var. *monticola.* Cabe (1995) published an extensive morphological study, including statistical analysis, which revealed variation both within and between populations. Cabe felt his evidence inconclusive, and he further allowed that some of the variation may be environmentally induced. As Cabe's structural variations did not correlate clearly with a geographic pattern, he suggested calling all the Virginia populations var. *virginianum* or "simply *Trillium pusillum.*" In a second, related study using isozyme evidence, Cabe and Werth (1995) obtained similar results and thus recommended all Virginia populations be considered a single variety until "further study." Cabe and Werth did not state whether or not they would maintain that taxon as var. *virginianum* or "simply" *T. pusillum.*

Buckley's var. *texanum,* while somewhat smaller than var. *ozarkanum,* and with generally narrower leaves and petals, varies in these respects considerably in the wild population we have seen. Palmer and Steyermark's var. *ozarkanum* rather consistently maintains a larger size, both in Ozark populations and in Kentucky. In our cultivation, the plants become quite robust, as does also *T. pusillum* var. *pusillum* (or is it var. *alabamicum?*) from northeastern Alabama.

What constitutes a species is, at least partially, a matter of personal opinion, but with this species complex we urge caution. Some of the characteristics that various authors have used to delineate their "variety" actually change with the age of the flower or the vigor of the plant, and are not very useful taxonomic characters at all. In uniform cultivation in the same soil in our gardens, all forms except var. *virginianum* and var. *texanum* become robust and essentially indistinguishable. Both of the latter varieties remain somewhat smaller and less vigorous in growth. All forms seed about spontaneously here.

Trillium pusillum and its varieties make excellent rock garden and wild garden plants, blooming as *T. nivale* fades and long before most trilliums flower. Rare, local, and frequently protected by law, this species should be propagated by seed, not collected from the wild. It seeds heavily in cultivation, and seedlings mature quickly. Practical commercial seed propagation should be possible without impinging upon wild populations. All wild populations should be rigorously protected.

10. *Trillium rivale* Watson

Synonymy: None
Common Name: Brook Wake-robin

Easily one of the most charming and beautiful of trilliums, Brook Wake-robin also grows in an area of exceptional beauty. Although highly local in its occurrence in the Siskiyou Mountains and small in stature, it is frequent enough that it can sometimes be seen from a moving automobile. The astounding thing is to see it growing under yellow pine on the edges of seeps and rivulets almost in the company of the carnivorous pitcher plant (*Darlingtonia* sp.) with prickly pear (*Opuntia* sp.) just a few feet away. A few miles away, at a lower elevation, it can be found not only on steep eroding banks and hills, but in thickets at the edges of redwood (*Sequoia* sp.) groves. Not a heavy clump former in the wild, it can, in cultivation in Scotland, form enormous clumps of up to 50 or more stems (see Plate 29). The specific name *rivale*, meaning "stream-loving," suits this species well, occurring as it does along rivulets, streamsides, and the steep valley walls of the rivers of the region.

Habit

Stem 4–15 cm tall.
Leaves distinctly petioled, the petiole 1–3 cm long; leaf blade ovate-lanceolate, acuminate, bluish-green, either entirely, or with a silvery-green pattern along the major veins, somewhat thick-textured, con-

Plate 28. *Trillium rivale,* showing some of the madder-purple flecking occasionally present on its petals. Photo by Fred Case.

tinuing to expand at and for a short time after onset of anthesis; 2.5–8 cm long, very rarely 1–3 cm longer, 1.8–6 cm wide.

Pedicel at first strongly erect, becoming somewhat recurved with aging, 2.5–11 cm long.

Sepals generally shorter than petals, green, apex essentially rounded-apiculate and weakly sulcate, 1.5–2.3 cm long, 4–8 mm wide, oblong or tapered toward rounded tip.

Petals white, sometimes pink, occasionally spotted with dark madder-
purple to rarely almost entirely madder-purple, ovate-cordate to almost circular, sides above middle tapered bluntly to the almost apicu-
late-attenuate tip, 1.5–2.8 cm long, 1–2.4 cm wide.

Stamens 5–12 mm long, the filaments about as long as the yellow
anthers.

Ovary flask-shaped, 3- weakly 6-angled but angles in close pairs or
fused, giving the impression of a 3-angled ovary, more or less 3-angled
to ovoid when mature, stigmas weakly lobed on adaxial surface.

Fruit small, greenish-white, pulpy, 3-angled, the berrylike capsule falling
from the basal attachment without splitting. In *T. rivale*, the entire
plant, after successful pollination, may enlarge and become more robust and turgid, with very glossy leaves.

Season

Late March into early May at higher elevations. Entire plant withers into
dormancy with onset of dry season in early to mid-July.

Distribution

The Siskiyou Mountains and southwestern Oregon. Also in the Klamath
Mountain Ranges, California (Hickman 1993).

Habitat

Open, even grassy hillsides, at edges and under
shrubbery, yellow pine groves and forests, edges of
redwood (*Sequoia* sp.) groves in the Lower Smith
River Canyon, roadside banks, ledges, and at higher elevations in the Siskiyou Mountains, on gravelly sliding slopes, especially if there is considerable old, rotted wood or peaty accumulation
mixed into soil. In borders of the redwood groves,
grows only where there is considerable sunlight
present at least part of the day. It does not occur in
the deep humus of dense redwood stands as *Trillium ovatum* does in the same region. Colonizes
road cuts and open, mildly disturbed soil rather
quickly, becoming a conspicuous element as the

Map 10. *Trillium rivale.*

Plate 29. *Trillium rivale* 'Purple Heart', in the garden of Mike and Polly Stone, Askival, Loch Ness, Fort Augustus, Scotland. Photo by Polly Stone.

various manzanita species mature and just as seedling conifers appear. It grows frequently on banks and edges of the abundant seeps of the Siskiyou Mountains in drier locations, but only a few inches to feet from colonies of the remarkable pitcher plant (*Darlingtonia* sp.) and among the many shrubs that characterize these rather open mountain forests.

Varieties, Forms, Hybrids

No botanical varieties listed in *Gray Herbarium Index* (1896). One or two horticultural names have been applied to collected forms, mostly with a great amount of the dark madder-purple speckling. These forms, while offered for sale, have not, to our knowledge, been formally named botanically.

Comments

To see this lovely plant in the wild is to experience one of the great thrills of plant exploring. Not only has the plant itself beauty and charm, but the beauty of coastal redwoods or at higher elevations, rugged scenery, open meadows and groves, ground covers of *Erythronium, Dodecatheon,* and even, in places, the orchid *Calypso* as a backdrop, is a setting not to be forgotten. While Brook Wake-robin occurs only in a very limited region and is not uniformly distributed within it, it is not extremely rare there, either.

In our experience, *Trillium rivale* is one of the few trilliums that retains seed viability from dried seed, even germinating after more than a year of dry storage. Propagation by seed should therefore be relatively easy. When a good tissue-culture procedure for *Trillium* has been perfected, commercial production of this species will be practical. This will relieve all pressure on wild populations from collection, a highly desirable situation.

Certainly this beautiful species has great garden appeal, especially in the rock garden. *Trillium rivale* can be cultivated in a sandy, peaty soil. While in the wild it withstands almost yearly seasonal drought, in cultivation (at least in the United Kingdom) it appreciates a moist but not wet substrate. It may not be rock hardy to cold in U.S. Department of Agriculture hardiness zone 5 or lower. In our garden we find it takes several years to acclimate itself before it will bloom and flourish. We grow it in a sand-peat and fir-bark bed among rhododendrons. Once established it will live and bloom well, but we feel most confident if we mulch the plants with large fir-bark particles and some pine needles over our rather severe and deep frost winters.

11. *Trillium rugelii* Rendle

Synonymy: None
Common Name: Southern Nodding Trillium (Patrick, undated)

This large trillium, not universally recognized by taxonomists and authors of floras, seems distinct in its features, although closely similar to *Trillium cernuum* at first glance. At least in part, *T. rugelii* may be responsible for the attribution of the range of *T. cernuum* var. *macranthum* (Radford et al. 1964) to the southern Appalachian Mountain region, where *T. cernuum* does not grow. The specific epithet *rugelii* honors botanist Ferdinand Rugel (1806–1878), an early plant explorer of the southeastern United States.

Plate 30. *Trillium rugelii,* the form common in the Great Smoky Mountain region. Photo by Fred Case.

Habit

Stem 1.5–4 dm tall, robust.

Leaves broader than long, 6–15 cm long, at least 6–16 cm wide, rhombic, bright green.

Plate 31. *Trillium rugelii*, from Alabama, showing the strongly reflexed petals characteristic of the region. Note also the large, dark stamens. Photo by Fred Case.

Pedicel 2–3 cm long, strongly recurved beneath leaves.

Sepals lanceolate-elliptic, green, very rarely red-streaked, 15–40 mm long, 7–17 mm wide.

Petals broadly ovate or elliptic, recurving from beyond the middle in most forms, some forms from Alabama with petals slightly narrower and *strongly recurved* from just above base: 2.5–5 cm long, 0.8–3.5 cm wide, normally white; bicolored rose and white, rose, dark rose-red and rose-red with a white center forms occur, usually in mixed colonies with *T. vaseyi* and apparently represent hybrids.

Anthers 12–16 mm long, *dark purple,* 3 to 5 times longer than the filament (Barksdale 1938).

Ovary flask-shaped, 6-angled, 14–17 mm long, purple-streaked, or maroon at anthesis.

Fruit a dark red-maroon, fleshy berrylike capsule.

Season

April in southern part of range, to late April and early May, blooming at end of the flowering of *Trillium erectum* and *T. grandiflorum* when they grow together.

Distribution

In the mountains of western North Carolina and South Carolina, extreme eastern Tennessee, southward into upland Georgia. What appears to be the same species in a strongly reflexed, narrower petaled form occurs along streams and rivers westward at least to Coosa County, Alabama.

Habitat

Rich deciduous forests; in the Great Smoky Mountains National Park, steep wooded hillsides, flats, streambanks; in the Pisgah National Forest of North Carolina, rich rocky wooded hillsides and flats along small streams. Occupies similar habitats in Georgia. In Alabama, the strongly reflexed petaled form occurs mostly in alluvial soils of both small streams and larger rivers.

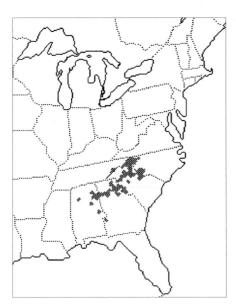

Map 11. *Trillium rugelii.*

Varieties, Forms, Hybrids

In the Pisgah National Forest near Brevard, North Carolina, we have found several obvious hybrid swarms between *Trillium rugelii* and *T. vaseyi*. Many of these possess beautifully colored petals, often bicolored. While not, to our knowledge, a named form, the plant from the riverbanks of central Alabama differs in having generally smaller leaves (but the leaves of these plants grow larger here in cultivation so size may reflect soil fertility), narrower ovate petals, strongly reflexed *from the base,* and strongly fragrant flowers with the odor of old-fashioned garden roses. Anther color and structure as in the mountain form.

Comments

This species has a wider range than implied in Barksdale (1938) and in that range occurs rather frequently. Colonies tend to be small and scattered, the plants robust. Unfortunately, the hidden flower renders the plant less than impressive. The flowers, however, are good sized and heavy textured.

This plant bears responsibility for much of the confusion over the distribution of *Trillium cernuum,* and especially for reports of *T. cernuum* occurring south of Virginia. The two species are, of course, quite similar when dried and pressed as herbarium vouchers. In life, *T. rugelii* is usually much more robust than *T. cernuum,* the petals broader, heavier textured, and less reflexed with larger dark purple, not pale lavender-purple anthers. Only the less robust specimens of the Alabama form more closely resemble *T. cernuum.*

In our opinion, there is so much hybridization among the trilliums related to *Trillium erectum* (of which *T. rugelii* is one) in the southern Appalachians and Blue Ridge that some specimens cannot be placed with certainty in any presently described species. In any species, there is a wide variation in plant size caused by age and vigor of the individual plant. Such variation further adds to the difficulty in identifying certain individuals. Hybrids of *T. rugelii* generally show a short declined pedicel often with color patterns from the other parent, making the nature of the hybrid fairly apparent.

12. *Trillium simile* Gleason

Synonymy: *Trillium vaseyi* var. *simile* (Gleason) Barksdale, *Trillium erectum* var. *vaseyi* f. *simile* (Gleason) Ahles
Common Name: Sweet White Trillium (Patrick, undated), Confusing Trillium.

This much-confused species is the least known and understood of any in the *Trillium erectum* alliance. Intermediate in some respects between *T. erectum* var. *album* and *T. vaseyi*, it also resembles many hybrid forms between those two species or some of the *T. sulcatum* × *T. flexipes* hybrids. Its confusing appearance makes the specific epithet *simile*, meaning "similar," particularly appropriate.

    Trillium simile is a grand species, with huge, showy, textured creamy-white flowers set off by the dark purple-black ovary. Along the Little River in Great Smoky Mountains National Park it can be found on roadside outcrops and in rich coves in large numbers. Its tendency to form clumps and its large flower size make it often the most conspicuous spring wildflower on the roadsides.

Habit

Stem 3–6 dm tall, usually 4–5 dm; commonly produces 2 or more scapes from a single rhizome terminus per season.

Leaves obrhombic, 10–18 cm long, 10–20 cm wide, short acuminate, medium green.

Pedicel 4–9 cm long, more or less erect, flower horizontally carried at top of peduncle, above the leaves.

Sepals oblanceolate-lanceolate, green.

Petals ascending, creamy white, heavy-textured, with faintly engraved venation on upper surface, broadly ovate to ovate-orbicular, acuminate, 4–7 cm long, rarely longer, 1.5–4 cm wide.

Anthers longer than ovary, slender, weakly recurved; anther sac longer than filament, yellow underlain with brown.

Ovary dark purple-black, pyramidal at anthesis, very strongly angled; stigmas mildly recurved, pale.

Fruit a dark purple-black somewhat fleshy orbicular berry about 1–1.5 cm in diameter.

Plate 32. *Trillium simile*, showing the gaping, three-dimensional nature of the flower. Photo by Fred Case.

Plate 33. A clump of *Trillium simile* in the Case garden. Photo by Fred Case.

Map 12. *Trillium simile.*

Season
April and May.

Distribution
Tennessee, from the environs of Gatlinburg, south into northern Georgia and eastward into western North Carolina, where it is commonly sympatric with *Trillium erectum* f. *album* with which it could be confused. In our experience, a plant of limited distribution largely in and around the Great Smoky Mountains. Plants reported from elsewhere may be other taxa.

Habitat
Rich coves under mature trees, in rhododendron (*Rhododendron* sp.) thickets

along streams, and at forest edges, frequently on outcrops partially exposed by road building. Likes underlying moisture and humusy soil.

Varieties, Forms, Hybrids

No forms or varieties described. *Trillium simile*, in the *T. erectum* alliance, hybridizes with others of that group frequently in the wild. Barksdale (1938) described a complex of forms that he considered the result of hybridization. We have seen such complexes near Marysville, Tennessee, where *T. simile* and *T. erectum* f. *album* occur together, where a full range of intergrades between the two species occur. Similar plants, not quite like either species, have appeared as spontaneous hybrids in our gardens.

Comments

An unusually attractive species, its huge creamy-white flowers make it as showy as *Trillium grandiflorum*, although it seldom forms such large colonies. The plant may be rare or merely inaccessible, growing in mature forest among the mountains. Its range is smaller than that of several related species. Clearly it is closely related to *T. vaseyi* and to *T. erectum*, but seems to be a valid if somewhat difficult species to identify when not in its most robust condition.

Trillium simile's habit of growth resembles *T. erectum* more closely than it does *T. vaseyi*, the species to which the name *simile* was intended to convey similarity. *Trillium simile* is a strong clump former, and its leaves are larger and scape shorter in proportion to the leaves than those of *T. vaseyi*. According to Patrick (1984), *T. simile* can be distinguished from similar species by viewing the flower from the side. In *T. vaseyi*, stamens and pistil will be visible, in *T. simile*, because the flower petals ascend, not reflex ("widely agape," Patrick 1984), those organs cannot be seen. In its most vigorous form, *T. simile* has immense flower petals. The ascending petal carriage and the leathery-textured, creamy-white flowers set off by the maroon-black ovary make this species extremely showy.

Small (1933) avers *T. simile* to be deliciously fragrant, a quality we have not noticed in our plants.

In horticultural promise, we consider this plant one of the finest. As a potential parent for fine garden hybrids, its flower carriage and size cannot be equaled. How it will actually breed is not yet determined, although we have hand-pollinated seeds in development.

13. *Trillium sulcatum* Patrick

Synonymy: None
Common Name: Southern Red Trillium, Barksdale Trillium (Patrick, undated)

This robust and splendid plant, we treat here, after Patrick (1984), as a distinct species, while admitting that there are, in northern Michigan, and especially where *Trillium erectum* mingles with *T. flexipes* or *T. cernuum, T. erectum* plants with petals and sepals fully as sulcate (boat-shaped) as those of Patrick's *T. sulcatum.* Because the other aspects of these plants—clumping, pedicel length and carriage, petal shape, and odor—are those of *T. erectum,* we consider the sulcate petals and sepals of these northern plants to result from introgression with *T. cernuum* and do not consider them compelling evidence for maintaining *T. sulcatum* as a variety of *T. erectum.*

Trillium sulcatum was first recognized by Barksdale in 1938 as a variety, but he did not properly typify it. The species generally occurs at lower elevations in Tennessee and the Carolinas than does *T. erectum,* often in very large colonies. The large size, long pedicel, and outward-facing flowers combined with a rich dark chocolate red-maroon coloration render the plant conspicuous. As a parent for garden hybrids this plant cannot be equaled, and both wild and our hand-pollinated hybrids possess outstanding characteristics. The plant is fully as variable in color as its relative *T. erectum.* The specific epithet *sulcatum* means "boat-shaped" and refers to the upturned margins of the sepal tips and petal margins so prominent (but not exclusive) in this species.

Habit

Stem strongly erect, 3–7 dm tall.

Leaves 13–20 cm long, 8–22 cm wide, subsessile, obovate to broadly elliptical, acuminate distally, narrowing toward basal attachment.

Pedicel straight, usually stiffly erect (or "almost horizontal but above the leaves," Patrick 1984), 6–11 cm long.

Flowers gaping, "relatively small and turned downward" (Patrick 1984), but in many plants of the Tennessee and Kentucky Cumberland Plateau, we find the flowers quite large, flattened, and facing outward.

Sepals usually streaked or entirely purple-maroon, occasionally wholly

Plate 34. *Trillium sulcatum,* from the Cumberland Plateau. Flower has broader petals with tips more strongly reflexed than plants from the type locality. Horti-culturally, this is a better form than the type. Photo by Fred Case.

green except on margins, 15–38 mm long, 9–15 mm wide; strongly sulcate-acuminate tipped.

Petals ovate to broadly ovate-overlapping, 18–50 mm long, 10–30 mm wide, dark red-maroon to purplish, carried somewhat forward to recurved spreading, heavy textured and veined, occasionally with the basal portion darker colored, occasional forms pink, white, greenish-cream, pale to rarely bright yellow, faintly to strongly sulcate-tipped.

Stamens about as long as the ovary or slightly longer, 15–18 mm long; anther about 2 times as long as the filament, purplish to yellow, the filament pink to white.

Ovary globose to flask-shaped, normally dark purple, 6-angled; stigmas recurved.

Flower odor faintly musty-fragrant, not unpleasant; Patrick (1984) compared it to that of fresh fungus.

Fruit more or less globose to pyramidal, red, juicy-pulpy.

Season
April and May, varying by up to two weeks on the Tennessee Cumberland Plateau, depending upon the season.

Distribution
Southern West Virginia, southwestern Virginia and northwestern North Carolina to eastern Kentucky (Patrick 1984) and southward mainly along the Cumberland Plateau to extreme northwestern Georgia and northeastern Alabama. Locally abundant on the Cumberland Plateau. Unlike *Trillium erectum, T. sulcatum* is absent from the Great Smoky Mountains and the other mountains of the Southern Blue Ridge Province (Patrick 1984).

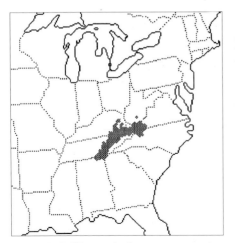

Map 13. *Trillium sulcatum.*

Habitat
Rich mesic woodlands often in company with *Trillium cuneatum, T. flexipes,* and *T. grandiflorum,* neutral to slightly acid, moist north and east-facing forested slopes, wooded ledges and streambanks. Frequent companion plants include *Aplectrum hyemale,* Jack-in-the-pulpit (*Arisaema triphyllum*), Dutchman's breeches (*Dicentra cucullaria*), golden seal (*Hydrastis canadensis*), *Iris cristata,* occasionally mountain laurel (*Kalmia latifolia*),

Rhododendron maximum, bloodroot (*Sanguinaria canadensis*), and eastern hemlock (*Tsuga canadensis*).

Varieties, Forms, Hybrids

forma *sulcatum*. The typical form described above.

forma *albolutescens* Patrick. Petals white, yellow-white, or creamy, occasionally greenish on the back (Patrick 1984). Found as an occasional
individual throughout the range of the species. We have two clones of
a magnificent butter-yellow flower color and two of a rosy-pink from
the Cumberland Plateau of northern Tennessee. These have not been
named.

Plate 35. A yellow form of *Trillium sulcatum* from the Cumberland Plateau.
Photo by Fred Case.

On the Tennessee Cumberland Plateau, *Trillium sulcatum* hybridizes with *T. flexipes*. We have seen two large hybrid swarms not far from the Kentucky border. Patrick (1984) also reported "intermediates" from the same region. The same range of colors described under *T. flexipes* for other hybrids prevails. Because of the very large size of the *T. sulcatum* plant, these truly command attention.

Comments

This beautiful species, one of the largest-leaved of the pedicellate trilliums, abounds on the Cumberland Plateau of Tennessee and Kentucky. Yet Barksdale (1938) in his original discussion mentioned only Surry and Wilkes Counties, North Carolina, where it is less common. We grow plants from the type locality and a large cross-section of plants from the Cumberland of Tennessee. Our plants from the type locality have smaller, more ringent flowers, with the petal tips thrust somewhat forward, giving the flower and pedicel, as Patrick (1984) put it "in profile resembling a long-handled candle snuffer." Most plants we have seen from the Cumberland Plateau, however, have distinctly broader petals, held flatter, with the distal portion somewhat reflexed. The sulcate (boat-shaped) sepals and petal tips, which Barksdale used in originally naming this as a variety, while present, occur to varying degrees in other species and therefore cannot be used alone to identify this plant. Used with the unusually long pedicel and the very robust stem and leaves, they form a useful identification feature (Patrick 1984).

Barksdale (1938) placed *Trillium sulcatum* as a variety of *T. erectum*. In many ways it does resemble that species although Patrick (1984) called that resemblance "superficial." In describing *T. sulcatum* in 1941, Svenson (quoted in Patrick 1984) said that *T. sulcatum* has "slender stems and elongate erect pedicels, quite different in appearance from the fleshy plant, usually with declined pedicels, which is common in the Northern States." In fact, *T. sulcatum* is generally taller, larger-leaved, and more robust of stature than *T. erectum*. In our experience, it has less tendency to clump, the stems are more erect, the peduncle is very stiffly erect in most forms, with out-facing flowers, while *T. erectum* flowers face upward or, on declined pedicel forms, downward.

Patrick, like most recent workers in *Trillium*, recognized a *T. erectum* complex. While he acknowledged that *T. sulcatum* belongs in this complex, he offered evidence of breeding compatibility with *T. flexipes* to suggest *T. sulcatum* is actually more closely related to *T. flexipes* than to *T. erectum*. *Trillium erectum* may hybridize with *T. sulcatum,* but no one has documented controlled crosses, and such a cross in the wild might easily be so similar to either parent as to go undetected.

Patrick (1984) suggested that this is a relict species related either directly or through progenitors to the Arcto-Tertiary Geoflora. He cited as evidence the species' compatibility with *Trillium flexipes,* a plant similar to the only Asiatic diploid trillium, *T. camschatcense.* Also, the species occurs on and around the Cumberland Plateau and in the New River drainage of North Carolina and West Virginia, both areas noted for relict species.

Trillium sulcatum can be a majestic plant, its color forms particularly clear and showy. As a garden plant or a breeding parent, it has great value.

14. *Trillium undulatum* Willdenow

Synonymy: *Trillium erythrocarpum* Michaux, *Trillium pictum* Pursh
Common Name: Painted Trillium, Striped Wake-robin, Painted Lady

Trillium undulatum is one of the more distinctive pedicellate species, having unique differences in coloring, structure, and behavior. Ranging far north and south in cool environments, it also demands a deep humus-rich strongly acid soil. In nature it seldom forms large clumps, but rather occurs as scattered individuals across available habitat. A late bloomer compared to other *Trillium* species in any given location, plants emerge from the soil and expand at a surprisingly fast rate; after a sudden warm spell, it can almost be a "not here today, in full bloom tomorrow" situation. Upon emerging from the ground and still quite small, the flower opens before completing its rapid expansion. If pollinated at this time, the petals, reacting to hormonal changes, quickly turn translucent and soon dry and fall. In such a situation the plant can be very disappoint-

Plate 36. *Trillium undulatum in* the wild. Photo by Fred Case.

ing compared to one which attains full size and development before pollination occurs. The specific epithet *undulatum* refers to the undulating or wavy petal margins that give much of the beauty to this flower.

Habit

Stem at full anthesis, 2–5, rarely 6 dm tall, dark green-maroon.

Leaves with a definite petiole, ovate-long acuminate, dark green underlain with maroon early, 5–18 cm long, 5–11 cm broad.

Pedicel erect, 2–5 cm long.

Sepals wine-red to dull maroon-green, lanceolate-acuminate, 13–37 mm long, 4–10 mm wide.

Petals oblong-ovate, occasionally lanceolate, widest just above the middle; proximal region tapering very gradually to attachment, not undulate, distal portion somewhat rapidly acuminate, the margins strongly undulate; when fully expanded 2–5 cm long, 1–2 cm wide, with an inverted V-shaped dark red mark, the red radiating outward along the major veins (hence the name painted trillium) except all white and lacking marks in forma *enotatum*.

Stamens 8–12 mm long, the dark anther sac longer than the white filament, erect or slightly spreading.

Ovary obtusely 3-angled, becoming obscurely angled-rotund in cross section when mature, white at anthesis; stigmas ascending from an obscure common style, then strongly recurved.

Fruit a scarlet, fleshy, obscurely 3-angled to cylindrical, *erect* berry, quickly deciduous upon ripening; 1–2 cm long.

Season

Late compared to sympatric species; late April to June, depending upon latitude and elevation; in Michigan and southern Ontario, from last week of May into early June; at northern end of its range near Sudbury, Ontario, Canada, blooms later.

Distribution

Local, from the "thumb" of Michigan and environs of North Bay, Ontario, to Quebec (absent in limestone-derived soils), and Nova Scotia, southward through New England, Pennsylvania and extreme eastern Ohio and Kentucky along the Appalachian Mountains and Blue Ridge, to the Carolinas and highest elevations of Georgia.

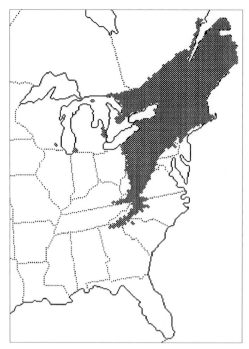

Map 14. *Trillium undulatum.*

Habitat

Always grows in strongly acidic, humus-rich soils: in the southern end of its range, in pine (*Pinus* sp.) woods, red spruce (*Picea rubra*) groves, mixed deciduous-conifer forests, and hemlock (*Tsuga* sp.) groves; in the northern part of its range, in second-growth low, moist red maple (*Acer rubrum*), birch (*Betula papyrifera*), oak (*Quercus velutina, Quercus* sp.), and sugar maple (*Acer saccharum*) cover, where it shows a definite preference for the proximity of old white pine (*Pinus strobus*) stumps. Plant companions at more northern stations include wintergreen (*Gaultheria procumbens*), pipsissewa (*Chimaphila umbellata*), royal fern (*Osmunda regalis*), cinnamon fern (*Osmunda cinamomea*), blueberry (*Vaccinium corymbosum* and related species), and pink lady's slipper (*Cypripedium acaule*). Southward, frequently found in proximity to "rhododendron hells," dense nearly impenetrable rhododendron (*Rhododendron* sp.) thickets often on steep hills or along streams. Also frequent in mountain laurel (*Kalmia latifolia*) thickets and shrubby borders of the "Balds" on the higher mountains, as well as in red spruce (*Picea rubra*) groves and under hemlock (*Tsuga* sp.). Often rare and local in the South.

Varieties, Forms, Hybrids

forma *undulatum.* The typical form described above.

forma *enotatum* Patrick. Petals lacking the red V and all other markings. This form has been reported several times across the species range. Radford et al. (1968, 1974) reported an occasional form with petals entirely suffused with red. We have seen a form with the red V present only as the faintest of red lines, but have not seen either of the other forms.

This species is not known to hybridize with other species. Its close relative, the dwarf *Trillium nivale,* is sympatric only over a minute part of the range of *T. undulatum.* Even there, the two species are isolated by differences in blooming dates and soil requirements. We have pollinated *T. undulatum* with stored pollen of *T. nivale.* The cross yielded ripe plump fruit and normal appearing seed, which has been planted. In spite of our emasculating the blooms, there is always the possibility of error; only time will tell if we were successful.

Comments

Cool soils seem a prerequisite for *Trillium undulatum:* only at very high elevations or at the extreme north of its range does it appear in well-lighted open situations. Its rhizome, whitish, not brown as in most pedicellate trilliums, lies deep in rich brown acid humus. It may lie in contact with mineral soil (usually sands) below, but there is almost always 4–6 inches of rich humus above.

Trillium undulatum has been reported from isolated stations west of its range in Wisconsin (Fernald 1950), upper Michigan's Porcupine Mountains (Braun 1950), and eastern Manitoba (Fernald 1950). The Wisconsin station is rumored to be an introduction, but we have no documentation for it. We have seen no herbarium specimens from these widely disjunct localities, although we have not made an extensive search of herbaria nationally. There are no herbarium vouchers for the Porcupine Mountains in the University of Michigan Herbarium. There is a specimen, without any exact locality data, from Berrien County, Michigan, in extreme southwestern lower Michigan, which is *Trillium undulatum.* The specimen is from the collection of E. J. Hill, a Berrien County botanist and an active exchanger of specimens. Lacking any other such vouchers from this well-botanized region, it is possible that the specimen represents a labeling error. On the other hand, the region is rich in suitable *T. undulatum* habitat. At least two other disjunct species (*Tipularia discolor, Woodwardia areolata*) frequently found in company with *T. undulatum* elsewhere occur in the region. The record of *T. undulatum* there may be valid.

Trillium undulatum is the most difficult eastern *Trillium* to cultivate outside its native habitat.

15. *Trillium vaseyi* Harbison

Synonymy: *Trillium erectum* var. *vaseyi* (Harbison) Ahles
Common Name: Sweet Beth, Sweet Trillium (Small 1933), Vasey's
  Trillium

One of the largest-flowered of our pedicellate trilliums, *Trillium vaseyi* remains poorly known and understood. Regrettably, botanists familiar with this plant mainly as dried herbarium specimens frequently lump it as a form of *T. erectum*. In the forest and in the garden the plant's aspect, size, habitat, structure, odor, and flowering season differ markedly from that of *T. erectum*. We consider it a distinct species. The specific epithet *vaseyi* honors George Vasey (1822–1893), an English-born American botanist.

Habit

Stem 3–6.5 dm tall, green, usually only 1 to 2 stems per rhizome terminus, green with little or no maroon undertone.

Leaves rhombic, 1–2 dm long, 6–20 cm wide, often wider than long, acuminate, tapered to base, the 3 bracts held closely, umbracular.

Pedicel 4–8 cm long, straight but declined or horizontal, carrying the flower beneath the leaves.

Sepals lanceolate-acuminate, 2.5–5 cm long, 6–18 mm wide.

Petals 3–6.5 cm long, 4–6 cm wide; inner petal surface with engraved veins, crimson, maroon-red, brownish-red, ovate-suborbicular, somewhat fleshy; outer surface paler, grayish-pink or rose.

Stamens 1.5–2.5 cm long, longer than pistil at anthesis, conspicuous; anther shorter than filament, slender, gray-purple, opening to expose bright yellow pollen, filament gray-purple to blackish-purple.

Ovary maroon or dark red-purple, conical-pyramidal, 6-ridged, 3–12 mm long; stigmas thickish, recurved, 2.5–6.5 mm long.

Flower odor faintly sweet.

Fruit relatively small, dark red-maroon, obtusely angled.

Season

Late April to early June, depending upon latitude and elevation; blooming later than *Trillium erectum* in a given district.

Plate 37. *Trillium vaseyi*, showing large size and nodding nature of the flower. Photo by Fred Case.

Distribution

Lower slopes and rich coves in the mountains of North and South Carolina, but absent at higher elevations; lower mountain slopes of eastern Tennessee, northern Georgia, and one or two stations in northeastern Alabama.

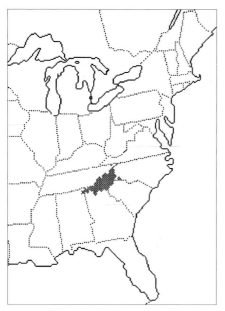

Map 15. *Trillium vaseyi.*

Habitat

Steep wooded slopes, ravines, stream-banks and especially deep rich moist coves at lower to mid elevations in Blue Ridge and Appalachian Mountains. Frequents moist shaded ledges, lower slopes, small stream-flats near and under rhododendrons. Shuns windy, exposed locations.

Varieties, Forms, Hybrids

White forms of *Trillium vaseyi* have been reported several times in the literature. C. F. Moore of North Carolina has grown such a plant. Some reported "albinos" may represent the somewhat similar plant *T. simile.* Double (that is, six-petaled) forms have also occurred very rarely. Apparently, none of these forms has been properly named. Barksdale (1938) described a colony of unusual trilliums in North Carolina which, after study, he concluded represents a collection of hybrids between *T. gleasonii* (synonym *T. flexipes*) and either *T. vaseyi* or its variety *simile* (synonym *T. simile*). Again, none of these forms seems to have been named. We have found several populations growing with *T. rugelii* in which numerous plants had the short, sharply recurved peduncle of *T. rugelii,* but had very large rose, pink, deep red, or bicolored broad petals. Almost certainly these represent hybrids between these two species.

We have produced heavy, apparently healthy seed in hand-pollinations of *Trillium vaseyi* by *T. flexipes,* but the two-year period required for seedlings to appear has not yet passed to prove these crosses viable.

Comments

But for its nodding or declined flower, this largest flowered of all the pedicellate trilliums would surely be the showiest of those bearing colored flowers. Even with the nodding habit, the plant is imposing, for its bloom, unlike that of *Trillium rugelii,* does not hide beneath the leaves. This species seldom forms large clumps or dense stands, but is widespread and scattered mostly as single stems or at most two stems per rhizome across suitable cover. From the horticultural standpoint of large size and color, this plant may prove of great interest to the hybridizer. Certainly its size and the very wide petals are desirable breeding characteristics, superior to the petal shape and size in *T. erectum* or *T. sulcatum.*

The Sessile Trilliums: Subgenus *Phyllantherum*

16. *Trillium albidum* Freeman

Synonymy: None
Common Name: None. We suggest White Toadshade, a translation of *albidum* (white), or Freeman's Trillium.

One of the showiest of the western sessile trilliums, this species grows in considerable abundance at some of its stations. Its large size and early flowering make it a conspicuous plant, even from some distance. Putative hybrids of *Trillium albidum* with *T. chloropetalum* var. *giganteum* growing near San Francisco are among the most attractive of sessile trilliums.

Habit
Stem erect, 2.2–5.8 dm tall, often several stems from the same rhizome terminus.

Leaves broadly ovate, 10–20 cm long, 12–15 cm wide, the leaf tip obtuse; weakly mottled with scattered darker spots (occasionally without spots or markings), spots often fading later in the season.

Sepals lanceolate, acute-tipped, 30–65 mm long, 12–15 mm wide, spreading.

Petals obovate, more lanceolate in young or weak plants, 48–78 mm long, 22–30 mm wide, widest at or just above the middle, usually erect or slightly spreading, tip rounded to acute, white to creamy white, often soft pink-rose near petal base, particularly in plants from the northern Napa Valley region, mostly plain white in northern California and Oregon.

Plate 38. *Trillium albidum,* growing in a grassy open grove in the mountains of northern California. Photo by Fred Case.

Stamens erect, 15–25 mm long, greenish-white with or without purple or red color present; anther sacs 11–20 mm long, opening to side (latrorse); filaments 3–4 mm long; connectives extended about 1 mm beyond anther sac, rounded.

Ovary ovoid, 6–11 mm long, rounded hexagonal, green or occasionally purple-stained; stigmas thickened 4–7 mm long, erect to spreading.

Flower odor fragrant; roselike (Freeman 1975).

Fruit ovoid to globose, green or purplish-green.

Season

Mid-March into late April. In March 1990, plants along streams near southern end of its range were in tight bud, but surprisingly, plants near

Plate 39. *Trillium albidum*, showing some color near petal bases. The ovary, typical of the species, was without any dark pigmentation. Photo by Fred Case.

Gold Hill, Oregon, were open. Elevation and slope angle affect bloom date. In the Trinity Alps, west of Redding, California, in 1973, plants were in full bloom in early April.

Distribution
From San Francisco Bay northward along the California coastal region to about Corvallis, Oregon. About 15 miles north of Corvallis, we found, along a muddy, sluggish river, a population of trilliums which fit neither *Trillium albidum* nor *T. parviflorum* clearly. Larger than *T. parviflorum*

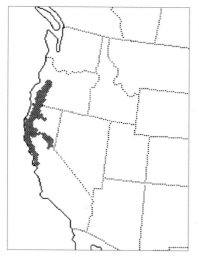

Map 16. *Trillium albidum*.

and smaller than most *T. albidum*, these plants had long, linear-lanceolate petals unlike either species. They probably represent hybrids or intergrades. From there northward plants bear smaller flowers; many or all may represent *T. parviflorum* Soukup. *Trillium albidum* also grows eastward in northern California to Placer County, in the Sierra Nevada Mountains. Locally abundant in the Trinity Alps. Frequent throughout its range.

Habitat

On moist slopes in mixed deciduous-coniferous forests or coniferous stands; in Trinity Alps growing in brushy thickets on flats, often coming out into open fields, pastures, and fencerows in moist soils; dense second-growth coniferous forests, floodplains along streams, rich deciduous slopes and floodplain of larger rivers (Rogue) in loamy soil (can reach very large size in such situations).

Varieties, Forms, Hybrids

Freeman (1975) recognized no varieties or forms. He pointed out that the ranges of *Trillium albidum* and *T. chloropetalum* overlap in the San Francisco Bay area. No white forms of *T. chloropetalum* occur south of that area. In the Bay region and northward, white forms of what is structurally *T. chloropetalum* occur, and plants of *T. albidum* may show purple coloring in the petal bases or on the ovary. Freeman suggested the possibility that these factors indicate introgressive hybridization or simply the occurrence of hybridization. We found a population just south of San Francisco that seemed to consist of *T. chloropetalum* var. *giganteum*, *T. albidum*, and direct hybrids. These hybrids possessed great beauty (see Plate 43).

Comments

Trillium albidum, seen in the central portion of its range, seems a very distinct and splendid species. At the southern end of its range, where it overlaps with *T. chloropetalum*, all sorts of identification difficulties arise. With the complex hybridization situation there, identification keys are to no avail. Petal shape in typical *T. albidum,* as we understand it, is strongly obovate (often almost diamond-shaped). At the northern end of the range of *T. albidum,* Victor Soukup has recognized the smaller, white-flowered plant growing exclusively there as a new species, *T. parviflorum.* We have seen four large populations of this smaller plant, and its flowers do, indeed, seem distinct. Except for the strange plants north of Corvallis in Polk County, we do not know if the change from *T. albidum* to *T. parviflorum* is a gradual, clinal change or an abrupt one in northern Oregon. Above the Columbia River, all plants we have seen belong to *T. parviflorum.*

Trillium albidum is the only western sessile trillium that has proven quite winter hardy and long-lived in our mid-Michigan garden. A few plants have persisted here for at least 18 years, although frost damage occasionally occurs.

17. *Trillium angustipetalum* (Torrey) Freeman

Synonymy: *Trillium sessile* var. *angustipetalum* Torrey, *Trillium giganteum* var. *angustipetalum* (Torrey) Gates, *Trillium chloropetalum* var. *angustipetalum* (Torrey) Munz, in part
Common Name: Narrow-petaled Trillium

This large *Trillium* species impresses for its plant size more than for its flower. Nevertheless, freshly opened flowers are large, dark red-purple, and relatively showy. The specific name *angustipetalum* means "narrow-petaled." The great length of the petals exaggerates their narrowness. As the flower ages, the petals become rolled longitudinally, making them quill-like and less showy.

Habit

Stem erect, 1.8–6.4 dm tall.

Leaves broadly ovate, spreading horizontally, 10–22 cm long, 8.5–15 cm wide, subsessile, leaf tip obtuse; blade often basally narrowed to a falsely petiole-like base 10–20 mm long; green, very sparsely mottled with dark green-brown or rarely all green.

Plate 40. *Trillium angustipetalum,* showing the extremely long, narrow petals. Photo by Fred Case.

Sepals linear to oblong-lanceolate, 35–47 mm long, 8–10 mm wide, acute-tipped, spreading.

Petals linear, 58–100 mm long, 7–14 mm wide, apex variously acute-obtuse, dark red-purple, glossy.

Stamens erect, 12–22 mm long; filaments 2–4 mm long, widest at base; anther sacs introrse, 12–18 mm long; connectives purple, slightly prolonged beyond anther sac.

Ovary ovoid-ellipsoid, 7.5–12 mm tall, 6-angled toward apex; stigmas thick, awl-shaped, 5 mm long, erect, purple.

Flower odor "spicy-musty" (Freeman 1975), "musty or fetid" (Hickman 1933).

Fruit subglobose, 6-angled, almost winged, dark purple.

Season
Early to mid-March to mid-April in the Pacific Coast part of its range; in its Sierra Nevada range, varies with season and snowpack from late April to May. Near Atascadero, California, we found many plants on wooded ravine slopes, but few with flowers. In other locations we saw many flowering plants.

Distribution
In the Sierra Nevada Mountains, from Fresno County north to Placer County, California (Freeman 1975); disjunct in the coastal mountains and hills of Santa Barbara and San Luis Obispo Counties, California. We have seen it in the Calaveras Grove of Big Trees and in several localities near San Luis Obispo. Not common.

Habitat
Big tree (*Sequoiadendron*) groves and other mixed coniferous-deciduous flatwoods in the Sierra Nevada, growing along slightly damper depressions under maples and deciduous shrubs. Near San Luis Obispo, in oak (*Quercus* sp.) groves in ravines in otherwise quite arid almost treeless chaparral, growing in a dark, quite humusy soil. Wooded canyon slopes and dense woods near streams in the coastal mountains. The plants tend not to be uniformly distributed through the habitat but clustered into small scattered groups.

Varieties, Forms, Hybrids
None.

Comments
Although some past botanists have considered this plant a form of *Trillium chloropetalum*, to us

Map 17. *Trillium angustipetalum*.

this is a very distinct and different species. It can produce huge, umbrella-like leaves that spread horizontally so that diameter across the leaf whorl can be almost 2 ft (60 cm). Strangely, in cultivation in central Michigan, the plants never get very large. *Trillium angustipetalum* grows often in rather dry open situations. When we explored the ravine copses in San Luis Obispo County, California, we did not at first believe we could possibly find trilliums in such habitat. Yet the largest and most vigorous plants we encountered grew there.

Like so many other western sessile trilliums, *Trillium angustipetalum* emerges too early in northeastern garden conditions, suffers severe, often fatal frost damage, and seldom persists more than a few years. We grew one plant in beech (*Fagus* sp.) humus and leaf mulch, which managed to persist for about 10 years, not appearing for a year now and then, blooming only a few times, then finally disappearing forever. We consider it a worthy plant, however, and will try it in a sheltered spot or perhaps a winter frame.

Byron D. Ness, author of the *Trillium* section of *The Jepson Manual* (Hickman 1993), lists *T. kurabayashii* as a synonym of *T. angustipetalum*. In leaf carriage, leaf coloring, texture, and petal shape, the two as we saw them are vastly different and certainly not the same species (see differences under *T. kurabayashii*).

18. *Trillium chloropetalum* (Torrey) Howell

Synonymy: Complicated; synonymy according to Freeman (1975) listed below under each variety.
Common Name: Giant Trillium

A handsome plant, *Trillium chloropetalum* surely holds the record for confusing the most people about its correct name and taxonomy. It was long confused with the eastern *Trillium sessile*, and many horticulturists continue that confusion to the present day. A much larger plant, far showier, and confined entirely to the West Coast, *T. chloropetalum* resembles *T. sessile* only in bearing a sessile flower. Because it has two rather distinct varieties and a host of color forms, not to mention putative

Plate 41. *Trillium chloropetalum* var. *chloropetalum*, liver-brown form. The dark brown color masks the yellow pigments always present in this variety. Photo by Fred Case.

hybrids with *T. albidum*, it presents many difficulties of identification to the naturalist, horticulturist, and botanist. Varieties of this species are among the most widely cultivated American trilliums in Great Britain and Europe. The specific epithet *chloropetalum* means "green-petaled."

Habit

Stem erect, robust, 2–6.5 dm tall (often taller in cultivation).

Leaves sessile (narrowing of leaf blade may give leaf a subsessile appearance), broadly ovate, 7–17.6 cm long, 7.4–17.7 cm wide, leaf tip obtuse-rounded, densely to weakly mottled in dark brown-green, var. *chloropetalum* more densely so, its leaf also with a bronze metallic overtone when young; blotching becoming more obscure to absent as leaf matures.

Sepals lanceolate, 35–65 mm long, 7–12 mm wide, apex obtusely rounded.

Petals somewhat variable in shape, but cuneate at base, apex variably acute to almost truncate, oblanceolate to obovate, 4.5–9.5 cm long 1.5–2.3 cm wide, greenish-white, bronze, liver-brown, purplish, dark purple-red, pink, clear white, or white with dark pink veining.

Stamens erect, 17–26 mm long; filament widest at base, about 4 mm long; anther sacs introrse; connectives purple, prolonged about 1 mm beyond anther sac.

Ovary ovoid, 6–12 mm tall, 6-angled, purple; stigmas thickened basally, divergent or erect.

Flower odor roselike (according to most authors); "sometimes more spicy" (Freeman 1975).

Fruit purple, ovoid, obscurely 6-angled.

Season

Late February to early or mid-April.

Distribution

See comments under each variety below.

Habitat

Variable; edges, openings in, and along ravines in redwood forest, thickets and tangles of cut-over forest, stream flats in deciduous woods, chaparral brushland, open wooded slopes on dunes (Point Reyes area), brushy islands in surprisingly open grasslands, but usually where soil remains moist most of the season.

Varieties, Forms, Hybrids

var. **chloropetalum.** The typical plant described above (Plate 41).

Synonymy: *Trillium sessile* var. *chloropetalum* Torrey, *Trillium sessile* var. *californicum* S. Watson, *Trillium giganteum* var. *chloropetalum* (Torrey) Gates

Distribution. From Monterey County, California, north to north side of San Francisco Bay to Marin and Sonoma Counties. Overlaps the range of var. *giganteum* and possibly *T. albidum* in the San Francisco Bay region.

var. *giganteum* (Hooker & Arnot) Munz. A larger variety (Plate 42).

Synonymy: *Trillium sessile* var. *giganteum* Hooker & Arnot, *Trillium sessile* var. *californicum* S. Watson, *Trillium giganteum* (Hooker & Arnot) Heller, in part, *Trillium sessile* var. *rubrum* Hort. ex Bailey

Distribution. San Mateo and Santa Clara Counties and the counties along the east side of San Francisco Bay, north to Napa and Lake Counties, California.

Map 18A. *Trillium chloropetalum* var. *chloropetalum*.

Freeman's study (1975) determined that var. *chloropetalum* differs from var. *giganteum* as follows: Petals yellow-green to deep purple, never white. Chemically, all plants of this variety have yellow pigment present in petals, whether or not it is masked by purple. Our quite limited field observations seem to indicate that plants of var. *chloropetalum*, at flowering, were somewhat shorter in stature than those of var. *giganteum*, and that the leaves showed a slightly metallic lustre at this stage of development.

Variety *giganteum* has petals white to deep red or garnet-purple, lacking all yellow pigments (Freeman 1975). The epithet *giganteum* means "gigantic" and refers to the plant's large size. In the populations we observed, var. *giganteum* was more robust and generally larger than var. *chloropetalum*. Narrow-petaled forms of var. *giganteum* occur occasionally in mixed populations with the wider-petaled ones, and in a

Map 18B. *Trillium chloropetalum* var. *giganteum*.

Plate 42. *Trillium chloropetalum* var. *giganteum,* in Navato, California, showing fairly typical color and petal shape for this variety. Photo by Fred Case.

few places almost exclusively. Freeman suggested that these could represent the "undiluted" var. *giganteum,* free from influences of hybridization, as the type specimen had narrow petals.

Descriptions by authors earlier than Freeman may have included plants of Freeman's *Trillium albidum* in var. *giganteum,* and in some,

Plate 43. A variety of *Trillium chloropetalum* or an intergrade between *T. chloropetalum* and *T. albidum*, south of San Francisco, California. Photo by Fred Case.

T. kurabayashii, so size structure, and even their habitat details may not properly apply. Freeman considered that these varieties differ from *T. albidum* in having introrse anther sacs (not lateral), and that the purple pigments present on anther and ovary tissue here are absent in *T. albidum*.

Comments

The variability of *Trillium chloropetalum* varieties can be astounding. The dark liver-brown forms and yellow-green forms south of San Francisco in the Santa Cruz Mountains seem a very different plant from the deep garnet-red forms north of the Bay. In the vicinity of the Big Basin Redwoods grow some beautiful pink, rose, and white pink-veined forms. In some locations, colors are uniform; in others, highly variable. In one station north of San Francisco Bay, we found white, green, yellowish, and dark red forms growing together.

These plants frequently grow in islands of forest or shrub, the habitats isolated in seas of grassland. Perhaps some of its abundant variation results from a current lack of gene flow between colonies and the consequent inbreeding of local mutations.

In some places, hybridization between *Trillium chloropetalum* and *T. albidum* certainly has taken place. A complete range of intergrades is present (Plate 43).

This species can be cultivated in the colder northeastern States and eastern Canada only with difficulty. It may possess full winter hardiness, but its habit of springing into growth too early in the season following a warm spell results in the plant sustaining severe frost damage year after year. Usually under such conditions the plants slowly decline and disappear. *Trillium chloropetalum* varieties fare far better in England, Scotland, and European maritime climates, where they are widely grown. There, under cultivation and fertilization, it attains sizes seldom if ever seen in the wild. Vast beds of *T. chloropetalum* and *T. kurabayashii* grow at the Royal Botanic Garden, Edinburgh, Scotland, making a splendid show in early April.

19. *Trillium cuneatum* Rafinesque

Synonymy: *Trillium sessile* var. *praecox* Nuttall, *Trillium underwoodii* Small, in part, *Trillium hugeri* Small, *Trillium viride* var. *luteum* (Muhlenberg) Gleason

Common Name: Whippoor-Will Flower, Cuneate Trillium, Large Toadshade, Purple Toadshade, Bloody Butcher, Sweet Betsy

Plate 44. A typical plant of *Trillium cuneatum*. Photo by Fred Case.

This largest of eastern sessile trilliums grows over almost as vast an area as any eastern sessile species. As one would expect, with so large a range, many forms, mostly unnamed, occur. Some of these forms can cause considerable confusion, if not downright grief, to the beginning *Trillium*

Plate 45. *Trillium cuneatum* in the Case garden, showing its clump-forming tendency in cultivation. Photo by Fred Case.

enthusiast, as they look superficially much like other species. *Trillium cuneatum* is most magnificent carpeting the forest floor over Ordovician limestone or shale bluffs in southern Kentucky, wooded hillsides in south-central Tennessee, and near Huntsville, Alabama. Its large size, rich dark flower, and strongly mottled leaves create an impression not to be forgotten. In some locations on the Kentucky-Tennessee border grow thousands of plants per acre. The specific epithet *cuneatum,* meaning "wedge-shaped," refers to the tapered shape of the basal half of the petal.

Habit

Stem erect, smooth to rough to touch near leaf attachment, 1.6–4.5 dm tall.

Leaves ovate, ovate-elliptic, occasionally ovate-orbicular with margins overlapping, 7–18.5 cm long, 7–13 cm wide, usually widest below middle, apex acuminate to acute, weakly to strongly mottled in shades of darker green, the mottling becoming less intense as the season progresses, or rarely leaves all green (in green- and yellow-flowered forms).

Sepals oblong-lanceolate, variably green, purple-streaked to all purple, rounded to acute tipped, 27–60 mm long, 7–13 mm wide, widely spreading.

Petals quite variable across range, generally cuneate with widest portion at or above the middle, tapering to the wedge-shaped base, or elliptic-obovate to oblanceolate, 30–60 cm long, occasionally longer, 9–27 mm wide at widest, maroon, maroon-purple, brown-purple, green-purple, clear green, yellow-green, pale lemon-yellow, or bicolored, yellow distally, with a purple base; in occasional clones flowers open or quickly fade to a bright copper bronze; the particular color pattern is consistent from year to year.

Stamens erect, 11–18 mm long; filaments 1.5–2.5 mm long, widest at base; anther sacs introrse or latrorse; connectives scarcely if at all prolonged beyond anther sacs.

Ovary including stigmas ovoid to vase-shaped, 12–15 mm long, with 6 weakly defined angles or ridges when mature; stigmas thick, erect slightly diverging at tips to spreading.

Flower odor generally pleasant, faint, spicelike, reminiscent of the odor of bruised Sweetshrub (*Calycanthus* sp.) leaves, occasionally musty-unpleasant.

Fruit ovoid, very obscurely angled or angles no longer apparent, green or with purple streaks, mealy or pulpy fleshy, not juicy.

Season

Early compared to other trilliums; early March in Alabama-Georgia populations, late March to mid-April at northern end of its range. Flowers long lasting, fading to browner or bronzer tones.

Distribution

Southern Kentucky, Tennessee west of the Appalachians, southwestward to Mississippi, eastward through Alabama south and east of the mountains into North Carolina, on Piedmont and Blue Ridge provinces. Very common in

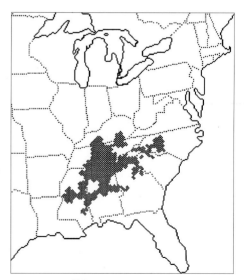

Map 19. *Trillium cuneatum.*

southern Kentucky and Tennessee, where plants carpeting hillsides can be observed from Interstate Highway I-75. A plant appearing to be *Trillium cuneatum* has been collected from Gratiot County, Michigan, and colonies of this and other exotic species have escaped from gardens and become established along the Grand River at Lansing, Michigan, and the St. Joseph River near Niles, Michigan. We assume that this situation has been repeated many times elsewhere.

Habitat

A wide variety of rich, mostly upland woods; most vigorous and impressive on limestone soils, but may grow on less calcareous sites. In northern Tennessee, it grows on both sandstone- and limestone-derived soils, but far more abundantly on the limestone. Capable of withstanding much competition, we have found it in open, grassy fields and on old coal mine tailings in full sun. Especially favors sloping land, rare on floodplains.

Varieties, Forms, Hybrids

forma *cuneatum.* The typical plant described above with maroon-purple flowers.

forma *luteum* Freeman. Floral parts yellow or yellow-green. This form occurs quite commonly as scattered individuals in an otherwise normal population. In some locations in southern Kentucky a *Trillium cuneatum* population containing many individuals of f. *luteum* grows with a population of *T. luteum*. At these locations, where hybridization seems also to occur, many plants cannot be placed in either species with certainty (Plate 46).

Comments

Perhaps the most vigorous and certainly the largest of the eastern sessile trilliums when in its best forms. Many petal color variations occur throughout the range of this species: bronze, red, yellow, yellow red-streaked basally, and clear greens.

Plants considered by most botanists to be of this species from the lower Piedmont of Georgia, Alabama, and Mississippi, in our observations, have smaller, narrower petals than material from northeastern Alabama northward to Kentucky.

Plate 46. A natural, wild grouping of *Trillium luteum* (back left), *Trillium cuneatum* (right), and the hybrid between them (left front), near Liberty, Kentucky. Note the intermediate petal shape and coloring of the putative hybrid. Photo by Fred Case.

For those in eastern North America who would use a sessile *Trillium* to provide color (flower or leaf pattern) in the garden, this certainly would be the logical choice. It possesses strong winter hardiness, vigor, good leaf colors, and enough size to make an impact. The plant seems to need complete dormancy with cold to grow properly. In mild continental European gardens it is not so easy. Instead, the California sessile species, which thrive and grow more vigorously than they frequently do in the wild, should be used.

20. *Trillium decipiens* Freeman

Synonymy: None
Common Name: Deceiving Trillium

At first glance *Trillium decipiens* appears to be only a very tall *T. underwoodii*. Indeed, Freeman (1975) named it *decipiens,* meaning "deceiving," primarily because of the superficial resemblance between these species. *Trillium decipiens,* however, is a much taller species. In *T. underwoodii,* the scapes are about 1 to 1.5 times longer than the leaves at flowering with the leaf tips just touching the ground; in *T. decipiens* the stems are 2.5 to 3 times longer than the leaves. The leaves of *T. decipiens* are, perhaps, the most highly colored and attractive of any of the sessile trilliums.

Habit

Stem erect, glabrous, 1.7–4.4 dm long.

Leaves ovate-lanceolate to lanceolate, rounded basally, widest at about one-third of length from the sessile basal attachment, tapered very gradually to an acute tip, 8–17 cm long, occasionally longer, 4.9–8.5 cm wide, usually very strongly marked with at least 3 shades of dark green, bronze green, and purplish-green, often with a light central strip, held horizontally not drooping.

Sepals lanceolate to ovate-lanceolate, 36–68 mm long, 12–21 mm wide, acute-tipped, divergent, green to maroon-streaked.

Petals obovate to oblanceolate, large in proportion to leaf size compared to many species, 50–90 mm long, widest at or just above the middle, 10–20 mm wide, maroon-purple, brown-purple to brown, greenish-streaked to green, rarely yellow, becoming brown, or occasionally bright copper bronze with age, long persistent; Freeman's (1975) key

Plate 47. *Trillium decipiens* in southern Alabama. Photo by Fred Case.

gave the petal color as mostly greenish, but the plants we have seen and grown are mostly dark maroon purple fading to brown tones.

Stamens erect or curving over ovary, 12–24 mm long; filaments 2–3 mm long; anther sacs 10–15 mm long, opening laterally (latrorse); connectives projecting 1–2 mm beyond anther sacs.

Ovary ellipsoidal, strongly 6-angled, 6–13 mm tall; stigmas short, recurved.

Fruit an ellipsoidal, strongly grooved and ridged, dark green to purple, pulpy-dryish berrylike capsule.

Season
Very early, from late January to February; in the northern or central Alabama part of its range, blooming February to April.

Distribution
South-central Alabama (southwest of Oak Hill), extending along the inner Coastal Plain at the Fall Line sparsely to eastern Georgia, Florida panhandle west of the Appalachicola River (Freeman 1975) and along the Alabama-Georgia state line northward to the Fall Line on either side of the Chattahoochee River. Local.

Habitat
Rich woods and bluffs in mixed deciduous forests of oak (*Quercus* sp.), red maple (*Acer rubrum*), beech (*Fagus* sp.), elm (*Ulmus* sp.), and others. Also in thinner upland oak (*Quercus* sp.) woods, in depressions and in ravines. Very abundant near Marianna, Florida, on low sandy-alluvial slopes to local rivers. Apparently tolerates a variety of soil types, but seems largest and most vigorous on calcareous sandy-alluvium. Usually grows as scattered individuals, often of two stems from a single rhizome tip. Companion plants include *Arisaema dracontium, Listera australis,* bluebells (*Mertensia virginica*), prairie phlox (*Phlox pilosa*), wild sweet William (*Phlox divaricata*), and poison ivy (*Rhus toxicodendron*).

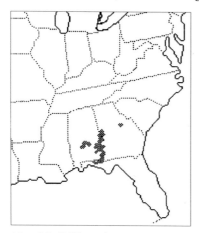

Map 20. *Trillium decipiens.*

Varieties, Forms, Hybrids
None. Possible hybrid swarms with *Trillium underwoodii* are discussed under that species. In April, we found plants near Oak Hill, Alabama, and elsewhere with petals that were a bright copper, almost orange-bronze. Whether they open that color or fade to it is uncertain. If they open so, they perhaps deserve designation as a special forma.

Comments

Near Marianna, Florida, we found large colonies in which every plant was attacked by a white, cottony fungus that damaged or destroyed the leaf whorl. We have not seen such extensive infection by any pathogen elsewhere. Plants from the southwestern part of the range of the species in Alabama were particularly large and robust. *Trillium decipiens* is an attractive species. Although the flower color is not brilliant, it is pleasant. The bronzy-copper colored forms seem to us more showy than the more common dark purple. In all forms the leaves are brilliant and eye-catching. If it never flowered, it would still be a useful plant in the garden for the unusual brilliance of its leaf mottling. Unfortunately, although fully hardy to winter cold in the North, its growth seems to be programmed as much by photoperiod as temperature; hence plants start growth too early in the North and frost kills them. Repeated frost killing, year after year, soon depletes the plant's food reserves and it dies.

Freeman (1975) reported no known instance where *Trillium decipiens* grew with *T. underwoodii*. We found such a colony along the Chattahoochee River north of Columbus, Georgia. While most of the plants there resembled *T. underwoodii*, small numbers of tall, typical appearing *T. decipiens* grew nearby. Some of the latter plants, brought to our Michigan garden, behave quite differently from the typical early-emerging plants described above. Rather, they thrive in a peaty rhododendron soil and emerge later than typical *T. decipiens*. We regard them as intergrades of *T. decipiens* and *T. underwoodii*. Only these putative intergrades seem able to persist here.

21. *Trillium decumbens* Harbison

Synonymy: None
Common Name: Decumbent Trillium

To first come upon a colony of this distinctive *Trillium* on a rocky northern Georgia or Alabama hillside can be a thrilling experience. First, the novelty of a *Trillium* with the leaves essentially flat upon the ground, growing in great massive colonies, is startling enough. Add the strongly mottled and patterned leaves and the very long, slightly twisted dark maroon petals with a faint sparkle from their crystalline texture and you

Plate 48. A colony of *Trillium decumbens* in a rocky, hillside woods in northern Georgia. Photo by Fred Case.

Plate 49. *Trillium decumbens*, fresh flower. Photo by Fred Case.

have a sight not to be forgotten. On vigorous plants, the large leaf whorl and long flamelike petals create the fleeting impression of an ancient Egyptian oil lamp.

Although still frequent within its somewhat limited range, large numbers of *Trillium decumbens* have been destroyed by strip mining for coal in northern Alabama. Whether the practice of grading and reshaping the land after strip mining will alter the habitat too much for the return of these trilliums and other localized plants as reforestation occurs is presently an unknown. The species epithet *decumbens* means "lying flat but with the end upturned."

Habit

Stem short, decumbent, usually by an S-shaped curvature, 5–20 cm long, somewhat stout, often about the same length as the leaves or occasionally shorter; densely puberulent, especially apparent just below leaves and on bases of main leaf veins below.

Leaves 4–12 cm long, 3.3–7 cm wide (Georgia plants larger than those in northern Alabama), sessile, ovate to suborbicular; strongly mottled in shades of green and bronze and with a silvery overlay (increased if plants become heavily frost-damaged during development); leaves *in good condition for only a few weeks after anthesis, dying back to semipersistent bases early.*

Sepals lanceolate, divergent, green or maroon-streaked, 22–48 mm long, 9–14 mm wide, diverging.

Petals linear-lanceolate or oblanceolate, acute, 40–80 mm long, occasionally longer, 7–10 mm wide, rigidly erect, twisted (but not spiralled), dark maroon-purple when fresh, fading especially distally to dull brown, greenish-brown, or with creamy yellow tones; (in the one anthocyanin-free plant we have seen, clear butter yellow).

Stamens straight, erect, 10–25 mm long; filaments very short, about one-third length of anther; anther sacs extrorse; connectives broad, extending to 3.5–4 mm beyond anther sacs.

Ovary oval, 6-angled, 5–10 mm long; stigmas subulate, divergent-recurved.

Fruit broadly ovoid to subglobose, crownlike, strongly ridged, dark purple berry, *present and enlarging on the now-naked scape until early autumn.*

Season

Leaves appear very early as frost leaves ground. Flowering mid-March to April.

Distribution

In the Ridge and Valley and Cumberland Plateau physiographic provinces from extreme southwestern Tennessee south of Chattanooga and southwestern Georgia, across northeastern and north-central Alabama to the vicinity of the Warrior River near Tuscaloosa.

Habitat

Prefers thin, open rocky wooded slopes, but also grows in mature deciduous woodlands. Often on rocky talus and disintegrating shale. Massive colonies occur locally on such shales along the Black Warrior River in Alabama. Also grows abundantly on the flats (floodplain) of small streams and the adjacent slopes near where these streams enter a larger river. We have seen plants in a canebrake on a floodplain below other colonies on steep sloping bluffs of the Warrior River. Occasionally at base of large limestone boulders in open, thin oak (*Quercus* sp.) woods. Colonies usually quite large. Companion plants include Jack-in-the-pulpit (*Arisaema triphyllum*), *Arisaema quinatum*, *Asarum (Hexastylis) arifolia* and others, ebony spleenwort (*Asplenium platyneuron*), *Hepatica acutiloba*, phlox (*Phlox* sp.), *Silene virginica*, and *Tipularia discolor*.

Varieties, Forms, Hybrids

None. We have seen a spectacular yellow-flowered form which appeared spontaneously in a garden in Birmingham, Alabama. Horticulturally this form would be a great garden plant. Many plants may appear to be yellow in bud, but the dark color develops rapidly as the flower reaches anthesis.

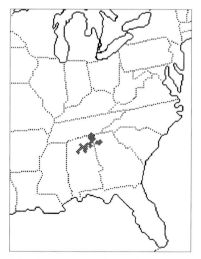

Comments

Few sessile trilliums have the charm and character of this species. It is a favorite of ours. It is completely hardy in our garden at Saginaw,

Map 21. *Trillium decumbens*.

Michigan, where winter temperatures can reach −23°F (−30°C). It seeds here and seedlings appear regularly. *Trillium decumbens* has a large deep horizontal rhizome, the growing point of which always faces down slope. The rhizome is rather easily broken in digging.

Although the plant is not yet threatened or endangered, it has been listed unofficially as "special concern" in Alabama. This is partly because of collecting from local colonies, but mostly because its prime range habitat is over the coal-bearing rock at the southern end of the Appalachian Mountain Chain in Alabama. The big threat to the plant is strip mining and possibly the new practice on commercial lumbering land of clear cutting, followed by a burn and herbicide treatment. Such practices seem to be having a very deleterious effect upon many native woodland plants.

This plant should not be commercially collected from the wild. The developing techniques of tissue culture should be used to produce massive quantities for commercial sale, as soon as such a technique can be adapted to *Trillium*.

22. *Trillium discolor* Wray ex Hooker

Synonymy: *Trillium sessile* var. *wrayi* S. Watson, *Trillium luteum* var.
    latipetalum Gates, *Trillium hugeri* f. *flavum* Peattie
Common Name: None, according to author of species. Patrick (un-
    dated) lists Pale Yellow Trillium and Pale Trillium. We suggest Small
    Yellow Toadshade.

Trillium discolor is one of the more attractive and distinctive of the sessile trilliums. Although it could not be described as a "dwarf," its lower stature in proportion to leaf size and shorter petals provides a contrast with the other comparatively large yellow sessile species, *T. luteum*. A plant of restricted range, *T. discolor* nevertheless can be very abundant locally within its native area. Indeed, along some slopes near the upper Savannah River, the soft creamy yellow blooms appear so thickly as to "light up the land." Although the specific epithet *discolor* means "pale," the soft yellow is quite showy.

Plate 50. A robust plant of *Trillium discolor*. Photo by Fred Case.

Habit

Stem erect, essentially glabrous, 1–2.2 dm tall.

Leaves ovate, elliptic to almost circular, acuminate-tipped, slightly drooping until anthesis, then held essentially horizontally, strongly mottled dark green over a lighter green background, mottling fading or blurring but not disappearing as the season advances, sessile, 6–13 cm long, 4–7 cm wide; occasional plants larger or smaller than typical.

Sepals oblong-lanceolate, spreading, shorter than the petals, 2–3 cm long, *acute.*

Petals spatulate, oblanceolate, clawed basally, 22–50 mm long, 9–15 mm wide, at least one petal strongly apiculate, the others apiculate-acuminate, soft pale yellow or greenish-yellow.

Stamens incurved-erect, 8–15 mm long, filaments 1–2.5 mm long; anther sacs introrse-latrorse; connectives extending beyond anthers 1–2 mm.

Ovary 2.5–8.5 mm tall, 6-ridged; stigmas short, divergent to erect.

Flower odor faintly fragrant, resembling that of sweetshrub (*Calycanthus* sp.), although authors do not state whether the resemblance is to the flower odor or to the bruised leaf odor of sweetshrub.

Fruit a subglobose berry, 6-winged (weakly), greenish-white at maturity, pulpy or mealy, dehiscing from receptacle when ripe.

Season

Flowers in mid-April to early May. Although early in phenology compared to sympatric species in the wild, its behavior in our Michigan garden is interesting. Here, the plants appear in leaf very early, but the buds remain tightly closed until most other species are well into anthesis or past, at which time the flowers open. This contrasts with its early flowering in the wild.

Distribution

Very distinctive: occurs only in the upper drainage of the Savannah River. In the Blue Ridge of North and South Carolina (in coves and stream flats at lower elevations), and on the upper Piedmont of South Carolina and Georgia in the vicinity of the Savannah River (both the Georgia and South Carolina sides), from Oconee County to McCormick County, South Carolina.

Habitat

A wide variety. In the Blue Ridge, rather acidic to clearly circumneutral or basic soils (Radford et al.

Map 22. *Trillium discolor.*

1968), often under oak (*Quercus* sp.), near rhododendron (*Rhododendron* sp.) thickets or near tangles of *Leucothoe* sp. on moist stream banks, higher slopes near streams and mixed deciduous forest on the Piedmont. We have seen it in company with the very rare oconee bells (*Shortia galacifolia*) and wandflower (*Galax* sp.), and with Jack-in-the-pulpit (*Arisaema triphyllum* varieties), lady's slipper orchid (*Cypripedium calceolus* var. *pubescens*), bleeding heart (*Dicentra* sp.), trailing arbutus (*Epigaea repens*), *Hepatica acutiloba*, bloodroot (*Sanguinaria canadensis*), Catesby's trillium (*Trillium catesbaei*), and sweet Beth (*Trillium vaseyi*).

Varieties, Forms, Hybrids
None.

Comments
A delightful species. In our experience, plants of the Piedmont generally grow larger in all details than those of the Blue Ridge coves. The Blue Ridge habitats tend to be of less fertile, acidic soils; perhaps this is what makes the size difference. In Pickens County, South Carolina, the plant occurs locally, but there are some good-sized populations. In one favored habitat it grows on the flats of small streams at the edges of thick tangles of fetter bush (*Leucothoe catesbaei*) or rhododendron (*Rhododendron* sp.). Here the plants occur as scattered individuals or small clusters, among eastern round-leaved violet (*Viola rotundifolia*), and numerous herbs. An almost constant companion in this situation is the pink-flowered form of Catesby's trillium (*Trillium catesbaei*).

In a wooded ravine and stream flat west of Greenwood, South Carolina, we found thousands of plants on lower slopes and in a rather open, sunny site for this species. Here the plants were very large, with almost round-apiculate petals of a very pale creamy yellow. It is not a clump former in the sense of *Trillium erectum* or *T. grandiflorum*, but at this spot many plants if not most had two stems from the terminal bud of each rhizome.

A horticulturally desirable species with a restricted natural range, this species should be propagated by tissue culture techniques or seed. It should not be commercially collected from the wild.

23. *Trillium foetidissimum* Freeman

Synonymy: None
Common Name: None. We suggest Stinking Trillium or Fetid Trillium.

In stature, at least, this species most resembles the widespread *Trillium sessile*. Its leaves, however, possess much stronger and more attractive mottling, often with almost iridescent bright green patches and bronzy tones. Locally frequent within its range, it occupies varied habitats. Some of the bluff habitats of mature beech (*Fagus*) with large numbers of *T. foetidissimum* scattered beneath were enchanting, particularly the bluffs just east of the Mississippi River in the vicinity of St. Francisville, Louisiana. The specific epithet *foetidissimum* means "extremely fetid" or "stinking." The foul odor is noticeable only within a few inches of the flower during warm, bright conditions.

Habit

Stem more or less erect, 9–30 cm long, usually between 10–18 cm, papilose basally.

Leaves 5–8.3 cm long, 3.8–6.7 cm wide, elliptic-ovate, rarely almost orbicular, sessile, apex obtuse-acute, light green, strongly mottled in dark green with a central light green stripe; leaves often carried quite horizontally.

Sepals lanceolate, acute, 16–40 mm long, 4–6 mm wide; spreading flat on same plane as leaves (but alternating with them), the tips weakly recurved.

Petals very gradually incurved from base to tip, narrowly linear-lanceolate, rarely more elliptic, acute at apex, pink-purple, red-purple, brownish-purple rarely yellowish, fading to brownish tones with aging.

Stamens 9–25 mm long, erect; filaments 3–6 mm long, dilated basally; anther sacs introrse; connectives prolonged 1–1.5 mm beyond.

Ovary ovoid 5–12 mm tall; stigmas erect.

Flower odor of putrid meat especially when in strong sunlight.

Fruit ovoid, 6-angled at least apically, purple-brown.

Season

From early March to early April, rarely February. Flowers last a long time in nature.

Plate 51. *Trillium foetidissimum* in woods near St. Francisville, Louisiana. Photo by Fred Case.

Distribution

Louisiana east of the Mississippi River, northward into the southwestern corner of Mississippi (Claiborne County to Hancock County; Freeman 1975). Rather frequent within this area.

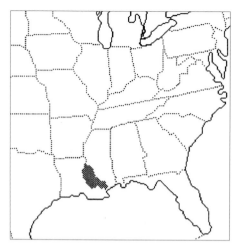

Map 23. *Trillium foetidissimum.*

Habitat

River bluffs, ravines, floodplains, low ground, in rich woods, even on roadsides and shoulders, in silts, sandy-alluvium, and loess soils. Companion plants include *Arisaema dracontium, A. quinatum, Erythronium rostratum,* American beech (*Fagus* sp.), *Magnolia* sp., wild sweet William (*Phlox divaricata*), and oak (*Quercus* sp.). Occasionally under spruce pine (*Pinus glabra*) in mixed woods. In one such dry oak-pine (*Quercus-Pinus* spp.) woods on a steep slope, we found scattered fetid trilliums in surprisingly dry forest, largely vacant of other herbs. The plants grew along an intermittent stream bed on a rather shaley outcrop and in talus. At St. Francisville, Louisiana, the plants abound in beautifully wooded ravines sloping down to small streams leading to the Mississippi River.

Varieties, Forms, Hybrids

forma *foetidissimum*. The typical form described above.

forma *luteum* Freeman. Lacking purple pigment in any floral organs, petals yellow to yellow green. Occurs as an occasional isolated individual mutation throughout the range of the species, rare.

Comments

In spite of its name which means "exceedingly fetid," this is a rather charming species. Its strongly blotched, horizontally held leaves give it considerable character, but the narrowly lanceolate-petaled flowers are not showy. We have not seen the yellow form of this species, but from Freeman's comments it is more conspicuous than the typical form.

The species seems tolerant of a wide range of soil moisture and soil types from low swampy woods to high, dry bluffs and ravine slopes. It is the only *Trillium* known to occur within its Louisiana range (Freeman 1975). Freeman considers *T. foetidissimum* to be closely related to *T. sessile*. Indeed. it is somewhat similar in size and growth habit, but with narrower petals and usually much more colorful leaves.

24. *Trillium gracile* Freeman

Synonymy: None
Common Name: Slender Trillium

Least familiar, perhaps, of all the sessile trilliums, this species also grows the farthest west of the Coastal Plain and Piedmont species. It was not recognized as a distinct taxon until Freeman's monumental work of 1975. It grows, in our experience, in sandier and sometimes drier, better drained habitats than most of its nearby congeners. Not clearly distinctive in its appearance, it differs from nearby species mostly in floral detail and in its later blooming season. The specific epithet *gracile* means "slender, graceful."

Habit

Stem erect, glabrous, 1.6–3.5 dm tall.

Leaves elliptic-ovate to obovate, 6–8.5 cm long, 2.6–4 cm wide, green, mottled with darker blotches; leaf tips obtuse or rounded, rarely acute.

Sepals lanceolate to oblong, 20–25 mm long, 4–5 mm wide, obtuse-tipped; widely spreading with recurved tips.

Petals linear-elliptic to oblanceolate, 20–40 mm long, 3–5 mm wide, acute-tipped, dark maroon-purple, rarely yellow.

Stamens erect, 12–16.5 mm long; filaments 2–3 mm long; anther sacs introrse; connectives very slightly extending beyond anther sacs.

Ovary ovoid, 3-angled, 5–8 mm tall; stigmas thickened basally, 2–4 mm long, spreading recurved.

Flower odor musty or funguslike.

Fruit ovoid, swollen enough to conceal its 3-angled nature, dark greenish-purple.

Season

Relatively late blooming from early to mid-April. *Trillium gracile* is in tight bud when *T. ludovicianum*, at same latitude, is in full flower. In our garden in Michigan, it is one of the last species of *Trillium* to flower.

Distribution

On upper Coastal Plain on either side of the Texas-Louisiana border. Occurs about two counties deep into either state. It occurs a bit farther

Plate 52. *Trillium gracile* near Nacogdoches, Texas. Photo by Victor Soukup.

northeastward locally into northern Louisiana. On lower Coastal Plain it is found between Beaumont, Texas, and Lake Charles, Louisiana. Particularly common in the Big Thicket area, persisting in very sandy soil, in one state park after brush and trees had been cleared in picnic and camping areas.

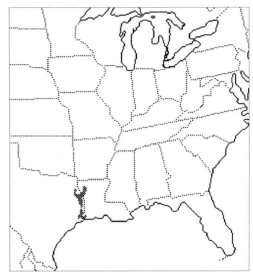

Map 24. *Trillium gracile.*

Habitat
Mature pine (*Pinus* sp.) and hardwood forests, particularly on higher banks and ridges of dissected small stream beds, often in rather dense shade; low sandy flatwoods along impoundments of the Sabine River, occasionally in very sandy open places.

Varieties, Forms, Hybrids
forma *gracile.* The typical plant described above.
forma *luteum* Freeman. Petals and all floral organs lacking purple pigment, yellow or yellow-green.

Comments
Freeman (1975) chose the epithet *gracile* because the plants appeared "graceful and delicate," and the relatively short leaves made them appear especially tall. When we visited this species, we were not particularly impressed that the plants appeared distinctively tall, slender, and graceful. Perhaps we were too early, as few plants were in flower. We found them to be taller than *Trillium ludovicianum,* but otherwise similar in leaf size. There is no question, however, that *T. gracile* blooms much later than its neighboring species. Its main distinctions lie in the technical details of its flower structure. In spite of its very deep southern range, the plant is at least fairly winter hardy here in central Michigan.

25. *Trillium kurabayashii* Freeman

Synonymy: None
Common Name: None

Masataka Kurabayashi, a Japanese cytologist and population geneticist who worked extensively with the genus *Trillium,* was first to suggest the presence of an unrecognized species on the West Coast of the United States. When Freeman's research proved Kurabayashi correct, Freeman (1975) named this taxon to honor him. This is a very large, attractive species frequently forming clumps and extensive colonies.

Habit

Stem erect, often 2 from a single terminal bud, 2.5–5.5 dm tall.

Leaves sessile, ovate to broadly ovate, 8–22 cm long, 12–17 cm wide, bright green (in early anthesis rather succulent in appearance) usually well-marked with lighter and darker green spots, occasionally obscurely or scarcely mottled: leaf tip acuminate.

Sepals lanceolate, divergent, green, purple-streaked, acute tipped, 4–7.5 cm long, 1–1.4 cm wide.

Petals oblanceolate, 55–110 mm long, 20–35 mm wide; dark red-purple, conspicuous.

Stamens erect, 15–26 mm long; filament short, 2–4 mm long, dark purple; anther sacs introrse, 13–24 mm long; connectives barely prolonged beyond anther sacs; pollen bright yellow.

Ovary ovoid, 8–15 mm tall, round to 6-angled, purple; stigma thickened basally, erect.

Flower odor spicy in fresh flowers, becoming fetid in older flowers (Freeman 1975).

Fruit ovoid to ellipsoid, or weakly angled, dark red-purple.

Season

Late March to early May, flowering earlier in western coastal range, later in the Sierra Nevada. We found the species in peak bloom near Klamath, California, on 19 March 1990.

Plate 53. Flower of *Trillium kurabayashii*, Klamath River, California. Photo by Fred Case.

Distribution
Coastal, from extreme southwestern Oregon (Curry County) southward in Klamath Mountains to Humbolt County, California. In Sierra Nevada Mountains from Butte County southward to Placer County, California.

Plate 54. *Trillium kurabayashii,* growing at the Royal Botanic Gardens, Edinburgh, Scotland. Photo by Fred Case.

Map 25. *Trillium kurabayashii.*

Habitat

Rich moist conifer-hardwood forest, slopes, especially lower slopes; predominantly deciduous flat woods along streams; edges of redwood (*Sequoia* sp.) groves, and alder (*Alnus* sp.) and fern thickets along streams, preferring older, higher flood terraces, not the lowest and wettest. Often forms large colonies. Grows in deeper humus and more sheltered forests than giant trillium (*Trillium chloropetalum*) or narrow-petaled trillium (*T. angustipetalum*).

Varieties, Forms, Hybrids

forma *kurabayashii*. The typical plant described above.

forma *luteum* Soukup. Flowers pale, translucent yellow-green, streaked with purple. Near Klamath River, California, we found several pallid-flowered plants in soft straw-yellow and green. Petals had small short darker streaks. Plants were interesting, but not particularly showy or striking.

Comments

Although the ranges of *Trillium kurabayashii* and *T. albidum* overlap, at no time did we see the two species growing together except in the Salmon River Mountains in northern California. Nowhere did we see what we would consider intergrades or hybrids. In April 1996, Viva Stansell (pers. comm.) informed us of the existence of a hybrid swarm of these two species at higher elevations in the coastal redwood region of northern California.

Trillium kurabayashii possesses rather conspicuous, large, fairly broad dark purple-red petals. Freeman (1975) called the color "lurid," but that is not the word we would use to describe it. The color, a cleaner dark purple-red than found in most of the purple-flowered eastern sessile trilliums, quite conspicuous, is not unpleasing. Freeman spoke of the plant as having "coarse, veiny (almost leathery) bracts." Our impression of plants in early bloom was more of a soft, succulent-wilty look, as of a plant grown-on too fast in a greenhouse. Freeman pointed out that *T. kurabayashii* grows much larger than the similar-appearing eastern *T. cuneatum.*

This showy clump-forming plant seems to be abundant in the heart of its range. With *Trillium chloropetalum* varieties and cultivars, it seems to be the plant grown extensively in botanical gardens in England and Scotland under the illegitimate name *T. sessile californicum.* It is winter-hardy in our mid-Michigan garden, but as with most of the western sessile species, emerges so early that it gets damaged by frosts and therefore never thrives.

26. *Trillium lancifolium* Rafinesque

Synonymy: *Trillium recurvatum* var. *lanceolatum* S. Watson, *Trillium lanceolatum* Boykin ex S. Watson
Common Name: Lance-leaved Trillium

This species, like prairie trillium (*Trillium recurvatum*), has a distinctive "look." In fact, the two species, which are related and similar in appearance, can be confused. The peculiar, interrupted distribution of *T. lancifolium* fascinates botanists and plant geographers, but the reasons for the distribution pattern have yet to be explained. The specific epithet *lancifolium* means "lance-leaved."

Habit

Stem smooth, erect, quite tall in proportion to the leaves, 1.5–3.2 dm tall, about 2.5 to 3 times longer than the leaves, arising from a very slender-elongated, white, very brittle rhizome.

Leaves sessile, lanceolate to narrowly lanceolate-elliptic, 5–8.3 cm long, 2–3.3 cm wide; mottled darker green, tapering to a blunt or acute tip.

Sepals spreading, lanceolate-acute, 13–20 mm long, 5–7 mm wide.

Petals linear to oblong or elongate-cuneate, often twisted, basally clawed, the claw about half as long as the expanded distal portion of the petal (limb), maroon-red, purple, greenish-tan or bicolored, the basal portion dark red-maroon, 2.8–6.6 cm long, 2–4 mm wide, widest above the middle.

Stamens 13–21 mm long; filaments equalling or slightly exceeding the anther sac; anther sacs and connectives weakly to strongly incurved, introrse; connectives extending 1 mm beyond the anthers.

Ovary 6-angled, ovoid-rhomboid, dark purple, 6–7 mm long; stigmas 3–4 mm long, linear, somewhat divergent-recurved.

Fruit a 6-angled berrylike capsule; the prolonged angle folds make the fruit appear almost winged.

Season

The disjunct distribution of this plant gives it essentially two blooming seasons: February and early March in the southernmost stations, and mid-April to early May in the northernmost districts. In Coosa County,

Plate 55. *Trillium lancifolium in* northern Georgia. Photo by Fred Case.

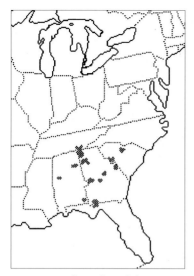

Map 26. *Trillium lancifolium.*

Alabama, we have found the plant blooming in early April; in northern Georgia, in mid-April.

Distribution

Florida panhandle near the Chattahoochee River and along the same river in adjacent southeastern Alabama and southwestern Georgia. In the vicinity of the Fall Line, across Georgia and North and South Carolina. A third area of occurrence lies from near Tuscaloosa, Alabama, northeastward to northwestern Georgia and Tennessee in the vicinity of Lookout Mountain. Most frequent in northeastern Alabama and northwestern Georgia (Freeman 1975).

Habitat

Prefers alluvial soils and reaches its greatest size and vigor on floodplains. Also occurs in rocky upland woodlands and brushy thickets. Freeman (1975) listed canebrakes as a habitat: we have seen it in such only once. Often grows in company with poison ivy (*Toxicodendron radicans*) in very wet soils. We have seen it both in heavy shade and in rather thin open woods.

Varieties, Forms, Hybrids
None.

Comments

In appearance, one of the most distinctive of sessile trilliums. Its choice of alluvial habitats often places the plant in unattractive situations. In its remaining habitats near larger cities in northern Georgia, it often grows near or in dumps and trashy woods. Late spring flash floods after downpours frequently inundate the plants and coat them with mud or batter them with waterborne debris. Yet the plant thrives. While rare in more upland situations, we have found it in such near Decatur, Georgia. On rich soil it may occasionally produce large clumps (perhaps offsets of one clone), but the plants tend to cluster in small scattered patches of single or a few stems of sporadic occurrence across the habitat, unlike other alluvial soil trilliums such as *T. ludovicianum,* which seems to be quite evenly distributed across favorable habitats.

Although rarely offered by plant nurseries, its distinctive, "lanky" appearance adds a special texture to the wildflower garden. Easily cultivated, it is, however, difficult to lift the plant's elongated and very brittle rhizome without breaking it into several pieces. If planted, however, each piece will grow and produce a plant, but it will take several years for the pieces to recover and develop food reserves before they will flower.

Trillium lancifolium is winter hardy in our garden at Saginaw, Michigan, where winter temperatures have dropped as low as −23°F (−30°C).

27. *Trillium ludovicianum* Harbison

Synonymy: None
Common Name: Louisiana Trillium

Anyone reading the pioneering taxonomic works on *Trillium* by Gleason (1906), Gates (1917), Freeman (1975), and others soon realizes how superficially similar most of the sessile trilliums can be, and will quickly understand why there has been so much written that is confusing or incorrect. One of these oft confused and misunderstood plants is *Trillium ludovicianum,* a species often taxonomically lumped with or misidentified as *T. maculatum* in the past. Once seen in nature, it becomes apparent the plants do not resemble each other closely in stature, petal shape, or color. Because this species grows almost entirely within the state of Louisiana, Harbison called attention to that fact with the epithet *ludovicianum,* which means "Louisiana."

Habit

Stem erect, smooth, 1.4–2.6 dm tall.

Leaves lanceolate-ovate, 5.3–9.5 cm long, 2.3–5 cm wide, sessile, the tip rounded-acute, strongly mottled in dark green and bronzy-green, often with a light stripe down the middle.

Sepals lanceolate-oblanceolate, 19–35 mm long, 2.7–4 mm wide, apex rounded or acute.

Plate 56. *Trillium ludovicianum* in central Louisiana. Photo by Fred Case.

Petals oblanceolate-linear, 3–4.7 cm long, 4–8 mm wide, faintly introrsely curved-erect, acute-tipped, thickened and somewhat clawlike at the base, pinkish-purple, purplish-green, or bicolored, the basal portion purple, the distal portion a peculiar dark grayish-silver green.

Stamens straight, erect, 10–18 mm long, filaments 2–3 mm long; anther
  sacs latrorse, connectives scarcely prolonged beyond anther sac.
Ovary ovoid, 6-angled, 8–9 mm tall, merging with the thickened bases
  of the stigmas; stigmas erect, with spreading tips 3–6 mm long.
Flower odor of carrion.
Fruit ovoid, 6-angled, tapering to basal attachment, dark purple-green,
  with the stigma bases apparent (Freeman 1975).

Season
Early March and April.

Distribution
Copiah County, in southwest-central Mississippi and the inner Coastal
Plain of central Louisiana, where it is local.

Habitat
Mostly low flatwoods, floodplains along streams, occasionally on steep
slopes leading to a floodplain. We have found it in nearly pure beech (*Fagus* sp.) stands and also in mixed deciduous floodplain woods. Freeman
(1975) stated that *Trillium ludovicianum* also can grow in a mixed pine-
beech (*Pinus* sp. and *Fagus* sp.) woods. We have not found it associated
with pines at our stations, but we are not as familiar with this species as
some others.

Varieties, Forms, Hybrids
None.

Comments
This species bears strongly marked
leaves. Indeed, the leaves are in many
ways more conspicuous than the petals.
Petal colors here, whether in the bicolored individuals or those entirely purple, are not particularly showy.

The range of *Trillium ludovicianum*
overlaps that of *T. cuneatum* in Mississippi and the two appear to intergrade.
To the west of *T. ludovicianum* in west-

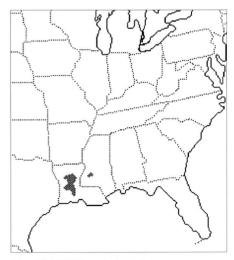

Map 27. *Trillium ludovicianum.*

ern Louisiana and Texas grows *T. gracile,* a relatively recently recognized species, which has also been confused in the past with *T. ludovicianum. Trillium foetidissimum* occurs just east of *T. ludovicianum* in eastern Louisiana and southern Mississippi. *Trillium ludovicianum, T. foetidissimum, T. gracile,* and the southwestern form and intergrades of *T. cuneatum* appear much alike in overall characters and make identification of trilliums from this region difficult. All these species except the western *T. gracile* grow near each other's ranges along the Mississippi River in southwestern Mississippi and bloom at about the same time. Those seeking to identify trilliums collected in this region must pay careful attention to the technical details of flower structure.

28. *Trillium luteum* (Muhlenberg) Harbison

Synonymy: *Trillium sessile* var. *luteum* Muhlenberg, *Trillium underwoodii* var. *luteum* (Muhlenberg) MacBride, *Trillium sessile* f. *luteum* (Muhlenberg) Peattie, *Trillium hugeri* f. *flavum* Peattie, *Trillium viride* var. *luteum* (Muhlenberg) Gleason
Common Name: Yellow Trillium, Yellow Toadshade, Wax Trillium

Because of its widespread use and availability in horticulture, more people recognize *Trillium luteum* than any other sessile species. Those who attend the Gatlinburg, Tennessee, wildflower pilgrimages see this plant by the thousands. It fills the forests, roadsides, even roadside ditches near the resort town just west of Great Smoky Mountains National Park. Elsewhere in its range it may not grow so abundantly, but it enjoys a fairly wide distribution. The specific epithet *luteum,* meaning "yellow," refers to the petal color.

Habit
Stem erect, smooth, 1.4–4 dm tall, rarely, taller.
Leaves sessile, variable, ovate-elliptic to almost orbicular-acuminate; strongly mottled at first, becoming more obscurely mottled as flower matures, 6.5–17 cm long, 6.5–9.8 cm wide.
Sepals oblong-lanceolate, lanceolate or oblong-elliptic, distinctly rounded-acute, 22–47 mm long, 8–9 mm wide, green.
Petals elliptic-lanceolate, lanceolate, oblanceolate, widest near base, ta-

Plate 57. *Trillium luteum* in the wild. Note the lanceolate petals. Photo by Fred Case.

pering to a long-acuminate tip, 34–66 mm long, 10–21 mm wide, greenish-yellow, to lemon-yellow, becoming more yellow with aging.

Stamens erect, 11–18 mm long, filaments 1.5–2 mm long; anther sacs introrse (or appearing lateral), connectives broad, not prolonged beyond anther sacs.

Ovary ovoid to spherical, 6-angled, 5–8 mm tall; stigmas erect, 3–4 mm long, the tips barely spreading.

Flower odor strongly of lemons.

Plate 58. A colony of *Trillium luteum* near Gatlinburg, Tennessee. Photo by Fred Case.

Map 28. *Trillium luteum.*

Fruit ovoid, 6-angled, green to greenish-white, occasionally with dark streaks, pulpy, separating in its entirety from receptacle, not opening along carpel sutures.

Season
April to May throughout range.

Distribution
Extreme western North Carolina and northern Georgia, west and northwestward through eastern Tennessee and a small area of east-central southern Kentucky. Green and yellow

forms of other sessile species account for the assignment to it of a much larger natural range in older literature.

Habitat

Deciduous forests, thin open woods, rocky streambanks and flats, rarely clearings and openings, old fields. Prefers rich mature forest on a calcareous substrate.

Varieties, Forms, Hybrids

Various authors give no named forms or varieties. We have seen obvious hybrids with *Trillium cuneatum* in Casey County, Kentucky (see Plate 46). The hybrids appear intermediate in stature, petal shape, and coloring of flower.

Comments

This species has been confused by botanists for a long time. Some, such as Radford et al. (1968), appear to lump it as a form of *Trillium cuneatum,* while others confuse it with *T. viride,* a more western species. Early botanists have confused *T. luteum* with the occasional individual or very local larger population of pallid color forms of other species. *Trillium cuneatum* rather frequently produces green, yellow-green, or pale lemon-yellow forms (but with a cuneate larger and wider petal) that mimic *T. luteum.* These forms, when growing with *T. luteum,* hybridize, leading to so many intergrades that many plants cannot be properly placed into either species with any confidence. For these reasons, almost no works older than Freeman's (1975) can be used reliably to plot distribution of *T. luteum.*

To make matters worse, *Trillium luteum* frequently escapes from gardens into the wild and may establish itself temporarily or permanently in the wild outside its natural range. Colonies occur in Michigan along the Grand River at Lansing, along the St. Joseph River near Buchanan, in an old-growth forest near Saginaw, and undoubtedly elsewhere.

Trillium luteum and *T. cuneatum* do not grow together over parts of their ranges. *Trillium luteum* is abundant in eastern Tennessee and along the Tennessee–North Carolina line, extending a short distance into North Carolina and Georgia. *Trillium cuneatum* is rare or absent from this region except along the Little Tennessee River (Freeman 1975); it ranges westward to western Tennessee west of the Cumberland Plateau, and from there north into Kentucky and southwestward into southern Mississippi, Alabama, and into the Piedmont of the Carolinas. In that vast region, *T. luteum* does not occur. Only in southern Kentucky, in southeastern Tennessee, and along the Little Tennessee River on the Tennessee–North Carolina border, where geological events have reduced their natural barrier (the Cumberland Plateau), do both species grow together abundantly (Freeman 1975). It is here that many forms intermediate in color, structure, and flower odor occur (Plate 46). For this reason, Freeman concluded, wisely, we feel, that these are two clearly different species, not varieties of the same species.

Trillium luteum enjoys great popularity with wildflower lovers and horticulturists, who frequently cultivate the plant. At the present time, most plants offered by nurseries are collected from the wild, a bad conservation practice. Under garden conditions, at least in Michigan, plants that in the wild had produced good clear pale yellow blooms tend, in most or all seasons, to produce lime-green or greenish petals with very little of the yellow coloring apparent.

29. *Trillium maculatum* Rafinesque

Synonymy: *Trillium sessile* Linnaeus, in part, *Trillium underwoodii*
  Small, in part
Common Name: Spotted Trillium

This conspicuous, attractive, large plant grows natively over a larger range than many of the more southern sessile trilliums. It may be found in both low ground and upland habitats. Long confused with other species, the plant nonetheless has distinctions which once learned make it fairly easy to distinguish in life. Unfortunately, in pressed herbarium specimens, the distinctiveness of this plant, like others of its ilk, is often obscured or destroyed, leading to confusion or error. In their *Manual of the Vascular Flora of the Carolinas,* Radford et al. (1968) made no mention of *Trillium maculatum* in their treatment of *Trillium,* without any

Plate 59. A typical red and a clear yellow form of *Trillium maculatum*. Photo by Fred Case.

explanation of why they omitted this species. *Trillium maculatum* is fairly widely distributed in southeastern South Carolina. The specific epithet *maculatum* means "spotted" and refers to the conspicuously marked leaves in some forms of this species. The best leaf color forms we have observed occurred in habitats near Augusta, Georgia.

Habit

Stem erect, smooth, 1.4–4 dm tall.

Leaves broadly ovate-elliptic to elliptic, sessile, apically rounded or barely acuminate, mottled, to varying degree, 7–15 cm long, 4.6–6.7 cm
wide.

Sepals lanceolate-linear, 2.2–5 cm long, 5–7 mm wide rounded-acute
tipped, spreading almost to horizontal, often suffused or streaked with
purple-maroon, the tips recurving slightly.

Petals 40–70 mm long, 7–17 mm wide, *narrowly to broadly spatulate-
cuneate, the widest point above the middle, and narrowing beyond middle rather triangularly to apex; petal margins slightly raised upward in
lower half, spreading-divergent when flower opens,* becoming more
erect and even touching in the manner of *Trillium cuneatum* when
older; deep clear red-maroon or purple, lacking the muddy or brown
tones of many purple sessile species, or rarely, purple basally and yellow toward apex, or clear sulfur-yellow.

Stamens erect, 12–20 mm long; filaments 2–3 mm long, widest at base;
anther sacs introrse on a broad connective; connectives essentially not
extended beyond the anther sacs.

Ovary ovoid, weakly 6-angled, the angles often obscured in a large turgid ovary, 8–11 mm long; stigmas thick, 2–4 mm long, awl-shaped,
erect.

Flower odor faintly spicy-fragrant; banana-like (Freeman 1975).

Fruit ovoid, obscurely, 3- to 6-angled, bearing the persistent stigmas,
dark purple-green.

Season

Early flowering compared to companion trilliums—from early February to early March in southern and outer Coastal Plain sites, and from
late March to early April in inner Coastal Plain and northernmost portions of its range.

Distribution

From Monroe County, Alabama, eastward and northeastward on the
Coastal Plain into the inner Coastal Plain of Georgia; thence extending
along the inner Coastal Plain and adjacent Piedmont into South Carolina. Abundant on bluffs and floodplains of the lower Savannah River

and along the South Carolina coast to the vicinity of Charleston. Also present in lower Coastal Plain of Florida in counties near the Chattahoochee River and eastward to base of the Florida Peninsula. Curiously absent, as Freeman (1975) pointed out, from the lower Coastal Plain of Georgia except along the Savannah River. Local, but locally abundant.

Prior to Freeman's work, many authors mistook *Trillium ludovicianum* for *T. maculatum*, in spite of its rather different petal shape and coloring, and attributed to the range of *T. maculatum* a western extension into Louisiana that does not exist.

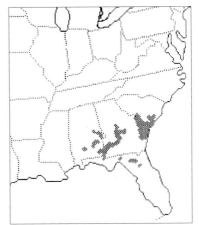

Map 29. *Trillium maculatum*.

Habitat

Rich mesic forests, particularly banks and bluffs of rivers; flood plains even of smaller tributary streams, often where quite brushy; beech (*Fagus* sp.) and oak (*Quercus* sp.) forests. Occurs on rich soils, calcareous soils and alluvium. Companion plants include *Hepatica acutiloba*, *Hexastylis arifolia*, deciduous *Rhododendron* species, bloodroot (*Sanguinaria canadensis*), wood poppy (*Stylophorum diphyllum*), and *Trillium* species. Usually at its best in fairly deep shade.

Varieties, Forms, Hybrids

forma *maculatum*. The typical plant described above with purple-maroon petals, carpels, and stamens (Plate 59).

forma *luteum* Freeman. All floral organs lack purple pigment; the petals are a beautiful clear, soft yellow (Plate 59). This is a particularly attractive form and worthy of horticultural propagation. Occurs very rarely with the typical form.

forma *simulans* Freeman. Petals yellow with purple bases; the stamens and carpel purple (Plate 60). Occasional throughout the species' range.

Comments

In our opinion, one of the most attractive of the sessile trilliums. Its colors, both the dark purple-reds and the anthocyanin-free yellows, are

Plate 60. *Trillium maculatum* f. *simulans.* Photo by Victor Soukup.

clearer and purer than their counterparts in the other species. In its more vigorous forms an imposing plant. We have found it in pure stands and growing with such rarities as *Trillium reliquum*; also with many of the well-known spring ephemerals of the South, including a charming dwarfish form of Bloodroot (*Sanguinaria canadensis*)

Unfortunately, *Trillium maculatum* does not possess great winter hardiness and emerges very early so that if it survives the winter's cold in northern latitudes, late frosts usually destroy its growth. Because it cannot resprout without a dormancy-breaking cold period, it remains dormant until the next spring when the process is repeated. Unless someone finds a hardier race or one that emerges later, *T. maculatum* may not perform satisfactorily in northern gardens. In the south and central latitudes, it makes a handsome garden subject, both in flower and in leaf.

30. *Trillium parviflorum* Soukup

Synonymy: None
Common Name: Small-flowered Trillium

One of the most recently described *Trillium* species, it seems first to have been recognized as different by a western *Trillium* expert and enthusiast, Edith Dusek, who brought it to the attention of Victor Soukup, another *Trillium* specialist. Soukup's studies led to his describing it as a new species.

We have observed this plant at three separate localities. It does indeed seem a valid species to us. As there is little herbarium material readily available to us, our description is based, in part on Soukup's (1980) original description, our observations, and limited herbarium studies. The specific epithet *parviflorum* means "small-flowered."

Habit

Stem erect, 1.7–3 dm tall.

Leaves subsessile, ovate, 6.5–16 cm long, 5–8 cm wide, larger in heavily shaded specimens, apex obtuse, bright green with a few widely scattered dark markings.

Sepals lanceolate, 16–25 mm long, 4–8 mm wide, tip variously obtuse to rounded.

Petals narrow, erect, linear to linear-lanceolate creamy white, occasionally purple-stained and cuneate basally, apex obtuse.

Plate 61. Flower detail of *Trillium parviflorum*. Photo by Fred Case.

Stamens erect, 10–15.5 mm long, filaments 1–3 mm long, white, greenish-white, or with purple stain; anther sacs lateral (latrorse), connective barely extended beyond anther sacs.

Ovary ovoid, 4–8 mm tall, obscurely hexagonal, at anthesis green or
green and purple basally; stigmas green, thickened, more or less divergent, outer surface purple.

Plate 62. *Trillium parviflorum in* southern Washington. Photo by Fred Case.

Flower odor spicy-fragrant; Soukup compares it to that of Trailing Arbutus (*Epigaea repens*).
Fruit dark red-purple or maroon, subglobose.

Season
Late March to early May. We found it in full flower in three localities in Washington near the northern limit of its range in mid-April.

Map 30. *Trillium parviflorum.*

Distribution

According to Soukup (1980), from Pierce and Thurston Counties, Washington, south into northern Oregon, reaching its southern limits in Polk County, Oregon, where we found apparent intergrades with *Trillium albidum.*

Habitat

Apparently tolerant of some variation. We found it in four very different habitats in our Washington localities. At one, a very mature fir (*Abies* sp.), spruce (*Picea* sp.), and hardwood stand, it grew in rich humus and mosses in company with western white trillium (*Trillium ovatum*), winter purslane (*Montia* sp.), and various fern genera—a distinctly moist and humid deeply shaded situation. At another site, we observed the plants in a rather open, somewhat grassy large grove of old oaks, with considerable underbrush, but rather few herbaceous companions. While some plants here grew in very moist soil, the overall impression was of a very dry windy habitat. Not far from some plants, in open very dry grassland, grew camass (*Camassia* sp.), shooting stars (*Dodecatheon hendersonii*), and many plants accustomed to going dormant and enduring strong drying during the summer. In the same area, in another habitat, in a tangled, wet streambank situation, the plants grew tall and vigorously amid alders (*Alnus* sp.) and grasses. In still another situation, plants grew in a rather greasy clayey soil on a hillside among shrubs, both in the open under power lines, and in nearby woods in humus and light shade.

Varieties, Forms, Hybrids

None. Along a river about 15 miles north of Corvallis, Oregon, in floodplain soils, we found a colony of plants larger than typical *Trillium parviflorum,* but with very long, very narrow linear white petals. The plants appeared to be either very long-petaled *T. parviflorum,* or an intermediate form with *T. albidum.*

Comments

In our observations of *Trillium parviflorum,* we have noticed a very broad range in overall plant size and stature, from very short small-leaved plants to tall, broad, umbrella-leaved giants. One thing stood out in all the plants: regardless of size of the leaf or plant height, the flower and petal size remained remarkably constant, with small, linear-lanceolate petals. Such is not usually the case with *T. albidum,* the species with which this plant is most likely to be confused. In *T. albidum,* the plants can be enormous, in which case the petals are very long, broad, and conspicuously obovate-diamond shaped. In the case of large clonal clumps the larger and more mature plants show the typical petal shape, while the smaller (presumedly youngest) offsets sometimes produced smaller, narrower petals more like *T. parviflorum.*

Trillium parviflorum seems to grow in drier soils in some of its locations than does *T. albidum.* Horticulturally, *T. parviflorum* is more a curiosity than an important species. Compared to *T. albidum,* it is far less showy, and, in the garden, the latter species will prove the more valuable. To the obsessive collector, of course, all trilliums are desirable. As *T. parviflorum* is rather rare and local, it is best left in the wild, at least until plants can be propagated by tissue culture which will not put a strain on wild populations.

31. *Trillium petiolatum* Pursh

Synonymy: *Trillium petalosum* Pursh ex Louis-Marie, Rev.
Common Name: Long-petioled Trillium, Purple Trillium, Round-
  leaved Trillium

To see *Trillium petiolatum* in the wild, early in April, before almost any other vegetation has commenced growth, is a shocking experience. Amid the sere, dry and dead grasses, or in a damp roadside swamp, appear the great plantainlike leaves, without question the least *Trillium*-like of all trilliums. One's first impression is of a swamp full of spindly specimens of *Caltha palustris* just pushing up their leaves. So hidden are the flowers below the leaf blades amid the grasses, that for a moment one fails to realize that the plants are in bloom. One could seek it in its windswept prairie grassland home and walk right by it, never recognizing it as a *Trillium.* The specific epithet *petiolatum,* meaning "petioled," draws attention to the very long petioles found in this distinctive species.

Plate 63. *Trillium petiolatum on* a rocky hillside in eastern Oregon. Photo by Fred Case.

Habit

Stem erect, smooth, often, but not always very short, 4–17 cm long, typically mostly subterranean (Mason 1975), arising from an essentially vertical, often very deep rhizome.

Leaves long-petiolate, 9–22 cm long, the leaf-whorl just at or slightly above soil; petioles 5–12 cm long; leaf blade ovate to elliptic, 7–14 cm long, 5.5–10.2 cm wide, medium green, without mottling, the tip obtuse or rounded; leaf with petiole strongly resembling leaves of *Plantago;* flower in axil of leaf whorl at or near ground level.

Sepals widely spreading, oblong-elliptic to oblanceolate, 22–47 mm long, 7–10 mm wide, apex acute.

Petals linear-lanceolate, acute, erect to incurved, light maroon red, purple, or greenish to yellowish, 30–55 mm long, 4–10 mm wide.

Stamens erect, 22–30 mm long; filaments 5–7 mm long; anther sacs opening laterally; connectives not extending beyond anther sacs.

Ovary ovoid, sharply angled, 4–9 mm long; stigmas essentially linear, divergent, the tips somewhat recurved, 7–20 mm long.

Fruit strongly angled/winged, ovoid.

Season

Depending upon the season, snow pack, and elevation, from very early April (earlier on south-facing slopes) to late May.

Distribution

Eastern Washington west to near Wenatchee, eastward into Idaho, southward to southwestern Idaho, and westward into Oregon. Most frequent in the general region of the meeting of the state lines of Washington, Oregon, and Idaho, in the Palouse Prairie Region of the upper Columbia River Basin (Freeman 1975) and the Blue Mountains. Local, but locally abundant.

Habitat

Occurs at about 5000 ft. elevation (Mason 1975) mostly on lower rocky hillsides just above stream flats, under brush; edges of forests, coniferous and

Map 31. *Trillium petiolatum.*

deciduous; open grassy glades, often on river-flats; and occasionally in surprisingly wet (for a *Trillium* species) seasonally swampy ground and edges of sloughs, often in rather compact colonies of many plants. Common companion plants include *Disporum hookeri, Equisetum telmatei,* spruce (*Picea* sp.), ponderosa pine (*Pinus ponderosa*), Douglas fir (*Pseudotsuga menziesii*), willow (*Salix* sp.), false spikenard (*Smilacina racemosa*) (Kawano et al. 1992, and present observations).

Varieties, Forms, Hybrids

None cited in the literature. Victor Soukup of Cincinnati, Ohio, has Kodachrome slides of a clear yellow-green form growing with the typical plant. We have photographed a plant with apple-green petals.

Comments

Kawano et al. (1992) considered the peculiar growth habit of *Trillium petiolatum* to be an adaptation to the somewhat xeric habitat and/or to volcanic activity, and especially to the severe drying that overtakes the habitat in summer. The deeply buried rhizome and scape (up to 30 cm; Kawano et al. 1992) certainly suggests adaptations to the dry habitat and perhaps to the effects of wind action. Only the habitat of *Trillium rivale* approaches that of *T. petiolatum* in exposure, openness, and seasonal dryness.

Kawano et al. (1992) stated that none of the species in their study (including *Trillium petiolatum*) reproduced vegetatively by offshoots. Yet in the Blue Mountains, Oregon, we found many massive clumps, up to 12–20 stems tightly massed, appearing as having formed from offsets of one very large mother rhizome. We did not dig these up and carefully examine them to see if offsets were being formed or whether any of the smaller side plants were attached to rhizomes. It is possible that they were not clonal, but rather represented either the mass germination of seeds from a single berry falling at that spot, or more likely, mass germination of an ant seed cache. We find such clumps of other species, often of mixed species in our Michigan garden. As the petals do not cluster tightly around the anthers and with the flowers at ground level sheltered by the overarching high held leaf blades, we suspect the plant is adapted for crawling insects to carry out cross-pollination.

Those in our acquaintance who have attempted cultivation of *Tril-*

lium petiolatum in our eastern climate consider it difficult or nearly impossible to keep. Although it resents excessive summer wetness, it surely possesses sufficient winter hardiness. It also appears too early in spring in our climate and late frosts cut it down. After several successive seasons of this pattern, the plants starve from lack of food production.

32. *Trillium recurvatum* Beck

Synonymy: *Trillium unguiculatum* Rafinesque, *Trillium unguiculatum* Nuttall, *Phyllantherum recurvatum* (Beck) Nieuwland, *Trillium reflexum* Clute
Common Name: Prairie Trillium, Toadshade, Bloody Noses

Trillium recurvatum, one of the truly easy-to-identify sessile trilliums, occurs over a large part of the Mississippi River basin, and is particularly abundant near the confluence of the Missouri and Ohio Rivers. Its stiffly erect stems and darkly marbled leaf patterns form an important feature of the spring woodlands. It is widely known to old-time natives, farmers, and those who roam the forests. The specific epithet *recurvatum* refers to the strongly recurved sepals, recurved under such strong turgor pressure that if lifted and released, they snap back forcibly.

Habit
Stem erect, usually stiffly so, glabrous, 1.5–4.8 dm tall, arising from an elongated, brittle rhizome that is white beneath the dead, dark sheaths.

Leaves strongly petioled, the petiole about one-fifth the leaf length; the entire leaf 6–18 cm long, 2.5–6.5 cm wide, ovate, elliptic, or lanceolate, acuminate; at first strongly mottled in darker green or bronze, fading with the seasonal expansion after anthesis, or rarely all green.

Sepals ovate-lanceolate, acute, strongly recurved and held against the stem by a considerable turgor pressure, 18–35 mm long, 6–18 mm wide.

Petals lanceolate to ovate, erect, 18–48 mm long, 9–20 mm wide, apex acute, the basal portion contracted into a claw; dark maroon-purple

Plate 64. *Trillium recurvatum.* Note the petiolate leaves, clawed petals, and the strongly recurved sepals. Photo by Fred Case.

to clear yellow, occasionally bicolored with a purple base and yellow apex, fading to brown-maroon with age.

Stamens 10–15 mm long, anthers strongly incurved above the erect filaments; filaments about one-third the total stamen length; anther sacs introrse; connectives projecting about 1 mm beyond the anther sacs.

Ovary somewhat 6-angled/winged, 7–10 mm long (about the same height as the stamen filaments, according to Freeman 1975); stigmas linear, divergent-recurved, 4–6 mm long.

Fruit 6-angled, rhomboid-ovoid, green, to white- and purple-streaked, pulpy, not juicy when ripe.

Season

Late March in northern Alabama to mid or late May in Michigan; flowers long-lasting.

Distribution

Southwestern Michigan west to Iowa and Missouri, southward to eastern Texas, northern Louisiana, northern Mississippi, and northern Alabama north to western Ohio. Locally abundant within range. Many Alabama plants are more slender, smaller, and more delicate in all parts and appear to grade towards *Trillium lancifolium* in appearance.

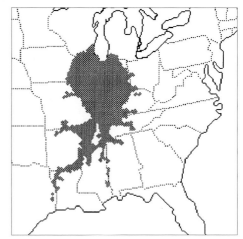

Map 32. *Trillium recurvatum.*

Habitat

Particularly abundant on rich clayey floodplain soils, the plants often temporarily inundated while in flower; rich moist woods and bluffs, most frequently on limestone derived soils, but occurring elsewhere. Frequently found with eastern camass (*Camassia scilloides*), false rue anemone (*Isopyrum* sp.), bluebells (*Mertensia virginica*), and sessile trillium (*Trillium sessile*). We have seen it in one Alabama location in a dryish upland, open woods in company with twisted trillium (*T. stamineum*) in a situation where one would not expect there was sufficient moisture for either *Trillium* species. Prickly pear cactus (*Opuntia* sp.) grew nearby.

Varieties, Forms, Hybrids

forma *recurvatum*. The typical plant described above when other forms are named.

forma *luteum* Clute. Applied to bicolored, faded, or possibly diseased individuals (Freeman 1975) in which purple pigment is lacking, allowing an underlying yellow tone to appear. Freeman (1975) feels there are so many color gradations to which this might be applied as to make use of this name impractical. It does, however, point out the problem with naming too many trivial color forms in the sessile trilliums: genetic color variations do occur, as also does fading with age while the petals remain turgid and otherwise fresh-looking; in rare instances hybridization produces intermediate colors. Mycoplasma disease in the pedicellate trilliums certainly affects colors, and while not much reported in the sessile trilliums, disease could produce color changes. We do not feel that diseased plants should be given formal names. Freeman's point is well taken.

forma *shayi* Palmer & Steyermark. In this form the petals and stamens are a clear yellow or greenish-yellow without any purple pigment apparent. This plant can be very attractive, is occasionally cultivated, and occurs as a so-called "albino mutant" occasionally throughout the range of the species. In the form given to me by the late John Lambert, the leaves also lacked the characteristic mottling of this species.

forma *petaloideum* Steyermark. Freeman (1975) reported it to be an abnormal, sterile form in which all sepals are petallike. We have not seen such a form in this species; however, similar individuals, in which all flower parts are leaflike, occur in mycoplasma-infected populations of *T. grandiflorum, T. cernuum, T. erectum,* and *T. undulatum.*

forma *foliosum* Steyermark. This form, in which all floral organs are replaced by leaves, may represent an infection in a sessile species.

Although we know of no published report of hybrids with *Trillium recurvatum,* in regions near and west of Louisville, Kentucky, where the range of *T. recurvatum* overlaps with that of *T. sessile,* we have seen many small, *T. sessile*-like plants that are slightly taller, with much narrower leaves than those typically found in pure populations of *T. sessile.* We suspect that these represent intergradation between these species.

Comments

Trillium recurvatum grows over a very wide range for a sessile species. Naturally, within that range there is considerable variation. In some districts the plants seem exceptionally tall, or darker flowered, or with wider petals. Plants in Blount County, Alabama, are smaller, delicate, and redder-flowered.

Plants are at their best when growing in rich neutral or slightly alkaline soil of floodplains or low woods. Very large colonies of robust plants often develop in central Indiana, western Kentucky, and on limestone slopes above rivers in south-central Missouri. Although rare and considered threatened in Michigan, large colonies occur on floodplains and slip-off slopes in Berrien County. The long, slender creeping rhizome located at the surface of the soil is very brittle. It is difficult to dig plants without damaging the rhizome.

Trillium recurvatum may be cultivated easily, at least in eastern North America, except perhaps in the very deep South. European gardeners tell us it is not easy to cultivate in their gardens.

33. *Trillium reliquum* Freeman

Synonymy: None
Common Name: Relict Trillium

This recently recognized species, when named thought to be extremely rare, local, and disjunct, has been collected in several new localities, and, while rare, may be of more widespread occurrence than formerly believed. It resembles *Trillium decumbens* somewhat, although it is less decumbent and differs in a number of structural features. We have seen it in several of its widely separated localities. The specific epithet *reliquum* means "relict."

Habit

Stem semidecumbent, decumbent, or weakly erect (especially in cultivation), glabrous throughout, 6–18 cm long.

Leaves sessile, horizontally spreading, ovate to elliptic, rounded tapered about equally from base to tip from widest point about at middle of leaf, 5–12 cm long, 6–10 cm wide, rounded or weakly acute at tip; strongly mottled on each side of a central light green stripe, in shades of light green, dark green, bronze-green, and dark purple.

Sepals divergent, somewhat recurved, 17–42 mm long, 5–9.5 mm wide, rounded-acute at tip, green, maroon-streaked.

Petals narrowly elliptic-lanceolate to oblanceolate, 25–55 mm long, 6–10 mm wide, acute-tipped, erect, dark brownish-maroon, green-purple, or streaked with yellow.

Plate 65. *Trillium reliquum*, plant habit. Photo by Fred Case.

Stamens erect, incurved, 12–20 mm long; filaments short, 1–2 mm long; anther sacs introrse; connectives extending 1–2.5 mm beyond anther sacs, the tips acute.

Ovary ovoid, 5–10 mm tall (about half of stamen height), 6-angled; stigmas short, recurved, linear.

Fruit ovoid, 6-winged/angled apically, dark maroon-purple berry.

Season

Mid-March to April. In one early spring, we found plants at the type locality already turning yellow and dying back in mid-April, while plants of *Trillium maculatum* nearby showed no signs of going dormant that early.

Distribution

Imperfectly known; Clay, Early, and Richmond Counties, Georgia, and Aiken County, South Carolina, along the Savannah River. Reports of other stations, including near Auburn, Alabama, indicate the plant may be more widespread but poorly represented in herbaria.

Habitat

Rich mixed deciduous forested slopes, bluffs and stream-flats. Often on lower slopes at edge of small stream floodplains near confluence with larger rivers. Near Aiken, South Carolina and at the type locality near Augusta, Georgia, we found the plants growing in company with *Hexastylis* sp., deciduous azaleas (*Rhododendron* sp.), bloodroot (*Sanguinaria canadensis*), spotted trillium (*Trillium maculatum*), and other members of the vernal flora. Especially near Aiken, the woodland floor was extremely rich in species with vigorous growth habit.

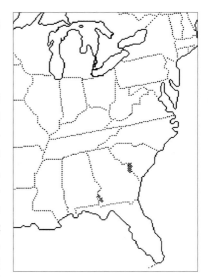

Map 33. *Trillium reliquum.*

Varieties, Forms, Hybrids

forma *reliquum*. The typical form described above.
forma *luteum* Freeman. Petals yellow to yellow-green. Known from the Chattahoochee River stations only.

Comments

Freeman (1975) reported a flower odor of putrid meat. We find this apparent only in freshly opened flowers. Most of the sessile trilliums produce musty or fetid odors at the time the stigmas are receptive to pollen. Fortunately, the odor is not strong and can be detected by the human nose only at very close range.

Listed as an endangered species in the United States, *Trillium reliquum* is too rare a plant to be collected in numbers from the wild, although individual colonies may have many plants. An interesting plant to the specialist both for its superficial similarity to *T. decumbens* and for its disjunct occurrences, *T. reliquum* is not particularly distinct or attractive as a garden subject. The plant has proved fully winter hardy in U.S. Department of Agriculture hardiness zone 5. It is hardier than many of the other trilliums of the outer Coastal Plain.

34. *Trillium sessile* Linnaeus

Synonymy: *Trillium longiflorum* Rafinesque, *Trillium rotundifolium*
Rafinesque, *Trillium isanthum* Rafinesque, *Trillium tinctorum*
Rafinesque, *Trillium membranaceum* Rafinesque, *Trillium sessile* var.
boreale Nuttall
Common Name: Sessile Trillium, Toad Trillium, Toadshade

Trillium sessile, the first sessile-flowered *Trillium* species to be named by
Linnaeus (hence the specific epithet), enjoys a very wide range across the
central and upper Mississippian Midwest region. An early appearing
species, it frequently gets covered by the late spring snows. In spite of a
fairly distinctive appearance, low stature, and definitive range, the plant
has a long history of confusion with other species. The confusion lies
mostly with horticulturists and a few early taxonomists who insisted on
calling any sessile trillium *T. sessile.* In particular, the western sessile species *T. chloropetalum* and its varieties, *T. angustipetalum,* and *T. kurabayashii* frequently are lumped together under the meaningless illegitimate name of *Trillium sessile californicum.* This error still persists in
European horticultural (and rarely botanical) literature. *Trillium sessile*
grows nowhere near California and is a very much smaller plant than
any of the West Coast sessile trilliums.

Habit

Stem somewhat stiffly erect, glabrous, from a brown, thickened horizontal rhizome, 0.8–2.5 dm tall, rarely taller.

Leaves sessile, rather broadly attached, oval to suborbicular, 4–10 cm
long, 2–8 cm wide; leaf size and shape varying with age of plant or district from green to bluish-green, occasionally with a silvery sheen or
overlay, strongly to sparsely mottled in darker green or bronze-green
tones at first (except in anthocyanin-free albinos where leaves are
plain green), the mottling rapidly fading as flowering progresses; leaf
apex rounded-acuminate to bluntly parallel sided-acuminate (especially around Louisville, Kentucky), rounded basally to its broad attachment.

Sepals lanceolate-oblanceolate, the apex rounded acuminate, 9–35 mm
long, 4–8 mm wide, spreading, green, variously streaked with maroon
purple to almost entirely purple in some individuals.

Plate 66. *Trillium sessile,* showing petal and leaf detail. Photo by Fred Case.

Petals oblanceolate to elliptic, occasionally almost orbicular, somewhat fleshy, 17–35 mm long, 7–20 mm wide, narrowed near basal attachment (but not truly clawed) gradually rounded-tapered to an acute tip, maroon, brown-maroon, green, or yellow-green, long lasting but fading to browner tones with age.

Stamens straight, anthers not curved, erect, 10–23 mm long; filaments broad, about one-third anther length; anther sacs introrse; connectives projecting 1–2.5 mm beyond anther sac.

Ovary 6-angled, ovoid to globose with maturity but pyramidally narrowed to the subulate stigmas, 4–8.5 mm tall; stigmas up to 2 times ovary height (Freeman 1975), erect.

Flower odor pungent, spicy in fresh flowers (Freeman 1975).

Fruit a dark green-purple berry, subglobose, the 6 angles somewhat winglike, fragmentally separating from the basal attachment on the receptacle.

Plate 67. A good color form, leaf, and petal of *Trillium sessile* from Indiana. Photo by Fred Case.

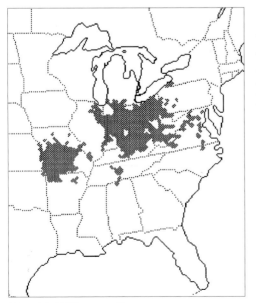

Map 34. *Trillium sessile*.

Season

March at southern part of range, April elsewhere, to mid-May in southern Michigan. Michigan native plants bloom later in our garden than collected material from farther south.

Distribution

Most abundant in Ohio, Indiana, northern Kentucky, and Missouri; strangely absent from most of Illinois (see Freeman 1975), present but rare in northeastern Illinois and occurring locally in Illinois along its southeastern and southwestern borders; rather widely scattered into Arkansas, extreme eastern Kansas, middle Tennessee to Alabama. Also widely scattered in West Virginia, Virginia, Maryland, and western Pennsylvania; barely reaching into southwestern New York and widely scattered in the southern tier of counties of southern Michigan. Not a rare plant in most of its range.

Habitat

Rich woodlands, particularly favoring limestone districts and calcareous soils, floodplains and riverbanks, on clayey alluvium. Occasionally on less fertile soils, sometimes in rather high, dry limestone woods. Persists under light pasturing, and in fencerows and brushy areas after lumbering. Grows with other local *Trillium* species, bleeding heart (*Dicentra* sp.), *Hepatica* sp., bluebells (*Mertensia virginica*), May apple (*Podophyllum peltatum*), wood poppy (*Stylophorum diphyllum*), and violet (*Viola* sp.).

Varieties, Forms, Hybrids

forma *sessile.* The typical plant of Linnaeus' description.

forma *viridiflorum* **Beyer.** Flowers yellow-green, some purple may be present on stamens and stigma. This rather frequent form occurs as an occasional individual among typical *Trillium sessile.* It has appeared as spontaneous seedlings in our garden. This is not a particularly attractive form. A good clear yellow form of *T. sessile* has apparently not been found and named.

Hybrids have not been identified scientifically so far as we are aware. We have seen what we believe to be intergrades or direct hybrids between *Trillium sessile* and *T. recurvatum* near Louisville, Kentucky, as the plants were intermediate in size and leaf shape, with petals somewhat clawed but closest to *T. sessile* in shape.

Comments

This rather small *Trillium* possesses ironclad hardiness both to temperature and to competition with coarser plants. It can be unbelievably abundant in favored woodlands near Louisville, Kentucky. Most forms have rather brown-maroon colored petals which fade to a dirty red-brown. A few fine clear deep maroon-reds occur. The same applies to the characteristic leaf mottling. Most plants have rather dull dark green or bronze markings that blur and fade with age. In the vicinity of Bloomington, Indiana, we have found plants with good flower colors and strongly marked and very attractive leaves that retain more color longer into the season than do most plants of this species. Such plants make the best garden selections.

Trillium sessile rather closely resembles *T. foetidissimum*. On several grounds, including stature and anther structure, Freeman (1975) considered the two closely related. Robust plants of *T. sessile* while infrequent may be as large as the smaller sizes of *T. cuneatum*, large enough to obscure its identity.

35. *Trillium stamineum* Harbison

Synonymy: *Trillium stramineum* Harbison ex Louis-Marie, Rev.
Common Name: Twisted Trillium

While this species is not showy, it is distinctive with its horizontally spread, twisted petals. Its very large and conspicuous crown of stamens seems to serve the function of the petals in attracting the carrion insects, which are presumed to pollinate this species. Although the flower produces, at close range, a foul, fetid odor, we have seldom seen it visited by carrion flies or any insects. The specific epithet *stramineum,* an adjectival form of the word *stamen,* calls attention to the prominent stamens of this species.

Habit
Stem erect, pilose, pubescent (Small 1933), 1.5–3 dm tall.

Leaves, ovate-lanceolate to broadly ovate, sessile, 6.3–7.6 cm long, 3.3–5 cm wide; pilose-pubescent on undersurface of larger veins (Small 1933), acute, light silvery or bluish-green with strong to more commonly faint mottling in darker greens, the mottling fading with age.

Sepals lanceolate-elliptic, 17–40 mm long, the tips acuminate; spreading like the petals to an almost horizontal position; upper surface with purple markings.

Plate 68. *Trillium stamineum*. Note the twisted, spreading petals, and the very large, erect stamens. Photo by Fred Case.

Petals narrow, lanceolate, rarely broader, 15–38 mm long, *spiral-twisted, spreading and carried in a horizontal position unlike any other sessile trillium,* very dark red-purple or brown-purple to rarely yellow, purple-streaked.

Stamens prominent, rather stiffly erect, 16–24 mm long, dark purple, filaments 2–4 mm long; anther sacs extrorse on coarse flat connectives; connectives not prolonged beyond anther sacs; pollen dark brown-purple.

Ovary short, oval, 6-angled, 5–7 mm tall; stigmas linear, spreading-recurved.

Flower odor of carrion, strong.

Fruit a purplish ovoid berry, strongly 6-angled.

Season

Late March to mid-May, mostly in April. Because the long axis of distribution is north/south, there is a wide difference in blooming dates at opposite ends of its range.

Habitat

Dry, upland woods of deciduous trees or in deciduous forest mixed with pines (*Pinus* sp.), often in soil on limestone outcroppings, mesic woods, and in central Alabama (at southern edge of its range) grows vigorously on sandy flats along medium streams under snowbell (*Styrax* sp.). North of Cullman, Alabama, large colonies occur on heavy clays on the floodplains of small streams with red buckeye (*Aesculus pavia*) and bluebells (*Mertensia virginica*). Also grows on steep wooded slopes and banks of larger rivers in west-central Tennessee. Occasionally found with whippoor-will flower (*Trillium cuneatum*) and bent trillium (*T. flexipes*). Other companion plants include eastern camass (*Camassia scilloides*), wild sweet William (*Phlox divaricata*), *Silene virginica,* and, in one location, dwarf trillium (*Trillium pusillum* var. *pusillum*).

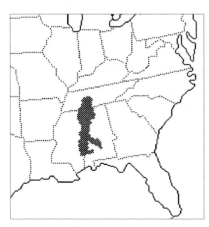

Map 35. *Trillium stamineum.*

Distribution

Along a north-south axis from northern west-central Tennessee southward to the upper Coastal Plain of central and western Alabama, and in eastern Mississippi in the counties bordering Alabama from the upper Coastal Plain northward into Tennessee.

Varieties, Forms, Hybrids

forma *stamineum.* The typical plant described above, when other forms are named.

forma *luteum* Freeman. Flowers yellow with no purple in any floral organs. We have a plant in which the petals are soft creamy yellow with purplish margins and some streaks, giving the plant the appearance of being illuminated from within. Bloom has been consistent over many years. Whether it deserves naming is debatable.

Hybrids with other species have not been reported.

Comments

With its horizontal spreading, spiralled petals, *Trillium stamineum* presents a rather different look than most sessile trilliums. One could not call it a truly showy species, yet it always catches the attention of those interested in native plants. It seldom forms clumps of even a few stems, but occurs as scattered individuals, sometimes in dense stands if the soil is heavy and fertile. It is fully winter hardy in Michigan.

36. *Trillium underwoodii* Small

Synonymy: *Trillium lanceolatum* var. *rectistamineum* Gates, *Trillium rectistamineum* (Gates) St. John

Common Name: Underwood's Trillium

This species has a long history of taxonomic confusion. In many ways, it looks like a vigorous but short-stemmed form of *Trillium cuneatum* or *T. decipiens.* One of its most distinctive features are the very large petals, much larger in proportion to its height than in most species. *Trillium underwoodii* grows rather commonly in woods within a few miles of the Coosa River in east-central Alabama. It chooses both high, dry Oak (*Quercus* sp.) forests and lower, richer forests of deciduous trees including Beech (*Fagus* sp.). The specific epithet *underwoodii* honors botanist L. M. Underwood (1853–1907).

Plate 69. *Trillium underwoodii* in an Alabama woodland. Note the stature, with the highly colored leaf-tip almost touching the ground. Photo by Fred Case.

Habit

Stem short, erect, smooth, 8–20 cm tall.

Leaves at anthesis usually drooping and touching the soil, sessile, ovate-lanceolate to obovate with an acuminate tip, ground color pale, silvery green, strongly mottled in 3 or more shades of dark green and bronze, sometimes with almost maroon markings, 6.5–12 cm long, 5–7.8 cm wide at widest point.

Sepals lanceolate, 4.5–5 cm long, 8–12 mm wide, rounded-acute, spreading.

Petals oblanceolate to elliptic, apex acute, 30–55 mm long, occasionally
   longer (possible intergrades with *T. decipiens?*), 1–1.5 cm wide, rich
   dark maroon-red or purple-red, rarely brown-maroon or yellow-green.
Stamens 14–17 mm long, more or less erect to weakly incurved; filaments 1–2 mm long; anther sacs latrorse; connectives prolonged 1–2
   mm beyond anther sacs, somewhat acute.
Ovary ellipsoidal, 6-angled, 6.3–11 mm long; stigmas short, linear, recurved.
Flower odor fetid, especially when first open.
Fruit an ovoid to obovoid, 6-angled (-ridged), purple black to dull greenish-maroon berry.

Season

Late February (in early seasons), or March in southern portion of range,
into mid-April in northern part of range. Blooms near Clanton, Alabama, in early to mid-April. In a given location, *Trillium underwoodii*
flowers open rather late, after other companion *Trillium* species mature
and begin to fade.

Distribution

Widely scattered across southern Alabama from Mobile County eastward, becoming more frequent eastward; northern Florida, especially
that region below the Alabama-Georgia state line, southwestern Georgia, and northward in eastern Alabama onto the Piedmont near the
Coosa River, where local large populations oc-
cur. Distribution of *Trillium underwoodii* is
much more restricted than that given in *Manual of the Southeastern Flora.* (Small 1933),
which indicates a range extending from Alabama to North Carolina and Arkansas. Freeman's work (1975) is the only accurate source
of population limits for most of the sessile
trilliums. A combination of the available
knowledge of the times, difficulty of travel,
and the frequency in trilliums of freakish
forms, color variations, and hybrids make earlier distribution accounts of *T. underwoodii*
essentially useless.

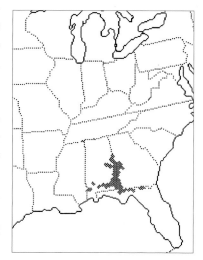

Map 36. *Trillium underwoodii.*

Habitat

Rich to dryish deciduous forests of mature or second-growth timber, dominated by oaks (*Quercus* sp.) or with beech-oak (*Fagus-Quercus* spp.), occasionally with scattered pines (*Pinus* sp.) present. Also on flat ground along streams where soil can be fairly moist and rich clay or sand. Although we have not tested the soil pH, the nature of the companion plants present suggests to us that it prefers a slightly acid substrate. Plants tend to occur as widely scattered individuals, not big clonal clumps.

Varieties, Forms, Hybrids

Named forms or varieties are unknown to us. We have found a single clear yellow plant of *Trillium underwoodii* in Coosa County, Alabama.

Near Columbus, Georgia, at a marina along the Chattahoochee River, we found a mixed population of *Trillium underwoodii* and *T. decipiens*. Freeman (1975) said mixed populations of these species were unknown to him. In this population occurred all variations in size and habit between the two species. We regard them as intergrades or a hybrid swarm. *Trillium decipiens* from that latitude normally fails in our garden by commencing growth too early and being destroyed by hard freezes, but the *T. decipiens*–like putative intergrades, like the smaller-statured *T. underwoodii*, come later and bloom and survive here. We feel that these plants are, indeed, of hybrid nature.

Comments

Trillium underwoodii can cause considerable confusion for the beginning *Trillium* student. In some ways it appears only as a low-statured *T. cuneatum*. As *T. underwoodii* continues to expand after flowering, it may become somewhat taller and then appear as a smaller plant of *T. decipiens*, which grows in parts of the same range. Its leaves do not always touch the ground at anthesis as various authors describe. *Trillium reliquum* also has vague similarities to *T. underwoodii* and grows sympatrically with it in parts of the *T. underwoodii* range. Only after one has seen the plants many times in a number of different stations can one feel confident that this truly is a distinct and valid species.

Because of its low stature, brilliantly marked leaves, and very large petals, *Trillium underwoodii* is highly suitable to rock garden use. It may not possess cast-iron winter hardiness in the coldest parts of North

America, but will certainly grow over much of the area. It is a desirable garden plant. As with most wild plants today, mass collecting from the wild is unconscionable, but selected collection of outstanding forms and tissue culture, once available, are the answer to having these plants without violating conservation principles.

37. *Trillium viride* Beck

Synonymy: *Trillium viride* auct. pro. parte, excluding *T. viridescens,*
   T. viride var. *luteum* (Muhlenberg) Gleason, and their synonyms
   (Freeman 1975), *Trillium cuneatum* sensu Mohlenbrock
Common Name: Green Trillium

Bird watchers shudder and shake at the mention of what they refer to as the "confusing fall warblers." *Trillium* enthusiasts and botanists have their own nemesis: the confusing green-flowered trilliums. *Trillium viride* is certainly one of these, long confused with *T. luteum, T. viridescens,* and, as Freeman has stated, almost any green-flowered trillium. In fact, seen in the fresh state in garden or wild, it has its own "look" and a number of distinguishing characteristics, but because its natural range is small and the plant is only rarely cultivated, it is one of the least familiar of trilliums to most people. The specific epithet *viride* means "green."

Habit
Stem erect, smooth to scabrous below the leaves, 2.3–3.4 dm tall, occasionally taller.
Leaves sessile, mottled at least at first, with a few faintly darker blotches, occasional without markings; narrowly to broadly elliptic, apex blunt to rounded acute, 8–20.5 cm long, 5–8 cm wide; sometime to the naked eye, and always under a lens, with the upper surface covered with numerous stomata seen as tiny white dots.
Sepals lanceolate-acute, widely spreading, 28–60 mm long, 7–9 mm wide.
Petals narrow, spatulate to linear-spatulate, 35–68 mm long, 5–15 mm wide, widest above the middle, narrowed and thickened below, more or less forming a claw, clear leaf green, yellow-green, yellow, or vari-

Plate 70. *Trillium viride* in northeastern Missouri. Photo by Victor Soukup.

ously purple streaked, especially basally (most we have seen are clear light green), petal apex obtuse, erect to widely spreading.

Stamens relatively straight-erect to slightly incurved, 15–25 mm long, the basally dilated filaments 3–5.5 mm long; anther sacs introrse-latrorse; connectives very slightly prolonged beyond the sacs.

Ovary ellipsoidal to ovoid, 5–12 mm long, deeply angled; stigmas 5–10
   mm long, spreading-erect with recurved tips.
Flower odor of decayed fruit (Freeman 1975).
Fruit ovoid, angled, green-white, somewhat pulpy.

Season
Late April to May.

Distribution
Districts adjacent to the Missouri River in northeast-central Missouri
and the corresponding region of southern Illinois.

Habitat
Rich woods, bluffs, rocky hillsides. Where we saw it, it grew in recently
cut-over brushy woods on steep and gentle hills where some limestone
outcrops were apparent. May apple (*Podophyllum peltatum*) grew nearby. Plants grew widely scattered, never in large groups, and frequently in
very open situations in woodsy, humusy soil over a fairly stiff clayey substrate.

Varieties, Forms, Hybrids
None.

Comments
This interesting plant has long been confused with *Trillium luteum* of
the Smoky Mountain region, though it
is far more slender and delicate than *T.*
luteum. Because the pallid forms and so-
called albinos of so many other sessile
trilliums as described in written accounts sound much like the description
of this plant, far too wide a range was
ascribed to *T. viride* by earlier writers
such as Gates (1917). The plant is
closely limited to the woodlands of the
counties adjacent to the Missouri River
in northeastern Missouri and southern
Illinois.

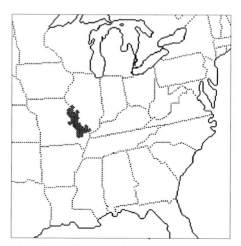

Map 37. *Trillium viride*.

Although its range and that of the very similar appearing *Trillium viridescens* do not overlap, both species grow in Missouri. Authors earlier than Freeman (1975) frequently combined the two into a single species. They are, indeed, quite similar, but if all other means of identification fail, the presence of numerous stomates, seen under magnification, on the upper leaf surface, will always separate *T. viride.*

While not overly conspicuous, *Trillium viride* makes an interesting display with its rather open, straplike clear light green petals. It is not an easy species to cultivate in thin sandy soils. Dealers seldom offer it.

38. *Trillium viridescens* Nuttall

Synonymy: *Trillium stenanthes* Rafinesque, *Trillium sessile* var. *nuttallii* S. Watson, *Trillium sessile* var. *viridescens* (Nuttall) Trelease
Common Name: Ozark Green Trillium, Ozark Trillium

This vigorous and attractive plant grows abundantly in rather heavy riverine and calcareous soils in the Ozark and Ouachita Mountain regions of Missouri and Arkansas and adjacent states. The specific epithet *viridescens* means "greenish." Because the species produces forms with dark purple, green and bicolored purple and green petals, the name has caused much confusion to botanists and naturalists alike. As is the case with several other species, nothing written before Freeman's work on *T. viridescens* can be depended upon because we do not really know whether the writers referred to *T. viridescens, T. viride,* or the green forms of other species.

Habit
Stem erect, often stiffly so, smooth to scabrous, 2–5 dm tall.
Leaves sessile, ovate, elliptic, to broadly so, 8.5–14 cm long, 6.8–9 cm wide, dark green, obscurely marked with a few to many darker blotches, lacking the numerous stomates on upper surface, acuminate.
Sepals lanceolate, spreading, green or variously purplish-marked, apex acute, 38–60 mm long, 5–12 mm wide.
Petals linear to narrowly spatulate, slightly thickened and clawed at base, erect, often slightly twisted, most commonly purple-black on claw,

Plate 71. *Trillium viridescens* in the Case garden. Photo by Fred Case.

greenish to yellow green distally; occasionally all dark purple-maroon forms occur (especially in areas of southwestern Arkansas), petals 40–80 mm long, 8–12 mm wide at widest point, petal tips rounded.

Stamens erect, connivent (clustered together, leaning upon each other), 16–25 mm long, filaments 2.5–5 mm long; anther sacs latrorse; connectives barely extending beyond anther sacs.

Ovary ovoid, 6-angled, 5.5–10 mm tall; stigmas about as long as ovary, linear, diverging-recurved.

Flower odor, if present, spicy or musty.

Fruit ovoid, obscurely angled, bearing the remains of the persistent stigmas, dark purplish-green or green, pulpy but not juicy at time of separation from the receptacle.

Season

Early April in southern part of range to mid-May in northernmost range. Plants were in early prime bloom in western Arkansas in last week of April 1981.

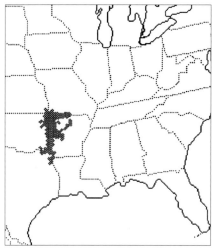

Map 38. *Trillium viridescens.*

Distribution

Extreme eastern Kansas and Oklahoma, west-southwestern Missouri, west and central Arkansas south into eastern Texas. Freeman (1975) stated that the species is most frequent in the Boston Mountains of Arkansas.

Habitat

Deciduous forests, usually quite rich, and on banks, bluffs, and floodplain alluvium, often growing there with cane (*Arundinaria* sp.), or on sloping banks just above normal flood levels in heavy clayey soils, growing with the common spring ephemerals of the region, *Hepatica acutiloba,* bloodroot (*Sanguinaria canadensis*), and violet (*Viola* sp.).

Varieties, Forms, Hybrids

None. While most plants we have seen in the wild produced bicolored petals—dark purple basally with the upper portion of the petal green, becoming lighter distally—we saw plants in the noted collection of John Lambert with extremely dark, all purple-black petals. Lambert told us there were extensive colonies of this color form south of Mena, Arkansas, on forested bluffs near a reservoir. To our knowledge this form has not been named, although it may deserve recognition.

Freeman (1975) considered that *Trillium viridescens* intergraded with ·*T. gracile* in northeastern Texas, and stated that these putative intergrades produce purple petals.

Comments

Trillium viridescens is a tall, robust and attractive, but not really showy plant. Like *T. viride* it prefers a rich fertile clayey soil or it does not respond well to cultivation. A degree of summer drying may be a requirement of good health for this prairie borderland species, as horticulturists in Europe report the plant to be very difficult to cultivate in their maritime, wet climate. It is easier for us, however, to cultivate this plant over a long period than to cultivate *T. viride* over the same time.

The Asiatic Trilliums

*A*sia contains far fewer *Trillium* species than North America. Most recent authors list five or six species, all belonging to the subgenus *Trillium*. One species occurs in the Himalaya Mountains, China, Taiwan, Korea, and Japan. The rest, far more restricted in range, occur in northeastern Asia, Kamchatka, and Japan, or are restricted entirely to the northern Japanese archipelago and Sakhalin Island. As with the North American trilliums, there is some disagreement among botanists about the number of species in Asia. In particular, some authors recognize *T. smallii* Maximowicz as a broad species encompassing the taxon *T. apetalon* (Ohwi et al. 1984). Others separate the two taxa as distinct species.

In this book, we follow in general the taxonomic treatment, nomenclature, and synonymy of Samejima and Samejima (1962, 1987) except for one species, *Trillium govanianum*. Authors of recent floras (Hara et al. 1978, Noltie 1994) treat *T. govanianum* as a member of the genus *Trillidium*. Although similar to *Trillium* in its rhizome structure, stem, and three leaves, *Trillidium govanianum* differs from *Trillium* in flower structure, having extremely narrow floral segments (tepals) all alike in size, shape and texture, and in its genome structure. We concur with these authors that the plant in question belongs to the genus *Trillidium* and thus we do not treat it in this book.

Much has been studied in Japan of the cytology and development patterns of Asiatic trilliums. Regrettably, much of the work is published only in the Japanese language or in scientific journals available only at the larger universities elsewhere. Whereas all North American trilliums are diploids (2n = 10), only *Trillium camschatcense* among the Asiatic species is diploid. The others range from triploid (2n = 15) to hexaploid (2n = 30). We give the ploidy number of each species with our species treatments.

Samejima and Samejima (1962, 1987) treated hybrids as if they were species, giving them full descriptions. Since hybrids, especially in wild populations, can be extremely variable with all the variation induced by backcrossing to either parent, or in crossing with sibling hybrids, we feel that long descriptions of hybrids are of little use or help to the beginning student of these trilliums. Therefore, while we mention the hybrids under the appropriate parental treatments, we provide minimal descriptions, except for the fertile and self-reproducing allopolyploid species *Trillium ×hagae.*

While we have seen all North American species in the wild, some in many localities, we have not seen the Asiatic species in nature. We have grown *Trillium apetalon, T. camschatcense,* and *T. tschonoskii,* at least briefly, in our gardens. For data, information, and documentation on the Asiatic species we rely upon the published scientific works listed above and in our bibliography, and a limited amount of herbarium material at the University of Michigan Herbarium. Our key was constructed from the data of Samejima and Samejima (1962, 1987), Hara (1966), Ohwi et al. (1984), and Noltie (1994).

The biology of the Asiatic species is essentially identical with that of the North American species in general features of growth, hybridization and seed behavior. Thus, the material in Part I of this book on the North American species serves also as introduction to the Asiatic species.

We have been unable to obtain information on the conservation problems, laws, or current conditions in Asia. Given the very large Asian human population, we assume that, outside of remote islands and mountain valleys, *Trillium* populations have been reduced locally, much as here in North America.

The Japanese trilliums possess full winter hardiness in mid-Michigan, but do not truly prosper in it. They do not die or emerge too early, but they languish and do not attain full size potential or flower for us in most years. Several acquaintances who grow them also report difficulty in their conditions. We suspect that in the milder East and West Coast climates of North America, or in milder (but not too hot) southern regions, these Asiatic plants may perform better.

A Key to the Asiatic Trilliums

1. Petals absent, sepals dark brown-red, purplish-red, green with reddish streaks or undertones, rarely all green. . . . . 39. *T. apetalon*

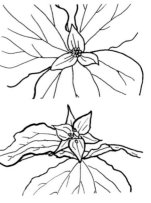

1. Petals present, sepals various. 2

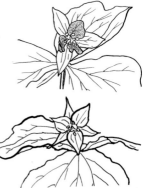

2. Petals 1–3, pinkish-red, reddish-purple, brownish-red, or dark red, perfect or variously deformed, one or more occasionally replaced by stamens; sepals purple, sometimes streaked with green. . . . . 42. *T. smallii*

2. Petals 3, white or pale purplish, normally shaped; sepals green. 3

3. Sepals acuminate, about as long as the petals. Petals white or pale purplish, ovate to oblong-ovate, narrowed or sulcate-narrowed near apex to a long-acuminate tip, especially in the Himalayan plants, petal bases more or less cuneate from below the middle, rarely obtuse. Leaves rhombic, depressed. . . . . 43. *T. tschonoskii*

3. Sepals obtuse-acute, shorter than the petals by about one-fourth length. Petals white, broadly ovate, ovate to ovate-orbicular, apex obtuse to acutish-obtuse, petal base more or less obtuse. Leaves various. 4

4. Petals broadly ovate to ovate, widest near base, petal apex obtuse-rounded to acute. Stamens taller than pistil, anther sac at least 3 times filament length. Leaves deltoid (especially so at south of range) to rhombic-oval, broadest at base, acute to acuminate.
. . . . 40. *T. camschatcense*

4. Petals broadly ovate to ovate-orbicular, apex obtuse. Stamens shorter than pistil or barely equal to it, anther sacs about 2 times filament length. Leaves rhombic to rhombic-orbicular, widest just below middle, short acuminate to subacute-acute. . . . . 41. *T. hagae* (6×), including *T. channellii* (4×)

39. *Trillium apetalon* Makino

Synonymy: *Trillium smallii* Maximowicz
Common Name: Enrei-so (Japanese for trillium)

Samejima and Samejima (1962, 1987) asserted this species, frequently lumped with or misidentified as *Trillium smallii,* to be a distinct species, but other authorities differ. For example, Ohwi (1984) listed *T. apetalon* as a synonym of *T. smallii.* The Samejimas say *T. apetalon* differs from *T. smallii* in leaf shape, pistil shape (not a wholly dependable character in our opinion), anther to filament length, and chromosome number (2n = 20). Because we follow their nomenclature generally in this book, we treat both *T. apetalon* and *T. smallii* as separate species. Whether they should be split or lumped together as varieties of a single species is a matter of taxonomic opinion. At whatever level, they are distinct taxa in cytology and flower structure. The specific epithet *apetalon* means "without petals," a consistent feature of the plant.

Habit
Stem glabrous, 1–3.7 dm tall, one to several, arising from a short thick rhizome.

Plate 72. *Trillium apetalon* var. *apetalon* on Hokkaido, Japan. Photo by Victor Soukup.

Leaves sessile, rhombic-ovate, abruptly acuminate-tipped, about as wide to slightly wider than long, 3–15 cm long, 3–15.5 cm wide.

Pedicel erect, 0.6–6 cm long.

Sepals variable, widely spreading, oblong, ovate-lanceolate, usually acute-acuminate apically, brownish-red, reddish-purple, or green, purple stained and streaked, 10–20 mm long, 6–12 mm wide.

Petals lacking.

Stamens erect, 5–10 mm long, about as long as the pistil; anthers 2–5 mm long, cream or pale purple, the filaments somewhat wider basally, variously reddish to cream.

Ovary 6-angled at anthesis, conical-globose, purple, reddish-purple, or with greenish streaks; pistils 5–11 mm tall; stigmas 3, widest basally, recurved, purple, persistent upon the ripe fruit.

Fruit a berrylike capsule, greenish-purple to purple, almost globose with the ovary ridges of anthesis almost obliterated by ovary expansion.

Season
April to June.

Map 39. *Trillium apetalon.*

Distribution

Northern Japanese Islands, Honshu, Shikoku, Kyushu, Hokkaido, Sakhalin Island, The Kuriles (Samejima and Samejima 1987).

Habitat

Mountain slopes, river valleys in deciduous forests, or subalpine mixed deciduous-coniferous forest. Frequent forest trees include elm (*Ulmus* sp.), alder (*Alnus* sp.), oak (*Quercus* sp.), ash (*Fraxinus* sp.), and magnolia (*Magnolia* sp.).

Varieties, Forms, Hybrids

var. *apetalon*. The typical plant when other varieties have been named.

var. *atropurpureocarpum* (**Makino**) **Samejima**. Fruit dark purple.

var. *rubrocarpum* **Samejima**. Fruit red.

var. *viridipurpureocarpum* (**Makino**) **Samejima**. Fruit green, purple-shaded.

forma *album* **Samejima**. Sepals green, stamens white.

forma *tripetalum* **Samejima**. A three-petaled form. Although Samejima and Samejima (1987) have named this a form of *T. apetalon* in their 1987 publication, they stated for *T. apetalon* "petals constantly 0." We wonder if some of the above color forms are truly genetically fixed and constant forms or varieties, or whether they might be merely ecologically induced by varying seasonal conditions and temperatures.

Trillium apetalon hybridizes with *T. tschonoskii* to form *T.* ×*miyabeanum* Tatewaki (2n = 20). The hybrid is intermediate in general characteristics between its parent species (Plate 73). Unlike *T. apetalon,* it usually produces dark red-purple suborbicular, apically obtuse petals, although these may be imperfectly shaped, or one or more may be absent. The hybrid appears in habitats occupied by both parents and is always sterile.

 Trillium apetalon also hybridizes with *T. camschatcense* to form *T.* ×*ye-*

Plate 73. *Trillium ×miyabeanum var. atropurpureocarpum*, a hybrid of *T. apetalon* with *T. tschonoskii*. Photo by Victor Soukup.

zoense Tatewaki (2n = 15). This sterile hybrid has red-purple petals with mucronate tips often irregular in shape, deformed, or one or more lacking. The petals may bear functional or partly developed pollen sacs. The plant occurs with both parents.

Comments

Trillium apetalon is fully hardy in mid-Michigan, but it is also a singularly unattractive trillium, owing to its lack of petals.

40. *Trillium camschatcense* Ker Gawler

Synonymy: *Trillium kamtschaticum* Pallas, *Trillium obovatum* Kunth, *Trillium erectum* var. *japonicum* A. Gray, *Trillium pallasii* Hulten
Common Name: Obanano enrei-so (means Large-flowered Trillium)

This species enjoys a fairly wide distribution in northern Japan, Kamchatka, and the regional islands, where it grows, apparently in abundance, and with considerable variation in flower size. It takes its specific name *camschatcense* from the Kamchatka Peninsula, the type locality from which the species was first described. In a general way, this species remarkably resembles *Trillium flexipes* of the central United States in habit, coloring, and flower structure. In common with all the North American trilliums, its chromosome number is 2n = 10. It shows a relationship to the *T. erectum* complex in the eastern United States: in experimental crosses with some members of the *T. erectum* group, it produces viable or plump, apparently viable seed, while when crossed with eastern U.S. species outside the complex, neither viable nor plump normal-sized seeds form (Haga and Channell 1982).

Habit

Stem 1–4 dm tall, one to several from the same thick, elongated rhizome, ribbed (Komarov 1968).
Leaves sessile, variable, broadly rhomboid to ovoid or deltoid-ovate, apices acuminate to acute, 3–16.5 cm long, 3–17 cm wide.
Pedicel erect, 0.5–8 cm long.

Plate 74. *Trillium camschatcense* growing in boggy ground with *Lysichiton* species (skunk cabbage), on Hokkaido, Japan. Photo by Victor Soukup.

Sepals pale green, oblong-broadly lanceolate, apices obtuse-acute, 20–40 mm long, 5–20 mm wide.

Petals white or creamy white, rather thick-textured, spreading, oblong-ovate, ovate, or oblong-lanceolate, apices more or less acute, 2–4.5 cm long, 0.8–3.5 cm wide, rarely larger or smaller.

Plate 75. Flower detail of *Trillium camschatcense*. Photo by Victor Soukup.

Stamens about equalling the pistils, erect, slightly recurved to straight,
cream or yellow, 10–24 mm long; anther sacs 12–15 mm long, much
longer than the filament (3–5 mm) yellow.
Ovary conical-ovoid, 6-angled, pale green to whitish, often marked especially at stigma bases with purple blotches or spotted throughout;
pistil 9–20 mm long.

Fruit globose, 8–28 mm long, 6–20 mm wide, greenish, or purple-spotted to rarely purple throughout when ripe.

Season
Variable, from early May to July, depending upon latitude and elevation.

Distribution
Manchuria, Korea, northeastern China, Commander and Kurile Islands, Sakhalin Island, Japan (Hokkaido and northern Honshu) (Samejima and Samejima 1987, Komarov 1968, and Ohwi 1984).

Habitat
Mixed deciduous forests on a variety of habitats, often with a moss-covered floor (Komarov 1968), under canopies of elm (*Ulmus* sp.), alder (*Alnus* sp.), ash (*Fraxinus* sp.), basswood (*Tilia* sp.), oak (*Quercus* sp.), and magnolia (*Magnolia* sp.). In subalpine situations often grows under birches (*Betula* sp.) (Samejima and Samejima 1987).

Varieties, Forms, Hybrids
var. *camschatcense.* Designates the typical plant when other varieties or forms are named.

var. *kurilense* Miyabe and Tate-waki. Found on the Kurile Islands and Hokkaido. Ovary and ripe fruit dark purple.

var. *soyanum* Samejima. Ovary yellow-green, apex green.

forma *plenum* Samejima. A fully double flower in which all floral organs have mutated into petals. In regions where the species prospers, this form would make a fine garden plant.

The taxa above are the only ones listed in the 1987 work of Same-

Map 40. *Trillium camschatcense.*

jima and Samejima; however, in their earlier monograph of 1962, they listed forma *polyphyllum* Samejima and included a drawing of it. In this form, all floral organs have been replaced with leaflike bracts, gradually reduced in size in the inner whorls. The effect is of symmetrically arranged leaves in nosegay style. This form occurs frequently in colonies of mycoplasma- infected *T. grandiflorum* and occasionally in populations of *T. erectum* and other species. Freeman (1975) listed *T. recurvatum* f. *petaloideum* Steyermark, showing the same condition. We wonder if *T. camschatcense* f. *polyphyllum* represents mycoplasma infection in *T. camschatcense*.

Samejima and Samejima (1962) also listed forma *violaceaum* Miyabe and Tatewaki, with very large pale violet petals, from open Hokkaido fields. Not listed in the Russian or Japanese floras cited above or in the Samejimas' 1987 work, we suspect it is merely a vigorous form from brightly lighted locations with aging flowers, or, as plants related to the *T. erectum* complex in America usually do not fade to rose or pink tones with age, one whose petals, responding to strong light, develop faint anthocyanin pigments from the onset of anthesis.

Trillium camschatcense is a parent of two natural hybrids: *T.* ×*yezoense*, described under *T. apetalon,* its other parent, and *T.* ×*hagae* Miyabe & Tatewaki, described under *T. hagae.* The other parent of *T.* ×*hagae* is *T. tschonoskii*. See also *T. Channellii* under *T. hagae.*

Comments

This wide-ranging species not unexpectedly shows wide variation in petal size and overall plant size. Color, however, is rather uniformly creamy-white. We have grown a plant or two of this species in mid-Michigan. In its habit, flower carriage, and structure, we could scarcely distinguish it from *Trillium flexipes*. It lacked the vigor of that species under our conditions, however, and it rarely flowered. Its ability to form fertile seed with certain American species shows its close relationship to the *T. erectum* complex here and renders it of great interest to evolutionary plant biologists, taxonomists, and biogeographers. If one were to key out a plant of this species but its provenance were unknown, it would key out to the American species *T. flexipes*.

41. *Trillium hagae* Miyabe & Tatewaki

Synonymy: None

Common Name: Shiroa-enrei-so (means White-and-Purple Trillium, referring to the ovary coloring)

Trillium hagae exists in two forms: as a sterile triploid hybrid between *T. camschatcense* and *T. tschonoskii* (*T. ×hagae*) and as a fertile allohexaploid reproducing plant (*T. hagae*). As such, it is comparable to the sundew, *Drosera anglica*, which occurs in the wild both as a breeding, self-reproducing tetraploid species and as a reoccurring triploid hybrid. Samejima and Samejima (1962, 1987) treat the hexaploid, fertile plant (2n = 30) as a full species, *T. hagae*. Ohwi (1964) did not mention it. As we have chosen to follow the Samejimas' treatment, both taxa are treated here. Our data is from Samejima and Samejima (1987), with some details furnished by Victor Soukup.

Plate 76. *Trillium hagae* on Hokkaido, Japan. Photo by Victor Soukup.

From the very limited material and photographs available to us, it appears that, at times, *Trillium hagae* produces very widely ovate-orbicular white petals. Both the fertile hexaploid (2n = 30) and the sterile triploid (2n = 15) are identical in appearance and can be differentiated only by chromosome counts or by the shape of the mature ovary, which fails to expand and develop normally in the triploid. In the fertile form, the ovary expands fully, forming an ovoid berry filled with plump, viable seeds at maturity. Plant habit and flower of both types appear alike.

Habit

Stem erect, 2–4.5 dm tall.

Leaves sessile, broadly rhombic-orbicular, the apex subacute, widest about half way between middle and base of leaf, 12–20 cm long, 11–19 cm wide.

Pedicel 2–4 cm long.

Sepals green, oblong-lanceolate, acute to slightly obtuse, 24–40 mm long, 10–15 mm wide.

Petals 3, white, ovate to ovate-orbicular, acute-obtuse, 25–48 mm long, 16–28 mm wide.

Stamens 10–15 mm long, shorter than the pistil; anthers 8–11 mm long; anther sac about 2 times filament length, yellow.

Ovary 6-ridged, green, occasionally with purple spots, 8–15 mm long, 6.5–10 mm wide; pistil 11–16 mm tall.

Fruit ovoid to ovoid-orbicular in the hexaploid fertile plant, undeveloped, lacking expanded seed, and deltoid-conical in the triploid hybrid.

Season
May to June.

Distribution
The fertile hexaploid race occurs in two disjunct areas: the north and southeast coasts of Hokkaido Island, Japan. The triploid, sterile

Map 41. *Trillium hagae.*

hybrid occurs on Hokkaido and northern Honshu Islands, Japan. Same-jima and Samejima (1962, 1987) also cite southern Sakhalin Island, but do not show any dots on their 1987 map of Sakhalin.

Habitat
Deciduous forested river banks, hillsides and mountain slopes.

Varieties, Forms, Hybrids
T. ×hagae (3×, 2n = 15) is the more widespread entity. It can be distin-guished from the hexaploid form by its failure to produce normal en-larged fertile seeds, hence the ovary fails to fully expand, retaining a deltoid-pyramidal form.

Comments
We have not seen living plants of this species. From book illustrations, it appears that it might be a garden-worthy plant. As a hybrid plant, it should possess more adaptable growing traits than some of the Asiatic species, which languish here. Time will tell whether the fertile hexaploid will appear outside its limited range or expand that range.

As this book was going to press, a new species, *Trilllium channellii Fukuda, Freeman & Itou,* was published (Fukuda et al. 1996). It occurs on a volcanic plain near Mt. Yuo, in the Kawayu area along Kussharo Lake, Kawakami County, Kushiro District, in eastern Hokkaido, Japan, and blooms slightly ahead of other trilliums in its district. Fukuda et al. (1996) believe this species, a fertile tetraploid, to be originally of hybrid origin. Although intermediate in many respects between *T. camschat-cense* and *T. tschonoskii,* and essentially identical in gross morphology with their hybrid offspring (*T. ×hagae, T. hagae*), *T. channellii* is not be-lieved to have originated as a hybrid between these two species. While *T. channellii* grows sympatrically with both *T. camschatcense* and *T. tscho-noskii* on eastern Hokkaido, the forms of *T. hagae* have yet to be found growing with *T. channellii*. Fukuda et al. (1996) suggest that the compli-cated chromosome structure of the various Japanese species and hybrids makes it unlikely that *T. channellii* arose as a hybrid involving most of these taxa. They argue that *T. channellii* most likely arose by the somatic doubling of chromosomes in a hybrid "between *T. camschatcense* and a diploid taxon that is either now extinct or may exist only as one or two genomes in *T. tschonoskii*" (Fukuda et al. 1996). *Trillium channellii* can be distinguished from the triploid and hexaploid forms of *T. hagae* "mainly by its tetraploid chromosome number and high degree of fertility" (Fukuda et al. 1996). From the practical standpoint and purposes of this book, *T. channellii* would be indistinguishable from *T. hagae* in gross morphology, would key out to it, and would require complex chromosome techniques under microscopic examination to make certain identification. For these reasons, and because the only information available to us is the single, recent research paper dealing with this taxon, we include *T. channellii* in the key under *T. hagae* and do not describe it here. For more information, the reader should consult the original paper.

42. *Trillium smallii* Maximowicz

Synonymy: *Trillium smallii* var. *maximowiczii* Miyabe & Kudo, *Trillium amabile* Miyabe & Tatewaki
Common Name: Kojima-enrei-so (means Kojima Island Trillium)

Samejima and Samejima assert that this species and the taxon *Trillium apetalon* constitute distinct species and treat them separately. Ohwi (1984) considers *T. apetalon* to be a variety or form within the concept of *T. smallii* and includes it in his treatment of that species. Because we have chosen to follow the nomenclature and treatments of Samejima and Samejima (1987), we treat each taxon separately. *Trillium smallii* is an allopolyploid (and hence fertile) species of hybrid origin between *T. apetalon* and an unnamed diploid *Trillium* species (Samejima and Samejima 1987). Its chromosome number is $2n = 30$. The specific epithet *smallii* apparently honors John K. Small, botanist-author of the *Manual of the Southeastern Flora* (1933), who was active at the time this species was described, but we can find no direct citation to this effect.

Habit
Stem erect, glabrous, without ridges, 1.5–4.5 dm tall, from a compact thick rhizome.

Plate 77. *Trillium smallii* on Hokkaido, Japan. Note the partial and deformed petals. Photo by Victor Soukup.

Leaves, depressed, ovate-rhombic to rhombic-orbicular, abruptly long-acuminate, its base slightly narrow-cuneate extended, 6.5–17 cm long, 6.5–18.5 cm wide.

Pedicel erect, or leaning, 2–5 cm long, rarely longer.

Sepals ovate-lanceolate to oblong-lanceolate, acute to subacute, brown-green to purple, 12–25 mm long, 8–15 mm wide.

Petals absent, or if present, 1–3, small, sometimes one or more deformed, dark red-purple, size variable on same plant, orbicular to orbicular-ovate, more or less 10–24 mm long and wide; petals occasionally mutated to additional stamens (Samejima and Samejima 1987).

Stamens 6–9, erect, dark purple, 7–12 mm long (Samejima and Samejima 1987), 25–30 mm long (Ohwi 1984); filaments 2.5–6 mm long, slightly longer than the anther sacs; anther sacs 3–6 mm long, purplish; pollen yellow or gray-purple.

Ovary 6-ridged, conical-globose at anthesis, 7–11 mm tall; stigmas separate, very short, recurved; pistil 9–12 mm tall.

Fruit globose, with persistent stigmas, dull green, 24–27 mm long and wide, edible when ripe (Ohwi 1984). We recommend caution in consuming any part of the plant, as trilliums contain powerful components used by native peoples to alleviate labor pains and may be dangerous.

Season
April to May.

Distribution
Southern Sakhalin Island and Hokkaido (Samejima and Samejima 1987); Hokkaido, Honshu, Shikoku, and Kyushu (Ohwi 1984, whose treatment of *T. smallii* includes *T. apetalon*).

Map 42. *Trillium smallii.*

Habitat
Deciduous forested hillsides at lower elevations. Occurs only on hillsides near "sea cliffs" (Samejima and Samejima 1987).

Varieties, Forms, Hybrids
var. *smallii.* The typical plant described above.

var. *atropurpureocarpum* Samejima. Ripened ovary is dark red-purple.

Comments

Because we have seen only a very limited amount of living and herbarium material of these species, we do not feel qualified to judge the merits of retaining *T. smallii* and *T. apetalon* as distinct species or one highly variable species. It must await the work of Japanese or other taxonomists who can work with large wild populations as well as extensive herbarium collections.

43. *Trillium tschonoskii* Maximowicz

Synonymy: *Trillium tschonoskii* f. *violacea* Maximowicz
Common Name: Miyama-enrei-so, Shirobana-enrei-so (means Mountain Woods Trillium or White Trillium)

This species is the only one of the Asiatic species (unless you consider *Trillidium govanianum* a true trillium) known to occur in the Himalayan Mountain region. It is similar in its general aspects to *Trillium camschatcense*. Its chromosome number is 2n = 20. The specific epithet *tschonoskii* honors Japanese botanist Chonosuke Sugawa (1841–1925).

Habit

Stem erect, 1.5–4 dm tall, glabrous, arising 1–2 from a single rhizome tip per season.

Leaves depressed, rhombic to rhombic-ovate, gradually rounded distally to an abrupt acuminate tip, 7–17 cm long, 6–18 cm wide.

Pedicel erect, 1–5 cm long.

Sepals ovate to broadly lanceolate, acute, 20–28 mm long, 5–15 mm wide, light green.

Petals white, slightly longer than the sepals, 1.5–3.7 cm long, 0.5–2 cm wide, ovate, oblong-ovate, rarely elliptic, narrowed near apex to a somewhat elongate-acuminate tip, basal portion with a straight, somewhat cuneate margin from just below the middle to its base.

Stamens 7–13.5 mm long, yellow-cream, barely exceeding the pistil; filaments 3–8 mm long; anther sacs yellow, 3.5–9 mm long; connectives pale green, slightly extended beyond anther sacs.

Plate 78. Flower detail of *Trillium tschonoskii* on Hokkaido, Japan. Note the somewhat abruptly narrowed and sulcate petal tips. Photo by Victor Soukup.

Ovary green, purple spotted, or all purple, 6–13 mm long, 4–8.5 mm wide, conical-ovoid in anthesis, 6-ridged; stigmas separate but closely grouped, basally thickest, short-recurved; pistil 6–13 mm long.

Fruit green, ovoid, with persistent stigma remnants prominent, shallowly 6-ridged or -lined.

Season
April to mid-June.

Distribution

Himalaya Mountains, China, Korea, Taiwan, southern Sakhalin Island, The Japanese islands of Hokkaido, Honshu, Shikoku, and Kyushu. Apparently absent from the Kuriles.

Habitat

Deciduous or mixed coniferous-deciduous forests up to subalpine levels; mossy woods.

Varieties, Forms, Hybrids

var. *tschonoskii.* The typical plant.

var. *atrorubens* Miyabe & Tatewaki. Apex of ovary at anthesis and in fruit dark red-purple. Endemic to Hokkaido Island, Japan (Samejima and Samejima 1962).

var. *himaliacum* Hara. The plant of the Himalayas. Hara (1971) considers this variety sufficiently similar to the Japanese species to be considered conspecific. He states that it differs in minor ways in having more rhombic leaves, shorter peduncles, less acuminate-elliptic sepals, and shorter stamens and anthers. In 1967 he collected plants at Pele La

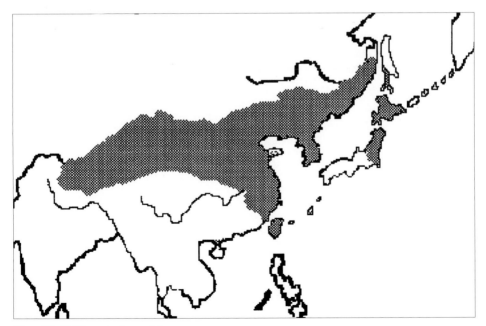

Map 43. *Trillium tschonoskii.*

that were smaller than typical *T. tschonoskii,* with purple petals. He does not state whether the flowers were freshly opened or aging. It is possible that the petals may have opened white and aged to purple.

forma *cryptopetalum* **Makino.** A rare form with extremely short petals found on Hokkaido and Honshu Islands, Japan.

Trillium tschonoskii hybridizes with *T. camschatcense* to form *T. ×hagae* (discussed under *T. hagae*) and with *T. apetalon* to produce *T. ×miyabeanum* (discussed under *T. apetalon*).

Comments

In Japan, where there is intense horticultural interest in all details of a plant's growth, much naming of forms has occurred. Whether these forms represent genetically fixed, constant forms and varieties, or result from ecological effects and vary from year to year, the authors do not state. In our American plants, individuals with darker ovary tips, redder fruits, and extra large petals generally are ecological forms, the color or extra size induced in some seasons by more than the usual light, a wetter season, or special fertility at that individual's site. In another season under differing conditions, they usually revert to typical plants. We feel that forms or varieties that are not genetically stable probably ought not to be named botanically, although in some instances, horticultural names or cultivar names might be appropriate.

Glossary

Abaxial. Away from the axis or stem, facing outward.

Abscission layer. A tissue layer in a plant with specialized, weak-walled cells that form a breaking point for the separation of a structure from the plant, such as the point at which leaf petioles break from the twig. In trilliums, the point at which cells at the base of the ripe fruit expand, become pulpy, and eventually disintegrate, separating the fruit from the receptacle.

Acuminate. Gradually tapered to a point.

Acute. Leaf apex convex or straight-margined and forming an angle between 45 and 90 degrees.

Adaxial. Towards the axis or stem, facing inward.

Adventitious roots. Roots not in a normal position. In trilliums, the feeder roots formed along the rhizome (underground stem); the only roots on adult trilliums.

Allele. One of several alternate expressions of a gene. For example, in eye color, one expression produces blue eyes, another allele produces green eyes.

Anther. The pollen-bearing portion of a stamen.

Anther-connective. The extension of the filament tissue between and sometimes beyond the anther sacs on a stamen.

Anther sac. The chambers of the anther containing pollen.

Anthesis. The time of expansion of the flower; as used here, the time when the flower is fully open and its organs functional.

Anthocyanins. Vacuolar plant pigments, usually red or blue.

Apex. The tip.

Apiculate. An extension of a leaf or petal midvein at least three times longer than wide, beyond the lamina of the organ. Used here for petals having a nipplelike extension of the midvein beyond the petal tissue.

Arcuate. Arching, moderately curved.

Axil. The angle formed between an organ and the stem or rachis to which it is attached.

Axis. The central region of a longitudinal support on which various organs are arranged, as the stem with its leaves.

Berry. A fleshy fruit with a fleshy outer wall and the seeds immersed in juicy or pulpy material.

Bract. A modified, often reduced leaf found in an inflorescence, frequently subtending a flower. In *Trillium,* the organs commonly referred to as "leaves."

Calcareous. Containing calcium; in soils, frequently used for those derived from limestone.

Calciphile. Lime-loving. Used to denote species which occur naturally only on calcareous soils.

Carotenes. Red, orange, or yellow pigments.

Carpel. The organ that bears the ovules; the female sporophyll.

Cataphyll. Small, dry, scalelike sheathing leaves along the nodes of the *Trillium* rhizome.

Chromosome. A body within a cell that carries the genetic instructions (DNA) for each cell.

Claw. The narrowed (often abruptly) and sometimes thickened tissue forming a basal stalklike portion of some petals.

Connective. The extension of filament tissue between and sometimes beyond the anther sacs or thecae.

Connivent. The coming together or converging of several organs, without actually uniting.

Cordate. Heart-shaped.

Cotyledon. Leaflike organs (seed leaves) borne upon the embryo in the seed.

Cross-pollination. The transfer of pollen from the anther of one individual to the stigma of another individual.

Crossover. The exchange of homologous sections of nonsister chromatids during meiosis. The process enhances the chance of variation of traits in a given offspring.

Cuneate. Wedge-shaped.

Cytokinins. Plant cell growth hormones.

Decumbent. Reclining upon the ground, but with the end upturned.

Dehiscent. Splitting open. Used of organs that split open along sutures, slits, or pores to discharge a product, as seeds from a pod or pollen grains from an anther sac.

Dichotomous key. An identification device composed of a series of contrasting couplets to which an unknown plant is compared. By selecting one of a pair that best describes the unknown plant's characteristics and following its lead to the next pair of couplets, one proceeds to eliminate choices until one is led to a specific identification.

Diploid. The condition of a cell or individual possessing the basic "normal" complement of species chromosomes, that is, one complete set from each parent. Usually designated as 2n.

Distal. Away from the point of attachment.

Elaiosome. An oily, fleshy outgrowth of a seed, similar to an aril or strophiole. In trilliums, the oils contain powerful ant attractants.

Elliptic. Oblong and equally rounded at each end.

Elliptic-ovate. Oblong, nearly equally rounded at each end, but with the basal end slightly wider.

Endangered species. Essentially any species population determined by scientific investigation to be so small as to be in danger of imminent extinction; also a legal status in the United States and some other countries.

Endosperm. Stored food tissue or material within a seed.

Epigeal. An embryo whose cotyledons and organs, upon germination, emerge from the seed coat and expand above the ground.

Erose. With the appearance of tattered, eroded margins, gnawed or ragged.

Extrorse. Facing outward. Said of anther-sac openings that face away from the ovary.

Fetid. An offensive odor, stench.

Filament. The support stalk of a stamen.

Fruit. A ripened ovary with or without accessory parts.

Genome. All the hereditary factors (genes) contained in one haploid (1n) compliment of chromosomes.

Germination. The resumption of growth of a seed.

Gibberellins. Plant growth hormones strongly affecting stem elongation.

Glabrous. Smooth, hairless.

Hybrid. An offspring from the mating of two different species. In genetics, one carrying different alleles for a single trait.

Hypogynous. Said of organs such as petals that are inserted on the flower receptacle below the ovary and not attached directly to it.

Introrse. Facing inward. Said of anther-sac openings that face towards the ovary.

Inversion. The breaking free and reattaching of a chromosomal segment end for end in the same chromosome.

Lanceolate. Lance-shaped, longer than wide, and widest toward the base.

Latrorse. Opening to the side, as anther sacs that open at 90 degrees from the ovary.

Leaf. The photosynthetic organ of a flowering plant. In trilliums, the bracts act as leaves in photosynthesis.

Limb. The expanded distal portion of a petal when a claw is present at its base.

Locule. The cavity or chamber of an ovary (or anther).

Meiosis. Cell division that produces haploid cells, gametes, in animals and plants.

Meristem. An undifferentiated tissue found in stem tips and cambium and capable of rapid division to produce cells that differentiate into the typical stem tissues and organs. Responsible for growth in length and width of woody stems.

Mutant. An individual carrying mutated genes.

Mutation. An abrupt, permanent change in a gene, which is then passed to future generations.

Mycoplasma. An organism smaller than a bacterium and larger than a virus that is unable to live except in association with a host cell or organism. Mycoplasma organisms are known to cause a variety of animal and plant diseases, including aster yellows disease, and the petal tissue–greening condition frequently found in *Trillium grandiflorum*. Mycoplasmas are believed to require a vector to carry the organisms between hosts. An ultimate parasite.

Mycorrhiza, mycorrhizal. A soil fungus–flowering plant association, usually considered symbiotic although it may be a complex parasite and host relationship, usually through the roots, and often occupying a specialized, combined fungus–root tissue mass (as in many terrestrial orchids).

Myrmecochory. The condition of having seeds adapted for dispersal by ants.

Node. The point on a stem where leaves, buds, or branches arise.

Oblanceolate. Lanceolate, but widest above the middle.

Oblong. Widest at the middle, with parallel sides.

Obovate. Egg-shaped, but with widest region above the middle.

Obtuse. Rounded or blunt at the tip.

Orbiculate. Circular.

Ovary. Ovule-bearing chamber, a part of the pistil.

Ovate. Egg-shaped, widest region below the middle, sides symmetrical.

Paraphyletic. A member of a group that does not contain all the descendants of a common ancestor.

Pedicel. A single flower stalk within a branched inflorescence. In trilliums, if the flower is borne on a stalk above the branch, it is regarded as a pedicel. Since the entire above-ground stalk is a flowering stalk, technically the main stalk would be a peduncle and that part above the bracts (leaves) a pedicel.

Petal. A division of the floral envelope which, in trilliums, consists of a large, oval, flattish colorful tissue.

Petiole. The stalk that attaches a leaf to a stem and supports it.

pH. Symbol used in chemistry for indicating the hydrogen-ion concentration of a solution; a measure of its acidity or alkalinity. As used here, it is used to measure the relative acidity or alkalinity of the soil.

Picotee. Petal color pattern in which the color is broken up into granules or islets, giving a grainy texture to the main petal lamina, but usually concentrated and therefore darker along its margins.

Piedmont. In physiography, formed at the base of a mountain by materials eroded from it. In geography, the region of the southeastern United States lying between the Appalachian and Blue Ridge Mountains and the Coastal Plain lowlands; this area is the center of occurrence of the sessile trilliums.

Pistil. The central organ of a flower, consisting of one or several fused ovaries and stigmas, the latter usually elevated on separate or fused stalks termed "the style."

Plastid. Cell organelles that produce or store food and usually contain distinct pigments. Those storing green pigments are termed chloroplasts, those storing yellow xanthoplasts, and so forth.

Pollen. A young male gametophyte.

Pollination. The transfer of pollen from the anther sacs of a stamen to a receptive stigma.

Polyploidy. The condition of a cell or individual having more than the normal diploid number of chromosomes in the cells. Usually designated as 3n (triploidy), 4n (tetraploidy), and so forth.

Praemorse. Appearing "bitten off." Applied to the posterior portion of mature *Trillium* rhizomes in which the old tissue slowly decays away.

Radicle. The part of a plant embryo below the point of its cotyledon attachments.

Receptacle. The platform of tissue on which the flower parts, sepals, petals, stamens, and pistils are inserted.

Recombination. Combinations of alleles in an offspring not present in the same pattern in either parent, which result from random assortment of chromosomes and genes during meiosis, meiotic crossover, mutation, or a combination of all the above during the reproductive process.

Recurve. Strongly curved downward or bent backward.

Rhizome. A modified, creeping stem, usually horizontal and underground.

Rhombic. An obliquely angled equilateral leaf.

Ringent. Gaping.

Scape. A flowering stem, without leaves, arising from the ground.

Sepal. The outermost ring of floral organs, forming the covering of the flower bud. Sepals may be green and leaflike in texture, or delicate and petaloid. In trilliums, they are green, leaflike, and fold away from the open flower petals.

Sessile. Attached to another organ without a stalk.

Shoot. One of two major body parts in complex plants, the root and the shoot. Generally considered an organ system distinguished by the arrangement of its parts (Villee et al. 1985).

Spatulate. Like a spatula, that is, oblong, with the proximal end narrowest.

Stamen. A pollen-bearing organ, the male sporophyll.

Stigma. The portion of a pistil adapted to receive the pollen.

Stomata, stomates. Gas-exchange openings on leaf surfaces, usually the under surface. Each opening is "guarded" by two bean-shaped guard cells that regulate the size of the opening.

Strophiole. An appendage from the hilum (point of attachment) region of a seed. Sometimes applied to the elaiosome of a *Trillium* seed.

Style. The narrow stalklike portion of a pistil adapted to elevate and position the stigmas.

Subsessile. Almost sessile, only a rudimentary stalk.

Subulate. Awl-shaped.

Sulcate. Boat-shaped.

Symbiotic. The condition when two species are codependent in some specialized manner and usually do not lead a life independent of the other.

Sympatric. The condition when two species occur together in one region, or the area where their ranges overlap.

Synonymy. In botany, the discarded names applied to a species incorrectly, either through misidentification, lack of priority, duplication, or other reasons.

Systematic fungicide. A fungicide that is absorbed into the plant tissue and carried throughout the plant.

Taxon. A classification (taxonomic) unit of any living thing at any rank.

Teratological, teratology. Pertaining to monstrous or deformed, as the study of monstrous or abnormal structures or individuals.

Undulate. With a wavy margin or surface.

Vernalization. An internal, cellular conditioning, usually by a specified period of exposure to cold, which breaks growth dormancy and prepares the plant or seed for new active growth.

Whorl. Organs, such as leaves, attached three or more per node like spokes from a wheel hub, as in trilliums.

Xanthophylls. Yellow plastid pigments in plant tissues such as leaves and petals.

Bibliography

Asbury, S. S. 1973. The anthocyanin pigments of sessile-flowered *Trillium* (Liliaceae). M.A. thesis, George Peabody College for Teachers, Nashville, Tennessee.

Barksdale, L. 1938. The pedicellate species of *Trillium* found in the southern Appalachians. *Journal of the Elisha Mitchell Scientific Society* 54: 271–296.

Barton, L. V. 1944. Some seeds showing special dormancy. *Contributions from the Boyce Thompson Institute.* 13 (5): 259–273.

Berg, R. Y. 1958. Seed dispersal, morphology, and phylogeny of *Trillium. Skrifter Utgitt av Det Norske Vidensk.aps-Akademi 1 Oslo 1.* Mat. Naturvidensk, K1, 1: 1–36.

Bodkin, N. L., and J. L. Reveal. 1982. A new variety of *Trillium pusillum* (Liliaceae) from the Virginias. *Brittonia* 34 (2): 141–143.

Braun, E. L. 1950. *Deciduous Forests of Eastern North America.* Blakiston Company, Philadelphia, Pennsylvania.

Brummitt, R. K. 1992. *Vascular Plant Families and Genera.* Royal Botanic Gardens, Kew. p. 782.

Cabe, P. R. 1995. The *Trillium pusillum* Michx. (Liliaceae) complex in Virginia. I. Morphological investigations. *Castanea* 60: 1–14.

Cabe, P. R., and C. Werth. 1995. The *Trillium pusillum* Michx. (Liliaceae) complex in Virginia. II. Isozyme evidence. *Castanea* 60: 15–29.

Case, F. W., Jr. 1981A. The Eastern American trilliums. Part 1. *Bulletin of the American Rock Garden Society* 39: 53–67.

_____. 1981B. The Eastern American trilliums. Part 2. *Bulletin of the American Rock Garden Society* 39: 108–122.

_____. 1982. The snow trillium, *Trillium nivale,* in Michigan. *The Michigan Botanist* 21 (1): 39–44.

_____. 1988. Trillium propagation and conservation. *Fine Gardening* 1 (2): 36–37.

_____. 1994. *Trillium grandiflorum,* forms, doubles, and diseases. *Bulletin of the American Rock Garden Society* 52: 45–50.

Case, F. W., Jr., and G. L. Burrows IV. 1962. The genus *Trillium* in Michigan: some problems of distribution and taxonomy. *Papers Michigan Academy of Science Arts and Letters* XLVII: 180–200.

Case, F. W., Jr., and R. B. Case. 1993. *Trillium erectum* and its hybrids. *Bulletin of the American Rock Garden Society* 51: 163–168.

Chase, M. W., M. R. Duvall, H. G. Hills, J. G. Conran, A. V. Cox, L. E. Eguiarte, J. Hartwell, M. F. Fay, L. R. Caddick, K. M. Cameron, and S. Hoot. 1995. Molecular phylogenetics of Lilianae. In P. J. Rudall, P. J. Cribb, D. F. Cutler, and C. J. Humphrie, eds. *Monocotyledons: Systematics and Evolution.* Royal Botanic Gardens, Kew. 109–137.

Deam, C. C. 1940. *Flora of Indiana.* Indiana Department of Conservation, Indianapolis.

Deno, N. C. 1991. *Seed Germination Theory and Practice.* Published by the author, State College, Pennsylvania.

Duncan, W. H., J. F. Garst, and G. A. Neece. 1971. *Trillium persistens* (Liliaceae), a new pedicellate-flowered species from northeastern Georgia and adjacent North Carolina. *Rhodora* 73: 244–248.

Edgren, M. 1993. Vegetative propagation of *Trillium chloropetalum. Bulletin of the American Rock Garden Society* 51 (3): 169–172.

Fenneman, N. M. 1938. *Physiography of the United States.* McGraw-Hill Company, New York.

Fernald, M. L. 1950. *Gray's Manual of Botany.* 8th ed. American Book Company, New York. 443–446.

Ferlatte, W. J. 1974. *A Flora of the Trinity Alps of Northern California.* University of California Press, Berkeley. 171–172.

Foster, H. L. 1968. *Rock Gardening.* Houghton Mifflin Company, Boston.

Freeman, J. D. 1975. Revision of *Trillium* subgenus *Phyllantherum* (Liliaceae). *Brittonia* 27: 1–62.

_____. 1995. The genus *Trillium* in the Southeast. *Newsletter of the Alabama Wildflower Society* L: 1–9.

Freeman, J. D., and T. E. Heinecke. 1987. *Trillium recurvatum* Beck forma *esepalum,* forma nova; a new sepalless form of the prairie wakerobin. *Rhodora* 89 (857): 17–20.

Friesner, R. C. 1929. The genus *Trillium* in Indiana. *Butler University Bot. Studies* 1: 29–40.

Fukuda, I., J. D. Freeman, and M. Itou. 1996. *Trillium channellii,* sp. nov. (Trilliaceae), in Japan, and *T. camschatcense* Ker Gawler, correct name for the Asiatic diploid *Trillium. Novon* 6: 164–171.

Gates, R. R. 1917. A systematic study of the North American genus *Trillium,* its variability and its relation to *Paris* and *Medeola. Annals of the Missouri Botanical Gardens* 4: 43–92.

Gibson, H. L. 1976. Some observations on the persistence and changes in green teratological forms of *Trillium. Proceedings of the Rochester Academy of Science* 13 (1): 1–16.

Glattstein, J. 1988. Trilliums. *Fine Gardening* 1 (2): 33–35.

Goodspeed, T. H., and R. P. Brandt. 1916. *Notes on the Californian Species of Trillium L. I. A Report of the General Results of Field and Garden Studies, 1911–1916.* University of California, Berkeley, Publ. Bot. 7: 1–24.

Gray Herbarium. 1896. *Gray Herbarium Index.* Gray Herbarium, Harvard University, Cambridge, Massachusetts.

Gunther, R. W., and J. Lanza. 1989. Variation in attractiveness of *Trillium* diaspores to a seed-dispersing ant. *American Midland Naturalist* 122: 321–328.

Haga, T., and R. B. Channell. 1982. Three species groups in American trilliums as revealed by compatibility with an Asian species. *Botanical Magazine of Tokyo* 95: 77–80.

Haga, T., and H. Watanabe. 1966. Chromosomes of a Himalayan *Trillium* in relation to the Japanese and American species. *Proc. Jap. Acad.* 42: 160–164.

Hall, M. T. 1961. Teratology in *Trillium grandiflorum. American Journal of Botany* 48 (9): 803–811.

Hanzawa, F. M., and S. Kalisz. 1993. The relationship between age, size, and reproduction in *Trillium grandiflorum* (Liliaceae). *American Journal of Botany* 80 (4): 405–410.

Hara, H. 1966. *The Flora of Eastern Himalaya.* University of Tokyo Press, Tokyo, Japan.

———. 1971. *Flora of Eastern Himalaya,* second report. University Museum, University of Tokyo.

Hara, H., W. T. Stearn, and L. H. J. Williams. 1978. *An Enumeration of the Flowering Plants of Nepal* 1: 80. British Museum (Natural History), London.

Hickman, J. C., ed. 1993. *The Jepson Manual (The Higher Plants of California).* University of California Press, Berkeley.

Hooper, G. R., F. W. Case, Jr., and R. Myers. 1971. Mycoplasma-like bodies associated with a flower greening disorder of a wild flower, *Trillium grandiflorum. Plant Disease Reporter* 55: 824–828.

Hoover, R. F. 1970. *The Vascular Plants of San Luis Obispo County, California.* University of California Press, Berkeley. p. 98.

Howell, T. 1897. *A Flora of Northwest America.* Library of Congress, Washington, D.C. 1: 660–661.

Ihara, H., and K. Ihara. 1978. A biosystematic study on the pedicellate-flowered species of the North American *Trillium.* (1) Geographical distribution of major groups and their gynoecium norms. *Journal of Geobotany* 25: 139–172.

Jepson, W. L. 1923. *A Manual of the Flowering Plants of California.* Assoc. Student Store, University of California, Berkeley. pg. 251.

Johnson, R. G. 1969. A taxonomic and floristic study of the Liliaceae and allied families in the southeastern United States. Ph.D. dissertation, West Virginia University, Morgantown.

Kato, H., S. Kawano, R. Terauchi, M. Ohara, and F. Utech. 1995. Evolutionary biology of *Trillium* and related genera (Trilliaceae). 1. Restriction site mapping and variation of chloroplast DNA and its systematic implications. *Plant Species Biology* 10: 7–30.

Kawano, S., M. Ohara, and F. H. Utech. 1992. Life history studies on the genus *Trillium* (Liliaceae). VI. Life history characteristics of three western North American species and their evolutionary-ecological implications. *Plant Species Biology* 7: 21–36.

Komarov, V. L. 1935. *Flora of the U.S.S.R.* 4: 361, 569–570. (Smithsonian) Israel Program for Scientific Translations (1968).

Les, D. H., R. Whitkus, F. A. Bryan, and L. E. Tyrell. 1989. Biochemical basis of floral color polymorphism in a heterocyanic population of *Trillium sessile* (Liliaceae). *American Journal of Botany* 76 (1): 23–29.

Mahotiere, S., C. Johnson, and P. Howard. 1993. Stimulating asparagus seedling shoot production with benzyladenine. *HortScience* 28 (3): 229.

Martin, J. N. 1935. The distribution and life history of *Trillium nivale* Riddell. *Proceedings of the Iowa Academy of Science* 42: 49–54.

Mason, G. 1975. Guide to the plants of the Wallowa Mountains of northeastern Oregon. University of Oregon Museum of Natural History, Eugene. p. 96.

Morgan, D., and S. McDaniel. 1979. *Trillium pusillum* (Liliaceae) in Mississippi. *Sida* 8 (2): 209–210.

Munz, P. A. 1959. *A California Flora.* University of California Press, Berkeley. 1355–1356.

Nesom, G. L., and J. C. La Duke. 1985. Biology of *Trillium nivale* (Liliaceae). *Canadian Journal of Botany* 63 (1): 7–14.

Noltie, H. J. 1994. *Flora of Bhutan.* 3 (1): 20–21. Royal Botanic Garden, Edinburgh.

Ohwi, J., F. G. Meyer, E. H. Walker, eds. 1984. *Flora of Japan.* Smithsonian Institute, Washington, D.C.

Patrick, T. S. 1973. Observations on the life history of *Trillium grandiflorum* (Michx.) Salisbury. M.A. thesis, Cornell University, Ithaca, New York.

_____. 1984. *Trillium sulcatum* (Liliaceae), a new species of the southern Appalachians. *Brittonia* 36: 26–36.

_____. 1985. *T. undulatum* f. *enotatum,* a new petal color form of the painted trillium. *Rhodora* 87 (850): 157–158.

_____. 1986A. The trilliums of eastern North America. Mimeographed handout, privately published. Knoxville, Tennessee.

_____. 1986B. The trilliums of Tennessee. Mimeographed handout, privately published. Knoxville, Tennessee.

Peattie, D. C., 1927. *Trillium* in North and South Carolina: a critical systematic reconnaissance. *Journal of the Elisha Mitchell Society* 42: 193–206.

Peck, M. E. 1941. *A Manual of the Higher Plants of Oregon.* Binford and Mort, Portland, Oregon. p. 210.

Piper, C. V., and R. K. Beattie. 1914. *Flora of Southeastern Washington and adjacent Idaho.* New Era Printing Company Press, Lancaster, Pennsylvania. p. 63.

Pringle, J. S. 1967. *The Trilliums of Ontario.* Rev. ed. Royal Botanic Gardens Technical Bulletin no. 5, Hamilton, Ontario, Canada.

Radford, A. E., H. E. Ahles, and C. R. Bell. 1968. *Manual of the Vascular Flora of the Carolinas.* University of North Carolina Press, Chapel Hill.

Radford, A. E., W. C. Dickison, J. R. Massey, and C. R. Bell. 1974. *Vascular Plant Systematics.* Harper and Row, New York.

Reed, C. F. 1962. The genus *Trillium* in Kentucky. *Castanea* 27: 143–155.

_____. 1982. *Trillium virginianum* (Fernald) Reed, comb. nov., in Maryland, Virginia, West Virginia, and North Carolina. *Phytologia* 50 (4): 279–285.

Roe, G. F. 1978. Additions to the range of *Trillium pusillum. Castanea* 43: 187–191.

St. John, H. 1963. *Flora of Southeastern Washington and of Adjacent Idaho.* 3rd ed. Outdoor Pictures, Escondido, California. p. 102.

Samejima, K., and J. Samejima. 1962. Studies on the Eastern Asiatic *Trillium* (Liliaceae). *Acta. Hort. Gotob.* 25: 157–257.

_____. 1987. *Trillium Genus Illustrated.* Hokkaido University Press, Sapporo, Japan.

Sernander, R. 1906. *Entwurf einer Monographie der Europaischen Myrekocho-ren.* Kungl. Sv. Vet.-Ak. Handl., 41 (7): 1–410.

Serota, C. A. 1969. The biosystematics of *Trillium rugelii* from Rutherford County, North Carolina. *Canadian Journal of Botany* 47: 445–452.

Serota, C. A., and H. B. Gryder. A morphological and karyotypic analysis of an isolated population of *Trillium gleasonii* Fernald. *Journal of the Elisha Mitchell Society* 83: 117–122.

Small, J. K. 1933. *Manual of the Southeastern Flora.* University of North Carolina Press, Chapel Hill.

Solomon, E. P., and L. R. Berg. 1995. *The World of Biology.* 5th ed. Saunders College Publishing, Philadelphia, Pennsylvania. 587–588.

Soukup, V. 1980. A new *Trillium* (Liliaceae) from the northwestern United States. *Brittonia* 32 (3): 330–333.

_____. 1982. *Trillium kurabayashii* f. *luteum. Phytologia* 50: 290.

Steyermark, J. A. 1963. *Flora of Missouri.* Iowa State University Press, Ames.

Stoutamire, W. P. 1958. Variation?, Why? *Cranbrook Institute of Science News Letter* 27 (8): 74–78.

Takahashi, M. 1983. Pollen morphology in Asiatic species of *Trillium. Botanical Magazine of Tokyo* 96: 377–384.

Takhtajan, A. 1983. A revision of *Daiswa* (Trilliaceae). *Brittonia* 35: 255–270.

Tatewaki M., and T. Suto. 1935. On the new genus *Kinugasa. Transactions of the Sapporo Natural History Society* 14 (1): 34–37.

Taylor, T. M. C., and A. F. Szczawinski. 1974. *Trillium ovatum* Pursh forma *hibbersonii* Taylor et Szczawinski, forma nova. *Syesis* 7: 250.

Utech, F. H. 1980. *Chromosome atlas of the vascular plants of western Pennsylvania. 1. Annals of the Carnegie Museum* 49: 265–305. Pittsburgh, Pennsylvania.

Villee, C. A., E. P. Solomon, and P. W. Davis. 1985. *Biology.* Saunders College Publishing, Philadelphia, Pennsylvania. 997–998.

Wherry, E. T. 1974. Note on *Trillium grandiflorum. The Green Scene* (March): 33.

Whitkus, R., F. A. Bryan, D. H. Les, and L. E. Tyrell. 1987. Genetic structure in a heterocyanic population of *Trillium sessile* (Liliaceae). *Plant Species Biology* 2: 1–7.

Wilkins, M. B., ed. 1984. *Advanced Plant Physiology.* Pitman Publishing, London. 409, 450, 460–462.

Zomlefer, W. B. 1996. The Trilliaceae in the Southeastern United States. *Harvard Papers in Botany* 9: 91–120.

Index

Boldfaced page numbers indicate main entries.